The Economic Transformation of Cuba

The
Economic
Transformation
of Cuba

A First-Hand Account
by Edward Boorstein

MR
PRESS

NEW YORK AND LONDON

TO COMANDANTE GUEVARA

Who gave me the opportunity to work for the Revolution

Preface

This book deals not with ordinary economics, but with the economics of a revolution. Few of Cuba's economic problems can be understood unless this is constantly kept in mind; little of anything in Cuba can be understood unless the parts are related to the whole—the Revolution. And the understanding of the Revolution cannot be verbal and formal. A true revolution has many aspects; it rearranges all of society. The richer the understanding of it, the stronger the light one can focus on specific problems. It would take an artist to do justice to a revolution, to evoke in the reader a feeling for the struggle and upheaval, for what it means to work within the turmoil. But even an economist cannot limit his analysis to specific problems; he must also discuss the Revolution—the setting in which the problems occur.

Several general themes about the Revolution will be developed: the irreconcilable conflict between American imperialism and the Cuban people;* the momentum and sweep of the revolutionary process; the inevitable untidiness of revolution.

The actions of the participants in the drama must be seen and judged against these characteristics of the revolutionary reality. Commentators—especially Americans—often find it difficult to face the sharp conflicts and choices laid bare by the Revolution; they want to soften things, and they base their analyses on alternatives that sound attractive and easy but have never really existed. Often the force exerted by the current of events on the leaders of the Revolution is unrecognized. When I was in Cuba I found that visitors or technicians from developed, highly organized countries would sometimes misunderstand the confusion, disorganization, and inefficiency they ran

---

* Throughout this English text the term "American" is used where the Spanish term would be *norteamericano*.

into because they failed to see them in perspective. But you cannot understand revolutions—or their economics—if you look at them through the eyes of a bank teller who has to tidy up all his small change and balance every little account every night.

My wife, our two children, and I arrived in Cuba in May, 1960. I worked for the first three months in the National Bank and from then on in the two government agencies responsible for the planning and administration of foreign trade—the Bank of Foreign Commerce and the Ministry of Foreign Commerce into which it was transformed. Economists were scarce and I held a variety of jobs in which I served as trouble-shooter for the Minister of Foreign Commerce, and for the Vice Minister of Economy, who was in charge of planning and the formulation of economic policy. My work in Cuba was the most satisfying work experience I have ever had. In September 1963, my family and I had to return to the United States for personal reasons. We left in a small freighter that sailed for Montreal from a little sugar port in eastern Cuba. Our stay of about three and a half years had covered the waves of nationalization in 1960, the invasion at the Bay of Pigs, and the missile crisis.

I am grateful to the Louis M. Rabinowitz Foundation for the grant that enabled me to write this book. I am indebted to Harry Magdoff for his help. To my friends in Cuba—Jaime, Carlos, Albán, Aníbal, Raúl, Cristóbal, Julio, Humberto, and the rest—*un fuerte abrazo de su amigo norteamericano.*

Contents

List of Tables

A revolution is not the same as inviting people to dinner, or writing an essay, or painting a picture, or doing fancy needlework; it cannot be anything so refined, so calm and gentle, or so mild, kind, courteous, restrained and magnanimous.

MAO TSE-TUNG

The
Economic
Transformation
of Cuba

I

The Prerevolutionary Background: Imperialism

The central fact about the Cuban economy before the Revolution was neither its one-crop concentration on sugar, nor the monopoly of most of the agricultural land by huge *latifundia,* nor the weakness of the national industry, nor any other such specific characteristic. Until the Revolution, the central fact about the Cuban economy was its domination by American monopolies—by American imperialism. It was from imperialist domination that the specific characteristics flowed. Unless this is recognized, the Cuban Revolution cannot be understood.

The specific characteristics of the Cuban economy can be handled as safe technical subjects, and even official reports by U.S. government or U.S. dominated agencies and books by respectable American authors deal with them. The *Report on Cuba,* published by the International Bank for Reconstruction and Development in 1951,[1] and *Investment in Cuba,* published by the U.S. Department of Commerce in 1956,[2] both speak of the concentration of the Cuban economy on the production and export of sugar, and recommend diversification. But what was keeping the Cuban economy from doing the obvious and diversifying—that is another story.

When the Revolution made it necessary to tell more, the boundary of respectability shifted leftward. A book like *Cuba: Tragedy in Our Hemisphere,* appearing in 1963, could comment favorably on land reform and touch on the power exercised by the U.S. ambassadors in

[1] Baltimore, Maryland, Johns Hopkins Press, 1951.
[2] *Investment in Cuba, Basic Information for U.S. Businessmen,* Washington, D.C., U.S. Government Printing Office, 1956.

1

Cuba.[3] But there was still a limit. A respectable book could not consider whether Cuba's problems were the inherent result of the presence of American monopolies. It could not examine imperialism as a system—and consequently could not explain the working of the Cuban economy as a whole. It could justify tinkering with the Cuban economy, but it could not follow through to an understanding of what was really necessary to solve Cuba's problems. It spoke of tragedy because it could not look a revolution against American imperialism in the eye.

Many of the specific characteristics of the Cuban economy are by now well known, so they can be summarized here in a few pages.

Sugar dominated the economy. Together with its by-products, alcohol and molasses, sugar made up about 80 percent of the exports and paid for the bulk of the imports. The sugar companies controlled 70 to 75 percent of the arable land; they owned two thirds of the railroad trackage; most of the ports and many of the roads were simply adjuncts of the sugar mills. The sugar industry employed about 25 percent of the labor force. The export of sugar and its by-products constituted 20 to 30 percent of the gross domestic product. But this last percentage does not give sugar its true importance: most of the rest of the gross product depended on sugar.

The sugar industry was seasonal, unstable, and stagnant, and it imparted these characteristics to the whole economy. It employed about four to five hundred thousand workers to cut, load, and transport the cane during the three to four months of the harvest season, and then left them to starve during the rest of the year. The price and demand for sugar rode up and down with war and peace and business cycles, taking the whole Cuban economy with them. Since export outlets for Cuban sugar were growing only slowly, the whole Cuban economy stagnated.

Even apart from sugar, there was great concentration in Cuban exports. When tobacco, minerals, and coffee are added, 94 to 98 percent of total exports is accounted for. Tobacco exports, next in importance

[3] Maurice Zeitlin and Robert Scheer, New York, Grove Press, Inc., 1963.

after sugar, also stagnated; they were about as high in 1957-1958 as in 1920-1921. The earnings from minerals and coffee were small and uncertain.

With exports stagnating, the only way the Cuban economy could have advanced was by increasing production for domestic use. But here again there was little progress. Diversification and growth of agricultural output was blocked by the landholding system. National industry—industry not just physically located in Cuba but integrated into the Cuban economy—was stunted, squeezed in a restricted national market by deadly foreign competition. Some new manufacturing industries producing for the Cuban market were being established, but they were foreign enclaves, appendages of the American or some other foreign economy, and did not help solve Cuba's economic problems.

Most of the land in Cuba was monopolized by huge *latifundia*—sugar plantations and cattle ranches—that sprawled across the countryside. Both sugar grower and rancher practised extensive agriculture which wasted land, limited employment opportunities, and kept agricultural output down.

The sugar industry used for growing cane only about half the total area it controlled; it kept the rest in reserve, either idle or as low-yield natural pasture. To cover fluctuations in the demand for sugar, the industry kept much more acreage under cane than was harvested. Little money was invested in irrigation, little fertilizer was used, and no attempt was made to improve cane varieties. Cane yields per unit of land were among the lowest in the world.

On the large cattle ranches a few cowboys handled enormous herds which roamed over thousands of acres of land. Pastures were not fertilized. There were no silos for storing fodder. In the wet season much grass was wasted; in the dry season when the grass became brown and sparse, the cattle lost weight and milk yields dropped sharply. Outside the Havana basin, most cattle were not milked.

Most of Cuba's rural population and part of her city dwellers subsisted on a diet of rice, beans, and two or three tubers such as *malanga*, with practically no milk or dairy products, eggs, poultry, meat, fruit, or vegetables. To boot, Cuba had to spend large amounts of foreign exchange to import foodstuffs—lard and vegetable oils, rice, beans, potatoes—whose domestic production could have been increased.

The underutilization of labor-power and land in the countryside was enormous. But the idle labor could not get at the idle land because it was monopolized by the *latifundia*. The sugar companies had no interest in the full employment of the rural population. Their interest lay in unemployment. They needed a huge army of labor in reserve in the countryside for the cane-cutting season. One of the reasons they monopolized so much land was to keep the sugar workers from it. If the sugar workers had had access to land they would not have been available at miserable wages whenever the companies needed them.

National industry in Cuba was limited to a few types of goods. There were local slaughterhouses, bakeries, and factories producing milk and dairy products, soft drinks, and candy. Local factories, shops, and cottage industries turned out shoes, clothing, furniture, brick and tile, and a few other clay products such as water jugs and flowerpots. A few factories were large and used modern machinery. But most characteristic were the hundreds of little shops and cottage industries.

How could Cuban national industry grow? The poverty which blanketed the countryside limited the effective demand: over a third of the population did not buy anything other than a few staple foodstuffs and articles of clothing. And into the truncated market that did exist, a flood of goods was poured by the giant corporations of the North.

Cuba's internal market was dominated by imports. Not only did the imports greatly exceed the domestic manufactures in value, but they were infinitely greater in variety. Every conceivable type of goods was imported—from cornflakes to tomato paste; from nails and tacks to tractors, trucks, and automobiles; from thread to all types of clothing; from goods for Sears and other department stores to accessories for the home, fertilizers and insecticides for agriculture, and materials and equipment for industry and construction.

The sugar mills, mines, and almost all the large manufacturing plants in Cuba were foreign enclaves. They pre-empted Cuba's best land, her mineral resources, her raw materials; they dominated the internal market for many products. But they could not give steady employment to a large number of people, and they prevented rather than promoted the creation of a national market.

These enterprises were foreign enclaves even though some of them were owned by Cubans. Whether foreign-owned or Cuban-owned, they were meshed with the American or some other foreign economy; they were dependent on foreign equipment, materials, or markets, and most of their profits were transferred abroad.

The sugar industry—counting the whole complex—employed a total of about half a million people, but it provided year-round work for fewer than 25,000. The nickel plant at Nicaro provided about 1,850 jobs and the copper mine at Matahambre, 1,250;[4] the other mines had fewer employees. For a few thousand jobs and some tax payments, all Cuba's mineral resources were taken over.

The foreign plants turning out cement, tires, paint, soap, detergents, toiletries, bottles, tin cans, paper, and oil and gasoline were typical of most U.S. investment in "manufacturing" in Latin America, and thus especially interesting. I have been through about 25 such plants in Cuba. In their economics, almost all were essentially the same.

They were mechanized or automated, turning out a large output with a small labor force. One plant, employing 30 people mostly engaged in watching instrument panels or sweeping and cleaning, turned out half the detergents consumed in Cuba, with a sales value of several million dollars. Three or four tire plants, each employing about 250 people, monopolized the Cuban tire market. The plants operated with foreign equipment and raw materials which were usually imported in a fabricated state. The tin can plant used imported tinplate; the soap and detergent plants imported fats, alkalis, and silica rock; the tire plants imported rubber, carbon black, etc. The profits were, of course, remitted abroad. And the products went to the upper 15 percent or so of the Cuban population; most Cubans did not have cars on which to put tires or paint, and could not afford canned tomatoes or a 40-cent package of detergent.

[4] *Investment in Cuba*, p. 73.

These plants were established in Cuba for a variety of reasons: to escape customs duties on finished goods, to get a more secure grip on the internal market, to be able to continue to use machinery that had already been written off as obsolete in the United States. They were technically impressive, even when the machinery was obsolete by American standards. They blew up the local production statistics. But they provided jobs for less than 3 percent of the Cuban labor force. Their economic effect was not much different from that of the packaging which a sales representative performs locally on goods brought in from abroad. These plants were little more than disguised American export operations.

The most striking examples of foreign enclaves in the Cuban economy were the three large oil refineries owned by Standard Oil, Texaco, and Shell. With their large control rooms full of instrument panels; their mazes of pipes, towers, tanks, and furnaces all operating automatically; their tankers, internal railroad systems, and trucks; their cleanliness and order, they were little communities unto themselves—marvels of technology. The value added by these refineries to the imported crude oil and other materials with which they worked was over $50 million a year, and this amount went into the statistics as Cuban output. Many an economic report has discussed the growth of "the Cuban economy" on the basis of these statistics. But in what sense was the output of these refineries Cuban? They employed fewer than 3,000 people, and most of those in the higher positions were foreigners.

The composition of Cuba's imports also reflected the basic split in the Cuban economy between foreign and national. Less than 20 percent of Cuban imports consisted of items serving the needs of the mass of the people, such as rice, lard, beans, codfish, cloth, and medicines. Little foreign exchange went for economic development. Eighty percent of Cuban imports went to the upper classes and the large corporations, whose products either went abroad or also to the upper classes. Tens of millions of dollars went for goods which, in a country as poor as Cuba, can only be classified as luxuries: passenger cars, air conditioners, record players, fancy foodstuffs. In 1957 when total imports were $770 million, $30 million were spent on passenger cars alone. Over $60 million went for petroleum to refine into gasoline to run the cars, and into fuel oil to produce electricity to run the air conditioners and other appliances.

The whole way of life of the Cuban well-to-do depended on American goods, and the market they formed was also an enclave. Most Cubans, and almost all rural Cubans, lived in a different world. A survey taken by the Catholic University in 1956 showed that average per capita income in the countryside, including homegrown food supplies, was less than $100 per year.

It is evident even from the telling that these characteristics of the Cuban economy were not accidents; they were interrelated. The sugar plantations, the sugar mills, the sugar railroads and ports, and the sugar boats were all links in a chain; so also were the large import houses, the foreign plants pumping goods into the Cuban market, the mines, the tourist industry, the banking business. And at the other end of the chain stood the giant foreign corporations—American imperialism.

It was the monopolies that geared the Cuban economy to sugar, dominated its resources, suffocated its industry with the goods they pumped in, and drained out its foreign exchange for luxuries.

The monopolies did not deliberately plot to strangle Cuba. They simply acted naturally. They made sure of the land and labor they needed, took control of mineral resources the way monopolies do everywhere, secured easy access into Cuba for their exports. They took control of resources and markets not only for their own use but to deny them to others. And just by being themselves, by taking normal advantage of their size and strength to promote their interests, the monopolies could not help but strangle the Cuban economy.

What could possibly be the result of competition for resources and markets between the giant corporations of the United States and the small economic units of Cuba? What sort of competition could Cuban workshops offer Westinghouse or General Motors? Just by selling goods in Cuba, the American giants were stunting the growth of Cuban industry.

It was inevitable that the monopolies would turn the Cuban economy into an appendage of the American economy. Their Cuban operations were only part of their total operations and their aim was profits—maximum profits on their operations as a whole. They were not interested in how their operations fitted into the Cuban economy, or how to develop that economy. They had to fit their Cuban operations into their total operations in the way that would make the most money.

What could the sugar companies be expected to do in Cuba other than what they did? Should they have produced a diversity of agricultural products for the Cuban market? They were in Cuba for a different purpose. They had positions of great value in the American sugar market, and to realize the most out of these positions, they needed control of a supply of sugar. The production of diversified products for the Cuban market was irrelevant to this need.

The corporations exporting to Cuba were also acting in accordance with business principles. Their job was to sell Cadillacs or whiskey, not to worry whether the importing country could put its foreign exchange to better uses than providing luxuries to a privileged foreign-oriented minority.

Decisions about investment in Cuba were also governed by the interests of the foreign corporations. Why put a plant in Cuba at all if the Cuban market could just as easily be supplied from the United States? And when a plant did get established in Cuba it was bound to be part of a broader complex. There were no good business reasons for setting up integrated, self-sufficient operations in Cuba. On the contrary, the plant which depended on foreign raw materials and spare parts was a safer risk against nationalization.

The very size and strength of the foreign corporations meant the loss for Cuba not only of her economic independence, but also of her political independence. Can there be any true independence for a poor country—especially a small one like Cuba—which has guests like United Fruit and Standard Oil?

Like the giant corporations, the U.S. government also acted naturally in Cuba. It pushed through reciprocal trade agreements so that American goods would have no difficulty entering Cuba. It promoted a monetary policy that permitted profits to be taken out with no trouble. It prevented Cuba from maintaining diplomatic relations with the socialist countries and pressured her into keeping trade with them at a minimum.

Throughout the years, the U.S. government promoted and defended American investment in Cuba, keeping a watchful eye on anything that might threaten that investment—attempts to limit the rights of foreign business, to increase tariffs or taxes, to lower electric power and telephone rates, to regulate the discharge of workers. The United States government used its influence to defeat Cuban legislation that was unfavorable to American business—or saw to it that if such legislation did happen to pass, it was not enforced. And it made sure of Cuban governments that were friendly to American business. What the United States government did in Cuba was no different from what it does in all countries to the extent that its strength permits.

Until 1934 the Platt Amendment, which had been forced into the Cuban constitution in 1901 by the United States, gave the United States the right to "intervene" in Cuba for "the maintenance of a government adequate for the protection of life, property, and individual liberty." There were many gross interventions. The United States landed troops in Cuba in 1906, 1912, and 1917.

In 1933, when the Cuban people began to move toward open revolt against Machado, "the Butcher," the United States sent Sumner Welles as a special ambassador to try to save his regime. Welles tried; he felt at first that the removal of Machado would mean "chaos"—the destruction of American property. But when he saw that Machado could not be saved, Welles employed a maneuver often used by the United States when it finds that a dictator it has supported has outlived his usefulness; he organized a palace revolt, a movement among army leaders and conservative politicians to replace Machado with someone else satisfactory to Washington. The maneuver worked for a while. Machado was removed by an army *coup d'état* which placed a conservative approved by Welles in the Cuban Presidency. But within a few weeks the new regime was overthrown. A "radical" government headed by Grau San Martín came to power and began to institute reforms. Washington found this government unsatisfactory and denied it recognition while Welles and his successor worked to replace it. A number of American warships were sent into Cuban waters and units of the Marines were mobilized. Again American officials connived with the Cuban Army and within a few months Batista was installed in power.

But United States intervention in Cuba did not really depend on the Platt Amendment. The United States has engaged in countless armed interventions—in Santo Domingo, Mexico, Nicaragua, and throughout the world—without Platt Amendments. Also, there is more to intervention than shows up when it becomes necessary to resort to armed force. There is the ordinary day-to-day action of the U.S. government and its embassies abroad—the exertion of influence and pressure in a thousand ways on local newspapers, businessmen, legislatures, government officials, and army officers. The United States was constantly intervening in Cuba.

The U.S. government was unconcerned about what it meant for the Cuban people to live under a dictatorship. What the U.S. government wanted in Cuba was the "order," "tranquility," and "favorable investment climate" required by American business. Whenever these conditions could best be attained by dictatorship the United States supported dictatorship. In Cuba this meant supporting dictatorship most of the time. The U.S. government only turned against a dictator when it was necessary to do so because he could no longer hold on.

Many liberal writers have commented on the intimacy with Batista of United States Ambassadors Arthur Gardner and Earl E. T. Smith, as though this were an idiosyncrasy of these individual ambassadors. These writers seem unaware that there were communications, a steady flow of instructions and reports, between Washington and Havana. Washington's repudiation of dictators after they have fallen means nothing. Its real attitude comes out in a publication like *Investment in Cuba*, written for businessmen without much demagogy. During the 1940's, complains this volume, "the whole machinery of government was geared to favor labor. . . . The situation improved materially during the period 1953-1955. A more balanced emphasis in government policy brought the interests of labor, capital, and the public into better focus."[5] The "balanced emphasis" came when Batista took over for the second time in 1953; the fact that he came to power through a *coup d'état* and was a dictator was not considered relevant.

For some writers, the central element in the development of the Cuban Revolution is American *policy*. William Appleman Williams, who has sympathies with the Revolution, writes: "Had American policy in action between 1895 and 1959 actually been successful by its own standards, then there would have been no Castro and no CIA invasion."[6] American policy in Cuba did not live up to its "professed morality," did not measure up to its "responsibilities." American power was used to stifle, rather than promote, development. Both the outbreak of the Revolution and the course it took are the results of "failure of policy."

Williams hardly deals with the role of the corporations either in holding down Cuba or dominating the U.S. government. For him, the U.S. government is "we" and its policy is "our" policy. "We" are moral, responsible people who will listen to a reasonable explanation of what we have done wrong. By providing such an explanation, policy can be changed and the problems solved.

But Cuba's problems—its underdevelopment and poverty, its lack of independence—did not result from any policy or failure of policy. They resulted from the simple presence of the U.S. monopolies and the monopoly-dominated U.S. government engaged in their normal business. They resulted from imperialism. Imperialism is not a policy; it is a system.

Imperialism was the framework on which everything in Cuba was built—not just the economy, but also the political and social structure.

[5] *Ibid.*, p. 21.
[6] *The United States, Cuba, and Castro*, Monthly Review Press, New York, 1962, p. 1.

"Until the advent of Castro," according to Earl E. T. Smith, "the United States was so overwhelmingly influential in Cuba that . . . the American Ambassador was the second most important man in Cuba, sometimes even more important than the president [of Cuba]."[7] Even this statement blurs the realities. The "sometimes" when the Ambassador was more important than the President was anytime something basic was at issue. American imperialism wielded the ultimate power in Cuba. Cubans were allowed a certain amount of choice —so long as they chose presidents and governments acceptable to the United States.

The class structure of Cuba was not just a matter of the traditional division into bourgeoisie, proletariat, and peasantry, but also of relations with imperialism. Cutting across the traditional divisions was the line between those who benefited from imperialism and those who suffered from it. The richest, most powerful groups derived their wealth and power from imperialism. Those groups which did not enjoy the favors of imperialism tended to be poor and weak.

All but a small part of Cuba's upper classes were dependent on activities tied to the United States. There were the magnates of the sugar industry, owners of the sugar centrals and *latifundia*. The big importers, the core of the urban oligarchy, had a magnificent source of income in the hundreds of millions of dollars worth of goods imported each year. The bankers depended for most of their business on the export of sugar and tobacco and on imports. The real estate operators depended on the oligarchy and the government for most of their business and on the United States for equipment and many construction materials.

Most retail stores, other than the small ones in wooden shacks, depended on imports. For block after block in Havana and on the main streets of the other cities, the window displays were filled with American goods: appliances, eyeglasses, toys, tools, Arrow shirts. Many restaurants depended on tourists for their business and on imports for the food they served. It is a mistake to equate the Cuban

<hr/>

[7] Testimony before the Senate Subcommittee to Investigate the Administration of the Internal Security Act, as quoted by Robert F. Smith in *What Happened in Cuba? A Documentary History*, Twayne Publishers, Inc., New York, 1963, p. 273.

storekeeper with the owner of an American store of the same type and size. In a poor country like Cuba, the storekeeper was much higher on the economic and social scale; but even more important, he depended—often for his very economic existence—on foreign imperialism.

For whom did the financially successful professionals work in Cuba? Where were the jobs and the money? The most expensive lawyers worked for the big companies, the big importers and commercial speculators, the real estate operators. The engineers and chemists worked for the large foreign-owned or foreign-oriented sugar companies, manufacturing plants, or mines. The architects worked for the real estate companies, the rich, or the government. And the doctors, dentists, and nurses served the rich and middle classes, most of whose income was tied directly or indirectly to imperialism.

Many employees and even some workers in the foreign companies got salaries and wages which by Cuban standards were high. In the capital-intensive, automated plants the cost of granting good pay was small. Many of these employees and workers developed a strong interest in their own favored position.

Now let us cross the imperialist divide in Cuban society. What can be considered a national bourgeoisie was weak and small; it did not have enough of a base in national industry and commerce on which to rest. The owners of the little—often family-operated—shops and factories turning out bread, shoes, dresses, furniture, etc., were not really in the same class as the sugar magnates, the big importers, and the bankers. And there were not enough of them to make up for their individual weakness, to make them in the aggregate into a force that could worry imperialism and its local partners.

There were thousands of small retail enterprises in Cuba—in wooden shacks or outdoor stalls and stands—selling fruits and vegetables, sugar cane juice, fruit drinks, peanuts, fried banana chips and pigskin, oyster and shrimp cocktails, handkerchiefs, shoelaces, and other cheap articles. The operators of these enterprises constituted a very different group from the owners of the conventional stores selling imported goods. Many of them had lower incomes and a more precarious economic position than the higher-paid workers in the foreign plants.

Outside the foreign enclave, the opportunities for professionals in Cuba were limited. The local cottage industry did not need technicians and the poor could not afford doctors. According to *Investment in Cuba*, Cuba had "slightly less than half as many professional, managerial, and service workers, proportionately, as the United States." Of the 70,000 people listed as professionals by the Cuban Census of 1952, half were primary school teachers; teachers accounted for twice as high a percentage of all professionals as in the United States.[8]

Most city workers, in the cottage industries and small shops, on the docks, and in the transportation system received much smaller wages than the elite in the large foreign companies. Nevertheless, they were better off than the vast majority of those engaged in agriculture.

About two thirds of Cuba's farmers were tenants, sharecroppers, and squatters. Historically, the peasants had been thrown off the land when the cattle ranches and sugar estates were formed. They had an interest in land reform, in the expropriation of the large estates, including the choice lands of the large foreign sugar companies.

Finally there was the largest, most homogeneous, and poorest bloc of the Cuban proletariat: the workers in the cane fields—a proletariat created by the sugar industry. Although the workers in the cane fields and those in the electric power industry were both proletarians, their positions differed greatly. The electric power workers enjoyed privileges which the foreign corporations had found it expedient to grant in order to soften the opposition to imperialism. But there could be no privileges for the sugar workers. The profits of the large companies and the functioning of the sugar industry required that they be kept in misery.

To what extent could the ills of the Cuban economy have been cured through reforms? How far could a Cuban government go in curing the Cuban economy without coming into conflict with American imperialism?

What reforms? Would a wage increase for the sugar workers who were unemployed six to nine months a year have solved any basic

[8] *Investment in Cuba*, pp. 182 and 183.

problems? With such heavy unemployment, could a meaningful system of social insurance have been set up? Suppose it had been possible to carry out a tax reform. What would it have meant?

Take economic development. How far could Cuba have gone with the standard recipes? It already had an excellent "investment climate." "The main manufacturing opportunities," said *Investment in Cuba*, "await the development of new and improved applications for sugarcane products. . . ."[9] But a few factories making paper or wax from cane would not constitute significant industrialization. Cuba's need for economic development could not be met by creating the type of development bank sponsored by the United States—a bank which can lend money only for nonindustrial projects, for projects outside the domain belonging to private enterprise.

Cuba needed land reform. But a true land reform is not a technical measure that can be accomplished to the satisfaction of everybody. A true land reform means taking the land away from the large estates and making it available to the people. A true land reform hurts; it changes the balance of political power; it begins a process of broader change. A true land reform is not a *reform*; it is a *revolutionary* measure.

Cuba could not afford artificial restrictions on its foreign market. Population was growing steadily. Unless the foreign market expanded, the Cuban economy would go backward. Cuba had to break the U.S. monopoly of its foreign trade.

Cuba needed full independence and sovereignty—not simply as a matter of justice and freedom, but also for practical economic reasons. The task of economic development is complicated enough for free countries; it cannot be accomplished by a country that is hamstrung by foreign domination.

Could the large foreign corporations in Cuba have been reformed? Could they have been prevented from acting according to business principles? Could they have been subjected to anything more than minor controls which would not have touched the heart of Cuba's problems?

What could a Cuban government have done to solve Cuba's prob-

[9] *Ibid.*, p. 8.

lems without touching some American interest? It could not have regulated public utility rates, touched the land, broadened foreign trade, imposed foreign exchange controls, increased taxes, raised tariffs, subsidized new industry. It could not have changed the charter and policies of the National Bank and tried to use it to promote development; nor could it have greatly increased public expenditures for education or medical care—such actions would have endangered the kind of monetary stability required by the foreign corporations. It could not have promulgated and enforced laws against racial discrimination because this would have interfered with the tourist business. American interests were so omnipresent in Cuba that if a Cuban government were to try to make any significant reforms, it was bound to collide with one or another of these interests. And given the nature of the United States government, what could be expected from it in the event of a collision?

No matter where you start probing the Cuban economy, if you cut at all deep you will hit the core of the malignancy—American imperialism. Cuba had many problems. But its chief problem was the United States. The precondition for being able to make a serious attack on Cuba's specific problems was the elimination of imperialism. A true revolution in Cuba had to be a revolution against American imperialism.

2

The Movement to Socialism

The kind of government necessary to make a serious attack on Cuba's problems could only be a revolutionary government, a government capable of carrying through the struggle against imperialism.

A liberal government simply could not have attacked the problems. Such a government would have had middle-class leaders and almost all middle-class leaders in Cuba were on the side of imperialism. The middle-class leaders were not ruffians like Batista. But what could they have done about the economy? Would they have had the interest and the vision necessary to confront Cuba's real problems, to say nothing of the stomach for a struggle with the United States? With the traditional army in existence they could not have waged such a struggle even if they had wanted to.

The key event of the Cuban Revolution was the capture of state power through an armed struggle by the people led by honest, resolute revolutionaries. Most of the rest of the development of the Revolution flowed from this event and Cuba's situation.

No one who has met, or closely observed, any of the leaders of the Revolution can have any doubts about their honesty or resolution. No fair-minded reader of Fidel's famous *History Will Absolve Me* speech of 1953 can fail to be impressed with its humanity, its fiery determinaion to get at Cuba's problems.

History Will Absolve Me is the speech of a revolutionary. It proclaims the right to rebel. It propounds revolution. It says that revolution does not mean "those small disorders which a group of dissatisfied people provoke in order to take from some their political plums or economic advantages." It means "profound changes in the social organism."

The revolution, says the speech, counts on the people. And "the people means the vast unredeemed masses to whom all make promises and whom all deceive." The people means the five hundred thousand farm laborers who work four months a year and starve for eight; the four hundred thousand industrial laborers and dock workers whose housing consists of one room, whose salaries go from the hands of the employer to those of the moneylender; the hundred thousand small farmers who live and die working on land that is not theirs; the thirty thousand teachers and professors who are so badly treated and paid; the twenty thousand small businessmen overwhelmed by debts; the ten thousand young professionals who come forth from school with their degrees, anxious to work and full of hope, only to find themselves at a dead end.

The speech lists the problems to be solved: land, industrialization, housing, unemployment, education, and health. And it says that these problems cannot be solved by mouthing phrases like freedom of enterprise, guarantees to investment capital, and the law of supply and demand.

When the leaders of the Revolution went into the Sierra, they already knew about imperialism. Only Americans can have any doubts about this; in Latin America, at the other end of the stick, all people who worry seriously about the problems of their countries know about imperialism.

Fidel—as he later pointed out—had studied Lenin's *State and Revolution*. In that book he read:

"The state is the product and the manifestation of the *irreconcilability* of class antagonisms. . . .

"A standing army and police force are the chief instruments of state power."

Every revolution "demonstrates to us how the ruling class strives to restore the special bodies of armed men which serve *it* and how the oppressed class strives to create a new organization of this kind capable of serving not the exploiters but the exploited."

A revolution must "regard the problem, not as one of perfecting the state machine, but one of *smashing* and *destroying* it." The oppressed classes must "smash the old bureaucratic machine at once and

. . . begin immediately to construct a new one." (Emphasis in original.)

Major Guevara was also deeply interested in the relationships between the state, the armed forces, and revolution. He had witnessed the use of the traditional army to overthrow the reformist Arbenz government in Guatemala in 1954 and had pondered the lessons of the experience.

Their understanding of the Marxist theory of the state and revolution is one of the master keys to the strategy and tactics of the Cuban revolutionary leaders from the early days in the Sierra to the economic reorganization of the government several years after they had come to power.

The tactics in the Sierra were flexible. To win, the Revolution needed the support of the masses. This support was there to be had: the people of Cuba were profoundly discontented, ready for revolutionary change. But though the revolutionary potential was deep, it was unformed; the people wanted change, but they were not clear just what change they wanted. As a result of American influence, many were prejudiced against socialism. The leaders of the Revolution had to know the people and talk to them in terms they were ready to understand.

At the time of the Sierra, there were many forces opposing Batista that were not revolutionary, starting with those who were against him simply because he had kept them out of his government. The problem for the leaders of the Revolution was to promote the broadest possible unity in the struggle against Batista without giving up essentials, or losing the leadership of the movement. Some weight had to be given to nonrevolutionary groups; sometimes compromises had to be made.

This helps to explain the first major political declaration from the Sierra, the so-called manifesto of 1957. This was a weak, watery document. For example, it talked about an agrarian reform that "tends to the distribution of barren lands . . . with prior indemnification of former owners." This manifesto resulted from a visit to the Sierra of Felipe Pazos, former president of the National Bank of Cuba, and

Raúl Chibás, younger brother of a respected political leader who had committed suicide in protest against the rottenness of Cuba's government. As Che Guevara tells it, Fidel tried to get them to agree to a more radical declaration on land reform, but they were adamant. "We knew," says Guevara, "that it was a minimum program which limited our efforts, but we also knew that it was not possible to establish our will from the Sierra Maestra and that we would have to reckon for a long period with a series of 'friends' who would try to use our military force and the great confidence that the people already felt for Fidel for their own macabre manipulations."[1]

But the leaders of the Revolution were far from pursuing unity at any price. A few months after the manifesto a number of Cuban exiles signed a so-called unity pact in Miami. Felipe Pazos and two others signed in the name of the 26th of July Movement, saying that they had authority to do so. When Fidel saw the pact, he sent a letter bluntly rejecting and denouncing it. "The important thing for the revolution," said the letter, "is not unity itself, but rather the bases of such unity." One paragraph is of special importance: "In the document of unity our declaration refusing any kind of military junta to govern the Republic has been eliminated. The most disastrous thing that could happen at this time is the replacement of Batista by a military junta, because it would be accompanied by the illusion that Cuba's problems would be solved merely by the absence of the dictator."

As the Revolution moved on, things changed. The Revolution itself began to revolutionize the people. The balance of force among the anti-Batista forces began to shift. In July 1958, Fidel was able to sign a satisfactory unity pact. One of its paragraphs agreed on "the adoption of a common strategy to defeat the dictatorship by means of armed insurrection, reinforcing, as soon as possible, all the combat fronts and arming the thousands of Cubans willing to fight for freedom."

Fidel explained later in his speech on Marxism-Leninism: "We were

---

[1] Ernesto Che Guevara, *Pasajes de la Guerra Revolucionaria*, Havana, Ediciones Unión, Narraciones, 1963.

always worried that since the revolutionary forces were not yet developed, a military coup would take place through the maneuvers of imperialism and reaction." So everyone was put on notice that "we would never accept a coup, that we reserved the right to clean out, reorganize, and rebuild the armed forces of the republic."

Sure enough, a last-minute attempt at a coup was made. When Batista fled, he left a letter of resignation appointing Carlos M. Piedra, a senior justice of the supreme court, President of Cuba. One of Batista's chief generals began to work immediately on setting up a military junta to be headed by Piedra. But Fidel quickly made a radio broadcast in which he instructed the commanders of the Rebel Army to continue fighting until the Batista forces surrendered unconditionally, and asked the people to prepare for a general strike against an attempt at a "counter-revolutionary coup."

Batista's armed forces began to crumble. One army surrendered to Major Guevara in Santa Clara. Fidel's army marched into Santiago and accepted the surrender of the forces at Fort Moncada. In Havana volunteer youths of the underground 26th of July Movement walked into the police stations and took over. Then, a day later, the Rebel Army arrived. Major Guevara took over the Cabaña fortress, across the bay from Havana, and Major Camilo Cienfuegos took over Camp Columbia, the army headquarters.

"Victory," writes Major Guevara, "cannot be considered as finally won until the army that sustained the former regime has been systematically and totally smashed . . . not even a skeleton of personnel from the former army can be retained."[2] The Rebel Army proceeded immediately to dismember the old army and to enlarge and reorganize itself for the tasks ahead.

Because the Revolution swept to power by defeating Batista's army and was backed by an aroused people, it had a firmer grip on state power than could have come from any election. Imperialism and its local allies held the financial and economic resources. Middle-class leaders in the opposition to Batista enjoyed some prestige, but it was

[2] Che Guevara, *Guerrilla Warfare*, New York, Monthly Review Press, 1961, p. 112.

eclipsed by that of Fidel and the other leaders of the Sierra. The Revolution had the Rebel Army. And it had a tremendous potential source of strength: it could arm the people.

From the time the Revolution came to power, there was no internal force in Cuba that could challenge it. The middle-class leaders in the early Revolutionary Government were there on the sufferance of the revolutionaries. A few people were against the Revolution from the beginning and more would fall out further along the march. But no internal opposition, counting on its own forces, could even dream of overthrowing the Revolution. The victory over Batista meant that the Cuban people had done away with the local overseer; now they confronted the owner of the plantation—American imperialism.

When the Revolution came to power in January 1959, the situation was essentially as follows: Between American imperialism and the Cuban people there was a fundamental and irreconcilable conflict of interest—a conflict that could only be settled by the Cubans surrendering their hopes for the future or by imperialism giving way. The leaders of the Revolution were determined men, backed by a courageous people who were fired by a growing vision of better things to come. The leaders of the U.S. government, while puzzled and troubled by the success of the Revolution, were confident that the overwhelming strength of the United States would enable it to control the situation. The drama began to unfold immediately.

The Revolutionary Government ran through most of the possibilities for reform in a few months. In January 1959, electric power rates for rural areas were cut in half. In February, mortgage rates were reduced. In March, rents on housing and telephone rates were lowered. This same month saw the creation of a National Institute of Savings and Housing (INAV) to build urban housing, and a National Tourist Commission (INIT) to promote tourism and expand tourist facilities. A Vacant Lot Law was passed to wipe out appreciation in the market value of urban real estate in excess of 15 percent.

Some of these reforms were radical, but they were still only reforms. This did not stop criticisms from the United States. From the time the Revolution took power, objections and complaints flowed in —against the trials of the Batista war criminals, against the reduction of electric power and telephone rates, against the law cutting down rents.

The United States government was warily watching the revolutionaries, trying to size them up. More than one official made up his mind early. Former Vice President Richard M. Nixon wrote: "I had had a three-hour conference with Castro when he visited Washington, back in April 1959. After that conference, I wrote a confidential memorandum for distribution to the CIA, State Department, and White House. In it I stated flatly that I was convinced Castro was 'either incredibly naive about Communism or under Communist discipline' and that we would have to treat and deal with him accordingly."[3]

With each new development in the Revolution, the people learned. Fidel spoke often, explaining things. Many who have little knowledge either of Cuba or its language have ridiculed the length of Fidel's speeches, but he was helping to educate the people—above all the simple people—in the meaning and problems of the Revolution.

Within six weeks after the Revolution had come to power, Fidel had covered a number of themes.[4] One of the first was simply that a Revolution was taking place. Fidel repeated this over and over. Batista was not overthrown by a *coup d'état* but by a revolution. A *coup d'état* is not a revolution. A *coup d'état* removes the president, removes the principal chiefs, but leaves the police, leaves the soldiers, leaves the old machinery of the state. *Coups d'état* are common in almost all the countries of Latin America, but revolutions have been rare. *Coups d'état* are the work of a few military leaders, but revolutions are made by the people. A *coup d'état* makes no basic change, but the Cuban Revolution means a total transformation of the nation. On January 2, 1959, the day after the Revolution came to power, Fidel said: The Revolution begins now. It will be difficult and full of dangers.

[3] Richard M. Nixon, *Six Crises*, New York, Pocket Books, Inc., 1962, p. 379.
[4] All of the paraphrases or quotations in the following paragraphs are taken from speeches made by Fidel from January 2 through February 17, 1959, given in *Discursos del Dr. Fidel Castro Ruz, Comandante en Jefe del Ejército Rebelde, 26 de Julio y Primer Ministro del Gobierno Revolucionario*, Oficina del Historiador de la Ciudad de la Habana, 1959.

Soon a second theme followed: Henceforth Cuba would be run by Cubans. The American press and the American international press agencies were waging a campaign against the revolutionary trials and executions of the Batista war criminals. Fidel first answered in a speech to the Havana Rotary Club on January 15, 1959. The purpose of this campaign is to discredit the Revolution; the so-called problem of the executions is just a pretext. Those who are carrying on this campaign are afraid of the Revolution; they are afraid of its hold on international public opinion, especially in Latin America. Fidel detailed some of the crimes that had been committed in Cuba. He referred to the war crimes trials held by the victors after the Second World War. The problem of the crimes committed under Batista is a Cuban problem; Cubans will settle it. The day of control of Cuba's destiny by foreigners is over. Fidel noted that an American magazine had said that American intervention in Cuba was not necessarily a thing of the past. If there is an intervention, answered Fidel, we will defend ourselves.

A week later in a speech to a crowd of over a million, Fidel returned to the subject. The Revolution, he said, will not weaken in the face of attack, but rather grow and become stronger. The international news monopolies never attacked Cuba when it was ruled by a dictator who made the most onerous concessions to foreigners, a criminal under whom 20,000 of our compatriots were killed, a thief who stole $300 million. There is Trujillo and his dictatorship of twenty-seven years; there is Somoza oppressing his country for more than twenty-five years—no press campaigns are organized against them. They are mounting a campaign against the people of Cuba because they know we are going to request the annulment of the onerous concessions that have been made to foreign monopolies.

Fidel also touched in this speech on the broader meaning of the Cuban Revolution. "I am only sorry to think of what would be the destiny of America if this Revolution is crushed. . . . How much do the peoples of our Continent need a Revolution like this one which has been made in Cuba!"

Fidel also discussed in those early weeks many of Cuba's specific problems—vice, unemployment, housing, industrialization. His approach was radical. "Many speak of unemployment, but few say what the remedy is. . . . Many speak of industrialization but also do not provide a solution. With public works, it is not possible to solve the problem of almost a million unemployed." Many of those who write on unemployment do not discuss the fundamental question of land reform, do not say that to get rid of unemployment it is necessary to liquidate the *latifundia*. But the Revolutionary Government, said Fidel, is preparing a land reform. "The United Fruit Company and all the *companies* [Fidel used the English word] which have thousands and thousands of *caballerías* of land will cry to the heavens when they have to part with them and then they will really be writing against us."

To the middle-class leaders in the early Revolutionary Government, who were really representatives of the oligarchy, this talk of revolution was anathema. They could only have swallowed such talk if it had been demagogy. To them it was simple immaturity and lack of realism for the Cuban Government to offend the United States. They could only become more and more uncomfortable as the Revolution moved on, as they saw that the revolutionary leaders would not give way before the United States, as the land reform came closer. They had no solutions to Cuba's problems, no true alternatives to propose. All they could do was pull backwards, promote disunity, and leave.

But the people were now in motion the other way. They first developed a general revolutionary spirit. They were ready to fight for Cuba's right to determine her own destiny before they knew what that destiny was to be. They were ready to begin tearing down the old system before they knew what to put in its place.

As the Revolution developed, those who had wanted the removal of Batista and little more turned against the Revolution. The Revolution lost a few in numbers but gained in depth. The people became ever more radical.

The first major economic measures of the Revolution were land reform and the diversification of foreign trade. The Land Reform Law was promulgated on June 3, 1959. Within days thereafter, action began on foreign trade, when Major Guevara set out for various socialist countries, as well as Egypt, India, and Japan, with the aim of broadening markets for Cuban products. In August 170,000 tons of sugar were sold to the Soviet Union and in October 330,000 tons more.

With the publication of the Land Reform Law, the United States sent a note expressing its grave concern and regretting that the Revolutionary Government had not consulted with American investors before promulgating the law. The first armed attacks by counter-revolutionaries came in June and small planes began to fly in from Florida and drop incendiary bombs on sugar mills and cane fields. At about this time, Cuba began to have difficulties in buying arms and airplanes: the United States was exerting pressure on other countries not to sell them to Cuba.

American objections were also voiced to the sale of sugar to the Soviet Union. In a speech on October 21, 1959, Fidel presented the position of the Revolution on foreign trade. "We have," he said, "a splendid future if we hold open all doors to the commerce of the world. . . . Because the last straw is to demand that a people not sustain relations with the rest of the world and at the same time threaten her with not buying what she produces. . . . This is to put a country in a position of political and economic subordination to another, since the truth is that there can be no political independence without economic independence."

Fidel's speech was made in an atmosphere of increasing hostility. The practical application of the Land Reform Law began with the taking over of the cattle ranches that got under way in the fall of 1959, and hostility grew sharper as this process went on. From the beginning, the Cuban leaders had been given to understand that Cuba depended economically on the sale of sugar to the United States. Now the Cuban sugar quota in the United States market was brandished more and more openly as a weapon of intimidation. The specter of a possible armed attack on the Revolution began to take shape, and in October the Revolutionary Government took the first steps toward the formation of a People's Militia.

Cuba's great waste of foreign exchange had always cried out for correction, but now the growing difficulties with the United States, and the possible loss of the sugar quota made the conservation of the dollar reserves doubly important. Major Guevara became president of the Cuban National Bank in November 1959, and on the 27th of that month a resolution establishing a system of import licenses was issued. Under this system the importation of a large number of nonessential goods was stopped. At about this time, American exporters, who had been granting ordinary short-term credit to Cuban buyers, began to insist on immediate cash payment.

Early in 1960, the doors to Cuban commerce really began to swing open. A mission from the Soviet Union, headed by Anastas Mikoyan, arrived on February 4, and ten days later trade, payments, and credit agreements were signed between Cuba and the Soviet Union.

The Soviet Union agreed to purchase one million tons of sugar in each of the years 1960-1965. The first million tons would be paid for completely with goods, the remainder 80 percent with goods and 20 percent with dollars. Among the goods to be delivered by the Soviet Union were oil, machinery and equipment, wheat, newsprint, and various chemical products. The Soviet Union granted Cuba a credit of $100 million for the purchase of plants and equipment. Interest on the credit was 2.5 percent a year and it was to be amortized over ten years.

This agreement constituted a virtual declaration of political and economic independence by Cuba. But more was involved than simply the achievement of sovereignty, about which Cuban patriots had brooded for so long. It had become fully clear that the Revolution was engaged in a life or death struggle with the United States. The agreement was also a preparatory measure against economic warfare by the United States aimed at choking the Revolution to death.

A series of transactions and agreements was also completed with other socialist countries. In January 1960, 50,000 tons of sugar were sold to China. This was, in a way, an even greater act of independence than the agreement with the Soviet Union, since in the eyes of U.S. imperialism China was, even then, a worse villain than the Soviet Union. In February trade and payments agreements were signed with East Germany, in March with Poland, and in June with Czechoslovakia.

During this period in which commercial relations with the socialist countries were being established, it was officially emphasized that the increase in commerce with other countries did not signify any intention of reducing commerce with the United States. The purpose was to increase Cuba's foreign commerce by broadening its base.

In 1960 Cuba was spending over $70 million on the import of oil and its products. This item alone constituted roughly 10 percent of total imports. To obtain oil for goods instead of dollars would greatly benefit Cuba's dollar balance. In April, 300,000 tons of petroleum were purchased from the Soviet Union under the trade agreement signed in February. But when the Cuban Government asked the three oil companies (Standard Oil, Texaco, and Shell) to accept Soviet crude oil at their refineries, they refused—a move which had clearly been concerted among themselves and with the U.S. State Department. In obvious preparation for battle, they were allowing their inventories of crude oil to fall and sending wives, children, and many American employees back to the United States. They were hoping to create an oil scarcity in Cuba. And they were counting on the use by the U.S. Government of even stronger weapons, if necessary.

When the companies persisted in their refusal to accept Soviet oil, the Revolutionary Government "intervened"—i.e., took over—the refineries in the last few days of June. Although the stocks of crude oil had fallen to dangerously low levels, a shortage of oil never developed. A few days after the interventions the first Soviet tanker sailed past the lighthouse of the Morro Castle into the Bay of Havana.

The situation was now moving to a climax, with a number of things developing simultaneously—U.S. action on the sugar quota, the threat of armed intervention by the U.S., trade talks with Soviet and Chinese officials, Cuban nationalization of American enterprises. The air of Havana had become electric.

In January 1960, a bill had been introduced in the U.S. Congress, giving President Eisenhower the power to eliminate the sugar quota. At the end of June, just as this bill was being finally approved, Prime Minister Castro announced: "They will take away our quota pound by pound and we will take away their sugar mills one by one." At the beginning of July, the Cuban Government gave the Prime Minister and President of Cuba the power to nationalize American properties in Cuba if the sugar quota was cut off.

On July 7, President Eisenhower eliminated the Cuban sugar quota for 1960, of which 700,000 tons remained to be sold. So ended an era and the idea that Cuba was tied to the United States and to her miserable lot by geography and fate. Until the Revolution almost no one would have found it conceivable that Cuba could survive without the sugar quota. But the Cuban people had come a long way in a short time. Now throughout Havana there appeared the slogan: *sin cuota, pero sin amo*—without a quota, but without a master.

Since the early spring of 1960, the menace of American armed intervention in Cuba had been growing. Richard M. Nixon wrote, as of the fall presidential campaign, that "for months the CIA had not only been supporting and assisting but actually training Cuban exiles for the eventual purpose of supporting an invasion of Cuba itself."[5]

In March 1960, Fidel thundered that Cuba was not Guatemala where the CIA had been able to overthrow the Arbenz government. In April he again talked of U.S. plans to overthrow the Revolution. And in his May Day speech he warned that the United States was preparing an armed aggression against Cuba, using as a pretext alleged Cuban preparations to attack Guatemala. "They want to destroy the Cuban Revolution," he said, "so that the example of the Cuban Revolution cannot be followed by the sister nations of Latin America."

On May 14, Secretary of State Herter denied that the United States had "plans for aggression against the government of Cuba." But he knew otherwise. Tad Szulc of the *New York Times* and Karl E. Meyer of the *Washington Post* wrote that "in the early spring of 1960, CIA agents on the island busied themselves with delivering weapons and radio transmitters" to plotters against the Revolutionary Government. "All these new anti-Castro groups had contact with the American embassy in Havana. . . . The CIA and the United States government had thus firmly entered the conspiracy to oust Castro."[6]

---

[5] *Six Crises*, p. 381.
[6] *The Cuban Invasion, The Chronicle of a Disaster*, New York, Ballantine Books, 1962, pp. 54 and 56.

In May and June comments on Cuba by U.S. public figures steadily mounted in hostility. Senator Smathers declared that the time had come for the United States to "do something" about Castro.

Fidel had warned of the danger of provocations. In the middle of June the Cuban government arrested a group, headed by a person called Chester Lacayo, that was preparing an invasion of Nicaragua from Cuba. *Lacayo* means lackey in Spanish. The Cuban government published information to show that this "lackey of the State Department" was engaged in a provocation: there was a photograph of Lacayo leaving the State Department building in Washington and a letter by him on an interview he had had with Secretary of State Herter and Roy Rubottom, Assistant Secretary for Inter-American affairs.

On July 9, two days after President Eisenhower had cancelled the sugar quota, Premier Khrushchev declared:

"I should like to call attention to the fact that the United States now obviously plans perfidious criminal steps against the Cuban people. . . .

"The United States is now not at an unattainable distance from the Soviet Union as formerly. Figuratively speaking, if need be, Soviet artillerymen can support the Cuban people with their rocket fire, should the aggressive forces in the Pentagon dare to start intervention against Cuba."[7]

Around Havana posters sprouted with the inscription, *Cuba no está sola*—Cuba is not alone. Tension began to subside. A feeling of quiet elation took its place.

On July 20, the Soviet Union agreed to purchase the 700,000 tons of the 1960 sugar quota which had been cancelled by the United States. And on July 23 a trade and payments agreement was signed with China in which she committed herself to buy 500,000 tons of sugar annually for the next five years.

Other actions were undertaken to counter economic warfare by the United States. The Bank of Foreign Commerce (*El Banco para el Comercio Exterior*), known familiarly as "Bancec," had been established in April. The title was a misnomer: the banking functions of

[7] *The New York Times*, July 10, 1960.

the new institution were secondary; it was actually a government foreign-trade agency. Now in July Bancec was instructed to import large quantities of goods as rapidly as possible, so as to reduce the impact of the embargo which the United States was expected to place on exports to Cuba. Bancec was responsible for ordering enough goods in various countries so that even with a U.S. embargo, shortages of import items would be minimal.

On August 6, everyone who had access to a television set sat glued to it as Fidel announced the nationalization of the key American properties in Cuba: the 36 American-owned sugar mills and their lands, the refineries and other oil properties, the electric power and telephone companies.

On September 17, the Cuban branches of American banks were nationalized. And in October nationalization was extended to the remaining sugar mills and banks (with the exception of two Canadian banks, soon purchased) and practically all other large or medium-sized industrial, commercial, and financial enterprises, as well as railroads, port facilities, and many movie houses and hotels.

The August and October nationalization decrees sharply accelerated the process of land redistribution which till then had been moving gradually. Less than 30 percent of the redistribution completed by the end of 1960 was carried out under the original land reform law. Some land had been obtained by purchase, and some under a law for recovery of property from officials who had illegally enriched themselves under Batista. Close to 50 percent of the redistribution resulted from the nationalization decrees.

In November the expected U.S. embargo on exports to Cuba was put into effect; all exports other than foodstuffs and medicines were forbidden. To replace the trade with the United States, a mission headed by Major Guevara set off for the socialist countries. The mission resulted in agreements for the purchase by the socialist countries of more than four million tons of sugar in 1961—about a million tons more than had formerly gone to the United States each year—and the sale to Cuba of the major part of the goods needed to keep the Cuban economy going.

For a while after the embargo, Cuba continued to buy some food-stuffs and medicines from the United States. But the commerce was continually harassed. For example, the companies selling lard, which had formerly received payment when they produced documents showing that the goods had been loaded on the ferry for Cuba, now insisted on payment as soon as the freight cars were loaded at the manufacturing plants; when the lard reached Florida to be embarked, it was often attached under court orders obtained by people with claims against Cuba. One after another the ferry lines to Cuba ceased operations, and in the summer of 1961, when the last line stopped running, Cuban imports from the United States dropped to practically zero. The United States permitted the import of Cuban tobacco for some time after other trade ended. But in February 1962, the tobacco trade was also cut off.

By the end of 1960, the Cuban economy was radically different from what it had been two years earlier when the Revolution came to power. Roughly 80 percent of Cuba's industrial capacity was socialized. But more important than the percentage was the fact that the state held the most strategic industries: sugar, petroleum refining, telephone and electric power, and cement, as well as the larger, more modern plants in all industries. Only the smaller plants remained private. The state plants produced more than 90 percent of Cuba's exports and accounted for most of its imports of industrial machinery and replacement parts and raw materials.

The state also held the banking system, the railroads, the ports, the airlines, the department stores, and an assortment of hotels, casinos, bars, cafeterias, and movie houses.

Socialized farms covered about 30 percent of the total farmland. But this 30 percent included most of the best land in Cuba. Cane cooperatives held 45 percent of the cane area, including the choice lands formerly held by the sugar mills. The socialized farms held between 15 and 20 percent of the total number of cattle. There were cooperatives for the production of rice, tomatoes, henequen, and charcoal.

Although Cuba did not want to reduce her trade with the United States, Cuban foreign trade had begun to swing around. Imports from the United States plunged downward from $577 million in 1957 to $23.7 million in 1961, and to less than $1 million in 1962. Exports dropped a shade less rapidly because of continued tobacco sales, but still were less than 1 percent of Cuba's total exports in 1962. Trade with the socialist countries climbed to replace that with the United States: it constituted over 70 percent of Cuba's foreign trade in 1961, and over 80 percent in 1962.

Although it would not be announced until the Bay of Pigs invasion in 1961, Cuba had become a socialist country.

Why was the Cuban Revolution so radical? Why did it move so quickly to socialism?

Why does an acorn give rise to an oak?

The Revolution could have avoided taking radical measures or touching American interests. But this would have meant not meeting Cuba's problems; it would have meant doing practically nothing. And failure to move toward solving the problems would have resulted in the disillusionment of the people, the loss of their willingness to fight for the Revolution. How, under these circumstances, could the Revolutionary Government have avoided becoming a prisoner of the United States, to be forced to behave or be overthrown, like so many other reformist governments in Latin America? The Revolution had no choice: it had to grow or die.

The growth could not be slow or even. Cuba could only solve its problems to the degree that it got rid of imperialism. But imperialism could not be nibbled away. At the slowest conceivable pace, it could only be removed in large chunks. And it formed an interconnected whole, no one part of which could be touched without affecting all the others.

If the United States had not reacted so violently to land reform and the expansion of trade with the socialist countries, the Revolution would have developed somewhat less quickly. But is this the only time that American imperialism has reacted violently to maintain its grasp? The United States reaction against Cuba was not an accident. And it speeded things up.

The properties of the American enterprises in Cuba covered such a large and strategic sector of the Cuban economy that their nationalization was willy-nilly a long step toward socialism. But the hold of American imperialism on Cuba was far more than a matter of ownership, and the break with the United States had effects that went beyond American-owned property.

The large Cuban-owned enterprises, which were so enmeshed with the U.S. economy that they might just as well have been American-owned, also had to be nationalized. What else could have been done with them? They had been separated from their markets, their sources of raw materials and equipment, and their commercial and financial connections. It would have been almost impossible to operate the Cuban economy as half public, half private. Could these enterprises have been left in the hands of their old owners while Cuba had to defend itself against economic warfare by the United States?

Nationalizing large industry meant nationalizing the railroads and ports. Nationalization of the sugar industry alone took in the bulk of the railroad lines and ports. Many of the other nationalized industries also had dock facilities and rail connections to their plants.

The very extent of the American stranglehold on Cuba meant that breaking it would have radical consequences. When the United States shut off its market, where could Cuba have turned to sell her sugar except to the socialist countries? The free world market could not have absorbed the three million tons per year set free by the elimination of the sugar quota, especially with the United States exerting pressure on other countries not to trade with Cuba.

The break with the United States struck the final blow at the big importers. Many of the goods in which they had specialized were no longer being imported; their trade connections no longer counted. What could be done with the buildings in which they had carried on their business, with the showrooms in which they had exhibited the fancy cars?

Foreign trade had to be nationalized. What role was there for private export and import houses sandwiched between the nationalized enterprises of Cuba and the socialist countries?

And so with hotels, department stores, etc. What could be done with hotels set up for American tourists who no longer could come? With stores geared to American goods?

As the Revolution developed, many Cuban businessmen became hostile and engaged in sabotage, so that there was no choice but to nationalize.

Fidel and the other leaders of the Revolution understood from the beginning that the choices they had to face were hard. They knew they were engaged in a life or death struggle with American imperialism. No one could foresee all the specific steps of this struggle. But the leaders of the Revolution had to think ahead; they had to try to anticipate moves and countermoves and to foresee how the process would end. Like everyone in Cuba, they could feel all around them the impetus of the Revolution and they understood to perfection the importance of maintaining this impetus. They knew what Lenin meant when he said: "When one makes a revolution one cannot mark time; one must always go forward—or go back."[8] And one could not go forward without arriving quickly at socialism.

Some people do not understand that a revolution must go forward. Theodore Draper, for example, argues that the Cuban Revolution was betrayed.[9] "Castro promised one revolution and made another. The Cuban Revolution was essentially a middle-class revolution that was used to destroy the middle class."

To support the betrayal thesis, Draper makes what he calls an "inventory of the promises" made by Fidel. For example, in his *History Will Absolve Me* speech in 1953, "Castro supported grants of land to small planters and peasants, with indemnification to former owners." He did not talk of encouraging agricultural cooperatives in general, but " 'cooperatives for the common use of costly equipment. . . .' These 1953 cooperatives," says Draper, "were clearly not the state farms of 1959."

Draper makes a show of the exhaustiveness and accuracy of his scholarship, yet he is unable to cite one thing: any promise by Fidel to

[8] John Reed, *Ten Days That Shook the World*, New York, Modern Library, 1935, pp. 270-271.
[9] Theodore Draper, *Castro's Revolution, Myths and Realities*, New York, Praeger, 1962. Also *Castroism, Theory and Practice*, New York, Praeger, 1965.

make a middle-class revolution. Fidel never made such a promise. He didn't promise either a middle-class revolution or a socialist revolution, but a revolution that would make a fundamental attack on Cuba's problems.

And it is precisely the problems which Draper ignores. Nowhere in his two books does he discuss what the revolutionaries should have done about unemployment, stagnation, illiteracy, etc. He is meticulous in the interpretation of texts, but he does not ask whether it is possible to make a meaningful land reform with indemnification to former owners, whether state farms are better for Cuba than cooperatives for the common use of costly equipment.

Even in the ordinary run of politics, statements and actions must be related to circumstances and events, but in times of turmoil and revolution, this is ten times more important. "Events themselves," said Karl Marx in one of his articles on the Civil War in the United States, "drive to the promulgation of the decisive slogan—*emancipation of the slaves.*" Lincoln started out with the aim of checking the extension of slavery in the territories; he ended by wiping out slavery throughout the United States. To say that Fidel Castro betrayed the Cuban Revolution by leading it to socialism makes no more sense than to say that Abraham Lincoln betrayed the Union because his election platform did not contain the Emancipation Proclamation.

3

First Efforts at Running the Economy

The first administrative arm of the Revolution was the Rebel Army. This army was never a purely military organization; it never existed just to fight; it was an armed force for carrying out the political tasks of the Revolution. Along with fighting went mobilizing, educating, organizing, and arming the people. The fighting could not be separated from the other tasks; it depended on them. Only by mobilizing the people could the fighting be carried through successfully to the winning of political power.

At first, the Rebel Army was a small band, struggling to keep from being destroyed. But as it carried through successful attacks on the military outposts of the dictator, as it explained its purposes to the people, it was joined by new recruits: here a few peasants fighting for land, there a few young people from a nearby town. After a while, it became, in the words of Major Guevara, "the head of a large movement with all the characteristics of a small government."[1]

Court trials were held for the administration of justice. Laws were promulgated—a penal code, a civil code, a land reform law. Small factories were established—to provide shoes for the rebel soldiers, to make explosives and repair weapons and equipment, to provide cigarettes and cigars, bread, clothing, etc. *Radio Rebelde* was set up. A newspaper was issued. Taxes were levied. Schools and hospitals were set up to serve not only the Rebel Army but also the civilian population: these were the first schools and hospitals ever to exist in the Sierra.

When Batista fled, the Rebel Army took over not only the forts and camps of the large cities, but the military posts and police stations ev-

[1] Che Guevara, *Guerrilla Warfare*, New York, Monthly Review Press, 1961, p. 74.

erywhere. It was not only the mainstay of revolutionary power, but the embodiment of revolutionary authority in the towns and countryside. The Rebel Army constituted a revolutionary administrative apparatus spread throughout Cuba.

The Revolution could not simply march in and, without further ado, make use of the old government apparatus. The old apparatus had many Batista collaborators and was not set up to do the work of revolution. "All the institutions that sheltered the former regime," writes Major Guevara, "should be wiped out."[2] Those parts of the old government that were allowed to exist temporarily, because reorganization takes time, could not be trusted.

When the Rebel Army swept to power, it exercised many of the functions of government. It established public order and did what was necessary to get things working. It occupied radio stations and arranged for the publication of newspapers. When food became scarce in Cuban households because the grocery stores had been closed by the general strike, the Rebel Army authorized the stores to open for two or three hours a day. In the countryside, it began the repair of roads and bridges damaged in the fighting.

The Rebel Army arrested those top officials of the Batista regime who had not been able to flee or take asylum in a foreign embassy. It searched for those who had tortured and killed under Batista. A Rebel Army commander was put in charge of reorganizing the national police force.

Congress was dissolved. The civil courts, with their many Batista collaborators, were suspended. The war criminals were tried by military courts under the penal code promulgated in the Sierra. The Rebel Army took charge of the property of Batista henchmen who had fled or were arrested.

Many actions were taken by Fidel as commander of the Rebel Army and leader of the Revolution. He proclaimed Manuel Urrutia President of Cuba. He announced policies and made decisions. Later when Fidel formally joined the government as Prime Minister, he continued to wear an army uniform.

In the countryside, the people brought their problems to the Rebel

[2] *Ibid.*, p. 112.

Army. It was to the Rebel Army they turned for justice against those who had oppressed them, for help in getting a damaged culvert repaired, for government in general.

The Rebel Army maintained and strengthened the links with the people that had first been forged in the Sierra. It released military camps and barracks for conversion into schools; it began to build public works; it helped out with farm work.

Finally, the Rebel Army provided personnel, ideas, and support for the other agencies of the Revolutionary Government. INRA (the National Agrarian Reform Institute)—the most important civilian agency of the Revolutionary Government—sprang from the Rebel Army and in its turn gave birth to other agencies.

One of the first consequences of the victory of the Revolution was the elimination of corruption from government. Corruption under Batista had been incredible. The revolutionaries immediately set about to establish absolute standards of honesty for public officials. It was made clear that drastic punishment would be meted out to anyone caught in wrongdoing. A Ministry for the Recovery of Illegally Acquired Properties was established. The traditional government subsidies to newspapers and newspapermen were abolished. The national lottery was cleaned up and converted into a source of funds for public housing. Thousands of ghost employees who never actually worked for the government were removed from payrolls.

The leaders of the Revolution set personal examples of austerity and dedication. "The guerrilla soldier," writes Major Guevara, "should be an ascetic." And "one of the great educational techniques is example. Therefore the chiefs must constantly offer the example of a pure and devoted life." This spirit carried over into civilian work. The leaders received low salaries, lived modestly, were informal and democratic with all around them, and worked during all hours of the day and night.

The change in the government was quick and dramatic. The honesty of public officials became a matter of revolutionary spirit, something you could clearly feel in dealings with them.

The Revolutionary Government also moved quickly in education, public health, and public works. First, there was the Rebel Army, continuing and expanding the work it had begun in the Sierra. It organized classes for soldiers and *campesinos*. It provided medical care to the *campesinos*, just as Major Guevara had when he was serving as first physician of the Rebel Army. It began to build schools, roads, and other public works.

Then came the Ministries of Education, Public Health, and Public Works. Here there were problems—not just of personnel who had served Batista, of corruption, and of organization, but of basic philosophy. These agencies had never served the people; they now had to be imbued with a new spirit. Everyone is entitled to education and medical care, not just those who count according to the standards of the respectable; public works are for the whole people, not just the foreign enterprises, the tourists, and the well-to-do.

The Ministries were taken over by the Revolutionary Government and the work of reorganization and reorientation begun. And before long, results began to appear. Thousands of new teaching positions and classrooms were created. Not only were camps and barracks converted into schools and hospitals, but also the mansions of the Batistianos and other structures that were suitable.

New parks, playgrounds, and sports centers began to spring up. Government expenditures for these purposes began to soar. Public expenditures on education rose from 74 million pesos in 1958 to 170 million in 1961, and were still higher later.

Yet the statistics do not tell the full story. The Revolution was beginning to bring education, medical care, and public works to the people, to the countryside. It was putting parks and playgrounds in the workingclass sections of the cities; it was bringing schools, hospitals, and roads to the most isolated, forsaken regions such as the Ciénaga Swamp and the mountains of Oriente.

These actions of the Revolutionary Government did not simply mean *improvements*; for large parts of the population, they meant the difference between education and no education, between medical care and no medical care, between being cut off from and being in touch with the rest of the world. These actions flowed from a truly radical sense of justice, a revolutionary spirit. This same spirit gave rise later in 1961 to the epic campaign in which the youth of the country—those from about 12 to 18 years of age—were freed of their own school-work for almost a year so they could go into the countryside to "alpha-betize" everybody, young and old. It isn't easy to grasp the full meaning of the actions of the Revolution in the backward areas of Cuba; on an international scale, the equivalent would be to start open-ing up the benefits of modern civilization to the inhabitants of the villages of central Africa.

The establishment of a National Institute of Housing (INAV) and a National Tourist Agency (INIT) put the government into addi-tional activities. Operating with money from the national lottery and social security funds, INAV started the construction of several thou-sand new apartments or one-family houses. In part the INAV projects were designed to counteract the decline in private construction activity which began in the wake of the government's measures to reduce rents and curb real estate speculation. The INAV projects reflected American middle-class standards rather than an attempt to meet the needs of a country as poor and as short of housing as Cuba. Individ-ual units cost about $8,000–$10,000 and were designed with an abund-ance of fixtures and gadgets, almost all of them of U.S. manufacture.

Tourism before the Revolution had depended heavily on prostitu-tion, gambling casinos, horse and dog racing, and the performance of abortions illegal in the United States. President Franklin D. Roosevelt had once advised the Cubans to free their tourist industry from these practices, and to base it on attractions "compatible with the dignity of man." Tourism had also depended on exclusiveness, on the enforce-ment of a color bar in hotels, restaurants, cabarets, and clubs, on keep-ing the ordinary people of Cuba out of the resorts and off the beaches. There were few public beaches and most Cubans could not get at their own waterfront.

An ordinary Cuban government, of the Batista type or otherwise, could not have followed President Roosevelt's advice, but the Revolu-tionary Government moved quickly against gangsterism and vice. It also immediately made clear its attitude on race prejudice: there was to be no color bar anywhere; all people were equal. And in April 1959, it passed a law opening all the coasts and beaches to public use.

For the people, it was like a fiesta. They could go everywhere as equals. Ordinary people all over Cuba began to use the sandy white beaches. Instead of having to dive into the rocky waters around the Malecón (the Sea Wall), Havana youngsters could now use the beach of the Havana Biltmore Yacht and Country Club where even Batista had not been welcome because he was partly colored.

INIT carried through an ambitious construction program. New public beaches with lockers, showers, and sometimes with pavilions, restaurants, and cottages, were rushed through. The construction of many new motels and hotels was begun. National parks were created in the mountains and around caves and other natural attractions. A project was undertaken for a large water park in the Ciénaga Swamp, with a number of interconnected lakes, a replica of an Indian village, a crocodile enclosure, cabins, and facilities for boating and fishing.

Most of the INIT projects, especially the beaches, were modestly designed. Some—the water park in the Ciénaga, for example—seemed to me personally to be extravagant. The rapidity with which everything was done led to a few downright mistakes, such as the placing of a new hotel on a coastal island which, after construction was well under way, was found to be unsuitable because there were mosquitoes, the waters had too many sharks to be safe for bathing, and transportation to and from the mainland was difficult.

The break in relations with the United States had a marked effect on the programs of INAV and INIT. An INAV project would require an elevator or electrical equipment from the United States that turned out to be unobtainable. Completion of the project was delayed —sometimes for a long time—while frantic efforts were made to get a replacement from some other country. INIT's early projects, in fact its whole way of thinking, were tied to the American tourist—and then the flow of tourism from the United States stopped.

The programs of INAV and INIT were begun in a period when the Revolution still had, in part, a middle-class aspect, when the full implications of the struggle with American imperialism had not yet become clear to everyone. They reflected the general revolutionary sweep, the rush to get on with the many things that were necessary for Cuba. "Don't waste time," said the signs in many Havana offices, "we have lost 59 years." The heads of these agencies were marked by their drive and their ability to get things done, not by their familiarity with the ins and outs of economics. Once the redoubtable, heavy-set lady who headed INAV stomped into my office at the Bank of Foreign Commerce, certain that a few words on her part would be enough to eliminate the restrictions on dollar imports for her projects. She simply refused to listen to the argument that it was necessary to ration dollars because there were not enough to allow the different agencies to import freely; the fact that allowing her agency too many dollars might mean that there would not be enough for some other important purpose, such as the purchase of medicines, did not trouble her; her job was to build houses, she was building good houses, and the problem of foreign exchange—which did not seem like a real problem, anyway, a tangible problem like building houses—was for other people to worry about.

The INAV and INIT programs were started at a time when Cuba was suffering from heavy unemployment, when construction was declining from an already low level and it was important to act quickly to counteract this decline. The true economic cost of the projects was much less than their nominal cost, since they were built with resources that would otherwise have been largely idle. American middle-class standards were inappropriate for a country as poor as Cuba, but there were no other standards familiar to the Cubans. To have devised different standards and pushed them through the bureaucracy would have taken a great deal of time. For all the imperfections and errors, the work of INAV and INIT brought obvious benefits, not only economic, but political; before the Revolution, no one had thought of building houses and beaches for the people.

The creation of INRA (National Agrarian Reform Institute) and the redistribution of the land gave the Revolutionary Government responsibility for agriculture—one of the crucial sectors of the economy.

But the importance of INRA went beyond this: INRA was no ordinary government agency; after the Rebel Army, it was *the* revolutionary agency. It was a second base from which the Revolutionary Government took control of the apparatus of the state.

INRA quickly divided the country into twenty-eight Agricultural Development Zones. These zones—midway between municipalities and provinces—were the territorial units through which the Agrarian Reform was carried out during the period of redistribution of the land. An INRA Delegate was set up as Chief of each zone. The authority and responsibility of the Chiefs were broad—in practice, without any clearly marked limits; they were to do everything necessary to carry out the land reform and make it work.

Most of the leading officials of INRA, both in Havana and the zones and provinces, were members of the Rebel Army. There were several reasons for this. The Army could provide tested revolutionaries, personally known to the leaders of the Revolution. It provided a country-wide administrative apparatus. And behind a revolutionary act like a true land reform lies force, and the army could, if necessary, provide force.

But the takeover of the land proceeded peacefully. The landholders protested against the land reform, both individually and through their associations. They tried to salvage as much as possible of their property and to sabotage the Revolution. They began to turn their physical assets into money to transfer out of the country. They increased the rate of cattle slaughter; cut down their expenditures on fertilizer; bought almost no new equipment; and neglected ploughing and planting. But they did not physically resist the takeover of the land; the power of the Revolution was too great.

The land taken over was not distributed individually among the landless rural workers. The small private farmers who had been working land they did not own received the ownership of this land. When their farms fell below the "vital minimum" of two *caballerías* (each *caballería* equals 33 acres), they were given enough additional land to bring them up to this minimum; sometimes they were allowed to buy more land up to five *caballerías*. But over 80 percent of the land held by the large estates was used to form collective farms. It went directly into socialized agriculture.

The large cattle ranches were organized into "direct administration farms" run by INRA; at the beginning of 1961 they became *Granjas del Pueblo* or "People's Farms," a form of state farm. The leaders of the Revolution feared that if the cattle were divided up among small farms the protein-hungry peasants would quickly eat them and deplete the supply. They had had experience with this when they were still in the Sierra, and almost all the cattle they had distributed had somehow managed to "break a leg" and require slaughtering. To have formed cooperatives from the large ranches in which a few cowboys took care of thousands of cattle would have been to form a class of rich cooperators.

The lands of the large sugar estates were used to form cane cooperatives. Cooperatives were also set up for the production of rice, tomatoes, henequen, charcoal (the main cooking fuel in the countryside), and other products. But the term cooperative was a misnomer. The administrators of the cooperatives were not elected by the members, but appointed by INRA. And although in theory remuneration of the members was to depend on the profits of the cooperative, in practice it quickly became a system of wage payments. Pay could not be held up indefinitely while someone undertook the impossible task of setting up or straightening out books and determining profits. Remuneration based on profits would have required a developed system of accountancy and accountancy depends on literacy, on the ability of most people to make out bills, reports, and records.

Toward the beginning of 1961 the cooperatives other than cane began to be changed into People's Farms, and in 1962 the cane cooperatives were also changed. Here and there a few cooperatives were left; but the People's Farms became the basic form of organization of Cuba's socialized agriculture.

There were other points in favor of People's Farms beside the fact that the cooperatives were never able to work as cooperatives. The farms varied greatly in soil, location, and ownership of cattle, machinery, and equipment. If the farms were organized and run as cooperatives, these variations would produce differences in profits and arbitrary differences in remuneration. There would be rich cooperatives and poor cooperatives; people working in different cooperatives would often find themselves doing equal work and getting unequal pay.

And with the great dependence of the whole Cuban economy on the export of sugar and the imports purchased with the proceeds—a situation that has no equivalent among the other socialist countries— Cuba's socialized farms cannot be allowed the degree of choice about what to produce that is normal for cooperatives. The government must be able to tell them how much sugar to produce.

As soon as it was set up, INRA became the most important government agency. It not only carried out the expropriation and redistribution of the land and the organization of farms and cooperatives; it also engaged in a variety of other activities. It set up People's Stores to sell goods to the *campesinos* at reasonable prices and to free them from usury; it built new housing, sometimes whole new villages, including community and sports centers; it built and operated schools and hospitals and sent teams of doctors and mobile medical dispensaries into the countryside; it built warehouses and factories to store and process agricultural products; it granted agricultural credit to farms and cooperatives; it constructed roads; it imported tractors, bulldozers, incubators, insecticides, fertilizers, animal foodstuffs, materials for constructing new agricultural installations, and chickens, pigs, and bulls for breeding; it carried out land clearing and reforestation programs; it sponsored courses on agriculture at Cuba's universities; and—to end the list which could go on further—it administered nationalized industries until the Ministry of Industry was formed, after which it still retained control of a few industries engaged in processing farm products.

INRA got into all these activities because it was the most natural instrument for carrying out revolutionary ideas and because neither the leaders of the Revolution nor the people trusted the old agencies of the state. INRA was run by several of the top leaders of the Revolution: Fidel was its President and Major Guevara was there. Many revolutionary ideas were either generated in INRA or developed there from ideas that had first been conceived in the Rebel Army in the Sierra. The carrying out of revolutionary ideas and programs could not be entrusted to the old agencies of the government with their entrenched bureaucracies and narrow vision; the best way was to assign them to revolutionary INRA where they could be sparked and supervised by the leaders of the Revolution. What old agency could be entrusted with setting up People's Stores, developing the fishing industry, or carrying through industrialization?

The agencies of the old government had built few rural schools, hospitals, and roads, and even now, though things were changing, INRA couldn't wait. And since the INRA Delegates were usually commanders of the Rebel Army—and even when not were general representatives of the Revolutionary Government—the people of the countryside brought them all sorts of problems, not just those having to do with agriculture.

Many of the new government agencies set up by the Revolutionary Government started in INRA—the Ministry of Industry, the Petroleum Institute, the Mining Institute, the Fishing Institute, the Agency of Hydraulic Resources. The People's Stores, created by INRA, formed an important part of the distribution network taken over by the Ministry of Internal Commerce when it was set up. When Major Guevara became President of the National Bank, he was both an officer of the Army and head of the Department of Industrialization of INRA; then he also became chairman of the commission in charge of the Bank of Foreign Commerce (Bancec) when it was formed. A number of key revolutionary officials of the National Bank, the Bank of Foreign Commerce, the Central Planning Board, and other agencies came from INRA. The current head of the Sugar Ministry served as Major Guevara's deputy in the Rebel Army, the Department of Industrialization of INRA, and the Ministry of Industry, before taking over his present post.

You could see and feel in the halls and offices of the INRA headquarters in Havana that it was a revolutionary organization. Here were not the prim, old-line functionaries of the National Bank or

Treasury, but bearded rebels in uniform, carrying arms. The working hours were not the 9-to-5 of the ordinary government worker. They were the irregular hours—the nocturnal hours—of the guerrilla fighter. Meetings could start at midnight and last till daybreak.

INRA was characterized by suspicion of and contempt for bureaucracy and paperwork. When a problem presents itself or a job needs doing, then resolve the problem, do the job. Don't raise questions about responsibility, coordination, and the like—that is for the old-line functionaries who are experts at telling you why you cannot do what the Revolution needs to have done, who are too full of professional vanity to be able to understand a revolution. *Es muy ejecutivo, sabe resolver*—he knows how to sail in and resolve problems. That was the highest praise at INRA.

The leaders of INRA were without experience in the administration of large organizations. They had little conception of how to delegate responsibility and still maintain control, how to use staffs which analyze problems and alternative courses of action to assist leaders in making decisions, how to issue policies and directives which can guide and control the work of large groups of people even from a distance. The idea of a large organization as a hierarchy in which each level has an appropriate range of authority and responsibility, in which the function of those at the top is to direct those below, not try to do all the jobs themselves, was foreign to the Cuban leaders at this time. Their experience had been in the guerrilla army in which the *comandantes* carried rifles.

Leaders at all levels operated as though the best way—almost the only way—of making sure something got done was to do it themselves. So they tried to be everywhere, and do everything, without ever seeming to have a moment to spare. On one day, Fidel and the other leaders of INRA might be working in Havana on questions of broad agricultural policy; on the next, they might be visiting cooperatives and farms, deciding how many breeding bulls this farm required, where the new housing on that farm should be located.

On paper there was an organizational hierarchy: there were provincial INRA Delegates, Zonal Delegates, and the administrators of the cooperatives; the "direct administration farms" were to be managed centrally from Havana—"one by one," according to a claim of INRA's Chief of Production. But it would be an error to assume that actual administration bore much resemblance to the organization charts.

Everyone by-passed different parts of the organization when it seemed quicker and more convenient to do so. Top leaders would by-pass Provincial Delegates to deal directly with Chiefs of Zone, or would by-pass the Chief of Zone to deal with the head of a cooperative or a construction project or with the local Rebel Army unit. Those below would often disregard the levels just above them on the organizational chain and bring their problems directly to INRA in Havana, preferably to one of the top leaders; then a decision might be taken without anyone's bothering to inform the intermediate officials of what had taken place.

Notwithstanding the organization on paper and the statement about centrally managing the state farms one by one, the administration of agriculture was in practice highly decentralized: decentralization simply imposed itself. INRA did not have the organization or knowledge to exercise systematic direction, review, and control of the cooperatives and state farms. There was highly centralized decision-making on specific problems, often on details. But it was sporadic; it touched only a fraction of the work of the farms. The responsibility for continuous everyday work and problems fell on the farms themselves.

During the many months in which the land was being redistributed, it was almost impossible for INRA to try to establish organized methods of work. It was constantly being buffeted by special tasks—new lands to be taken over, new cooperatives and state farms to be set up. This process, which kept INRA from settling down to ordinary agricultural administration, began to subside only after the second batch of nationalizations in October, 1960—about a year and a half after INRA was first created.

Although they worked in the countryside, Cuba's rural proletariat had little experience in farming and little knowledge of diversified agriculture. They knew how to cut cane and pick coffee, but not much about raising crops and livestock, combating plant and animal diseases, handling machinery. They didn't have the thousands of bits of empirical knowledge which American or Canadian farmers, for example, pass down from father to son. Large numbers of them couldn't read: they could not have made use of little how-to-do-it pamphlets such as the U.S. Department of Agriculture puts out, even if such pamphlets had existed in Cuba. And almost none had experience in management or administration.

But the people went to work with a will. They set about clearing thousands of acres of land under *marabú*, a soil-robbing weed. On formerly idle land, they planted import-saving crops such as rice, potatoes, cotton, peanuts, and soybeans. They built.

The countryside began to sprout with new facilities: spanking modern sheds for raising chickens and pigs, stalls for giving cattle prepared food, eliminating the need for them to roam around the pastures. At Los Pinos, about three hours drive from Havana, a large hydroponics installation for growing tomatoes and peppers without soil was built. Near Trinidad, in the south of Cuba, a cooperative chicken hatchery was set up; each of its ten incubators bore the name of a Cuban national hero such as José Martí or Antonio Maceo, except for one which was named after Abraham Lincoln. New housing, community centers, schools, hospitals, and People's Stores sprang up.

The change wrought in the countryside was more than a matter of increased production and new facilities. A new world opened up for Cuba's rural population. The *campesino* achieved a dignity and hope which showed in his bearing. And as the area under cultivation expanded and the work of constructing and operating the new facilities got under way, rural unemployment declined—faster than anyone at the time realized.

There were also errors. The hatred of *marabú* was carried too far; sometimes the newly cleared land had only a thin soil cover that was easily subject to erosion. Occasionally the *campesinos* slaughtered valuable breeding animals for food at the same time that foreign exchange was being spent to import additional stock. The new facilities followed standards appropriate for a rich country like the United States, not a poor one like Cuba; simpler, cheaper facilities would often have been better.

The specific errors were innumerable. A cooperative would grow a large crop of tomatoes for export, but in the revolutionary rush the materials necessary to package it would be overlooked. Everyone knew that foreign exchange could be saved by growing more potatoes, but no one foresaw that for Cuba to supply itself during the whole year instead of just the few months of its own harvest season, storage facilities would be required.

For the first two or three years, INRA's financial controls were primitive. An incident that occurred during my stay at the National Bank in the spring of 1960 illustrates how things worked. One day Major Guevara's economic assistant and I were visited by a former guerrilla fighter who was now in charge of a thousand new People's Stores—about half the total. His stores were in financial difficulties and he was applying for a loan of 16 million pesos. He had brought no papers, but simply explained that if the credit were not granted the stores would begin to run out of merchandise within about four to six weeks. My co-worker and I suspected from the beginning that the loan would have to be granted, but to find out how frequently the problem might recur if nothing were done about it, we asked a few questions about the financial methods by which the People's Stores were being operated. How much credit were they extending to their customers and to what extent was it being repaid? How were prices fixed? How did they compare with costs? The administrator answered our questions in a friendly manner but with a touch of impatience. Yes, the People's Stores had been extending a large amount of credit to customers, a good part of which was not being repaid. But what could he do about it? Before the Revolution the *campesinos* had been gouged by the country stores; their indebtedness had been used to help control them. Now the People's Stores were *their* stores and had to avoid the slightest resemblance to the old stores; time and patience were required to bring the problem of credit under control. And no matter what—the People's Stores could not be allowed to run out of merchandise. My co-worker and I decided to recommend that the loan be granted, even though it did not exactly fulfill the textbook norms of central bank lending.

To enable the Chiefs of Zone to carry out their many tasks, they were allowed to draw large sums of money from INRA in Havana over whose use they enjoyed wide discretion. The money was used for many things: to clear the *marabú*, to set up People's Stores, to help the new co-ops meet their expenses, to buy cattle, to build and improve roads. Between June, 1959, and the end of 1960, the Chiefs of Zone drew 156 million pesos from INRA and returned less than 15 million.[3] There was no systematic accounting of the expenditures and no close checkup of costs—there could not have been.

To find that there was error and waste during the early years of the land reform is—as a Cuban might say—to discover the Mediterranean. Everyone knew that there was error and waste. To call attention to a technical error was 10 percent of the battle. The main problem was direction and organization: how to release the energy and initiative of the masses and at the same time keep the error and waste down.

At the time the land reform started, it was necessary to act quickly, to get people engaged, to begin putting the idle resources to work. The revolutionary enthusiasm of the masses is a tremendous force. But masses of people cannot operate with the calm and precision of a few technicians doing a specialized job in a small office. Even from a narrow economic point of view, the benefits of rapid, mass action far outweighed the error and waste. Politically, the benefits were immeasurable.

There was no comprehensive, detailed, and finished agricultural policy when INRA began, nor could there have been. There were many ideas. And there was also the method that Napoleon explained when he was asked how he determined the tactics to be followed in a battle. "*On s'engage, et puis—on voit.*" You get into the action, and then—you see.

Much of the action in the early period of the land reform was simply a reaction against the obvious faults of the previous agricultural

[3] Jacques Chonchol, "La Reforma Agraria Cubana, 2a parte," *Panorama Económico*, No. 288, marzo 1962 (Santiago, Chile: Editorial Universitario, S.A.), p. 38.

setup. Land was being wasted and people were unemployed: put the land and people to work. There was overconcentration on sugar; therefore diversify. Foreign exchange was being spent to import products which could be produced in Cuba: grow more rice, cotton, and potatoes; start pig raising so Cuba could begin to save on the $25 million she was spending each year on the import of lard.

Then, as the agricultural program got under way, more ideas sprouted. Some technicians pointed out that to prevent the losses of the dry season, silos should be built—if need be, they could be simple and crude at first. Cattle, which in the area outside the Havana basin were raised mainly for meat, should be used for milk as well. René Dumont, a visiting French agronomist, argued that the large collective farms should combine cultivation of crops with the raising of livestock; in this way, steady work would be provided for agricultural labor, and the by-products of the crops could be used to help feed the livestock. Fidel proposed that each cane cooperative should have two hundred milk cows for the use of its members. Different experts agreed that conditions in Cuba were propitious for cattle-raising, thus opening a perspective for a great future cattle industry, which would not only provide much-needed meat for the people of Cuba, but export earnings as well.

These ideas had their weaknesses. Most of them were enveloped in an over-optimism which intoxicated almost everybody, Cubans and foreigners alike. Do thus and so and you will quickly have big increases in cane yield, the supply of chickens, or meat production. Practice was to show that things are never that easy.

The analyses and proposals were made from limited perspectives, not a general view of the whole economy. The unemployed resources were so great that one could increase the production of, say, rice, tomatoes, or cucumbers without interfering with other parts of the economy. No one worried about the choices that would have to be made when the resources became scarce. No one worried whether the over-all supply of labor would be large enough to do everything that was being proposed; whether tomatoes or cucumbers might interfere with sugar.

And yet the answers to the most important agricultural problems depended not just on agriculture, but on the whole economy. The direction in which agriculture should be developed depended on how this development would fit in with the balance of payments, industry, the standard of living, etc. Take even the seemingly technical problem of whether farms should be mixed or specialized. Dumont's maxim—"never a crop-farm without livestock, never a cattle farm without crops"—has most validity when there is a surplus of labor, and loses validity rapidly as labor becomes scarce. With a short labor supply but abundant pasture land, it may be right to maintain many extensive, specialized cattle ranches in which there are many cattle, few cowboys, and no crops.

For all their limitations, however, these initial ideas were of great value. They were sensible responses to the agricultural situation confronting the Revolution during the first few years of the land reform. Many benefits resulted from applying them. Some of them—for example, the idea of greatly developing the cattle and meat industry—so proved themselves even in changing circumstances that they became a central part of long-run agricultural policy.

But more than this: they began the process of grappling with the problems. "Even a poor hypothesis," Charles Darwin said, "is better than none at all." The initial ideas, including those that later had to be altered or discarded, began the testing of hypotheses, the piecing together of interrelations between different parts of the economy, the attainment of a view of the whole, through which a long-run agricultural and economic policy was worked out.

As factories were "intervened" or nationalized, the Revolutionary Government acquired the responsibility for running them. A number of plants—including some sugar mills, a textile factory, construction firms, the telephone company—were taken over during the first year and a half after the Revolution came to power under the "ill-gotten gains" law, because their owners had abandoned them or were not keeping up operations, or because of disputes about wages or prices. But at the end of July 1960, most industry was still in private hands.

Then came the waves of nationalization set off by the dispute with the oil companies, and within three months the Revolutionary Government found itself with the greater part of Cuban industry on its hands. It had to keep this industry going. But who would run it?

Most of the top administrative and technical personnel in the American-owned plants had been American. Foreigners had directed the oil refineries, while Cubans took care of the maintenance and cleaning, operated the cars and trucks, and served as mechanics. The American technicians at the Nicaro nickel plant lived in a large, barbed-wire compound that was designed like an American military camp, with a post movie house and similar facilities. You could always tell where the American administrative and technical personnel had lived in the *bateyes* of the American-owned sugar mills—they had had the best houses, the ones with the private beaches whenever the *batey* was near a waterfront.

There were also Cuban administrators and technicians, many in the Cuban-owned plants, some in the American ones. But these Cubans were a United States-oriented elite, almost as distinct from the rest of the population as the Americans.

By October 1960 most of this administrative and technical personnel had left Cuba. The Americans and some of the Cubans were withdrawn by the home companies of the plants for which they worked. Other Cubans left of their own accord: they found themselves unable to understand the struggle with the United States, unwilling to accept the new way of life that was opening up before them.

The Revolutionary Government had to keep the factories and mines going with only a minute proportion of the usual trained and experienced personnel. A few examples can perhaps best give an idea of what happened.

Five of us from the Ministry of Foreign Commerce, on a business visit, were being taken through the Moa nickel plant. In the electric power station—itself a large plant—which served the rest of the complex, our guide was an enthusiastic youngster of about 22. He did an excellent job as guide, but his modesty as well as his age deceived us and only toward the end of our tour did we realize that he was not some sort of apprentice engineer or assistant—he was in charge of the plant. I noticed that he spoke English well and asked him if he had lived in the States. "Sure," he answered, "I studied engineering at Tulane." As soon as he finished, he had come back to work for the Revolution and had been placed in charge of the power plant.

In another part of the complex, the head of one of the key departments was a black Cuban who had about four years of elementary school education. He had been an observant worker and when the engineer of his department left he knew what to do—although he didn't really know why, or how his department related to the others in the plant. Now to learn why, he was plugging away at his *mínimo técnico* manual—one of the little mimeographed booklets which had been distributed throughout industry to improve people's knowledge of their jobs.

And so on throughout the Moa plant. The engineer in charge of the whole enterprise, who had a long cigar in his hand and his feet on the desk as he gave us his criticisms of the way our Ministry was handling his import requirements, was about 28 years old. His chief assistants were about the same age and some of them were obviously not engineers.

Yet Moa was made to function. Even laymen are struck with its delicate beauty—a testament to American engineering skill. *Es una joya*—it's a jewel, say the Cubans. It is much more impressive than the larger but older nickel plant at Nicaro. Shortly after the nickel ore is clawed out of the earth by giant Bucyrus power shovels, it is pulverized and mixed with water to form a mixture 55 percent ore and 45 percent water. From then on all materials movement is liquid, in pipes, automatically controlled. The liquids move through the several miles of the complex, in and out of the separate plants, with their reducers, mixing vats, etc. Everything depends on innumerable delicate instruments, and on unusual materials, resistant to exceptionally high temperatures and various kinds of chemical reaction. The margin for improvising in repairing or replacing parts is small—much smaller than in the mechanized rather than automated Nicaro plant. Yet the Moa plant was in operation when we were there: two of the four main production lines were going—and all four would have been going if it had not been necessary to cannibalize two lines to get replacement parts for the other two.

Except that Moa was an especially complex and difficult operation, it was typical of what happened throughout the mines and factories, and for that matter in the railroads, banks, department stores, and movie houses that had been taken over. The large oil companies had expected that the Cubans would not be able to run the oil refineries. But they were wrong. When a co-worker and I talked to the young administrator of the now combined Esso-Shell refineries across the bay from Havana, he said, only half-jokingly, that he was about two lessons ahead of us in his understanding of how the refinery worked— and I wondered how it was kept going. But we had been around the refinery ten minutes earlier and there it was—going.

A textile plant was placed in the charge of a bearded young man of about 23 who had impressed Major Guevara with his courage and resourcefulness in the Rebel Army. The former Procter and Gamble plant, which each year turns out several million dollars worth of soaps, detergent, and tooth paste, was run by a former physician who, besides being generally able, knew some chemistry. For many months, the Matahambre copper mine was in the charge of an American geologist, a friend of mine. After coming to Cuba to work for the Revolution, he had been pressed into service, though he was not a mining engineer and had never run a mine, because he was still the most qualified person available. He had to educate himself rapidly in mine ventilation; this was one of Matahambre's biggest problems at the time. I went through the mine with him once and it was obvious from the way the men treated him that he had gained their respect for the way he was handling his job.

Once an economist from the Ministry of Industry and I visited a large plant near Matanzas that produced rayon for tires, textiles, and export. We sensed at the plant that the harassed, outspoken administrator, almost the only engineer left, was all but sustaining the whole operation by himself. We got into a conversation about him with one of his assistants. It turned out he had a bad leg of some sort which was giving him trouble; his father, who had owned valuable property in the nearby swanky bathing resort at Varadero was out of sympathy with the Revolution; and his brother, also an engineer, had left for Venezuela or some such place. But there he was, holding a meeting with his staff at 11 P.M., using all his energy to help keep the *rayonera* going.

When you walked through a Cuban factory, you didn't need to be told that it was under new management—you could see and feel it everywhere. In the Pheldrake plant for producing wire and cable, formerly owned by Dutch and American interests, the whole office of administration was filled by men in shirt-sleeves who were unmistakably workers; the engineers had gone and the workers had taken over. On the main floor, a group of them were struggling—using baling wire techniques—to repair one of the extrusion machines so that the wire required by the Cuban telephone industry could be kept coming. In a large tobacco factory, the administrator was black; in the metal-working plant formerly owned by the American Car and Foundry Company, the head of a department turning out chicken incubators was black. Black people had not held such positions before the Revolution.

It was the same in the Ministry of Industry itself. In early 1961, just after the Ministry had been formed, I attended one of its staff meetings. About 40 people were present, including the Minister—Major Guevara—the Vice Ministers, the heads of the Petroleum and Sugar Institutes, and the administrators of leading enterprises or groupings of them. There were a few technically trained and experienced people: the head of the Petroleum Institute was a Mexican engineer; a Chilean economist was in charge of economic investigation. But most of the people present were young revolutionaries, with little training or experience for their new jobs. The chief Vice Minister, Major Guevara's deputy, was a tough, outspoken young officer of the Rebel Army; the head of the Sugar Institute was a former union organizer; an elderly former salesman, sympathetic to the Revolution, served as liaison officer with the Ministry of Foreign Trade.

Along with the problem of finding people to run the mines and factories, came that of obtaining replacement parts and raw materials. The extreme domination that the United States had previously exercised over the Cuban economy now increased Cuba's vulnerability to the American embargo. Almost everything, from the large boilers in the sugar mills to ordinary electric sockets, was built and worked according to American designs and specifications. The identification plates on the machinery and equipment bore such names as General Electric, Westinghouse, Minneapolis Honeywell; the electric current used was the same as that in the United States; the system of measurement was inches and feet, not centimeters. And most of the larger factories—except for sugar mills and tobacco plants—worked with raw materials imported from the United States, sometimes specifically designed for the machinery and processes in which they were to be used.

Just as an automobile can be put out of commission for lack of some small, inexpensive part—say a gasket for a brake cylinder worth three dollars—so the operations of a large factory or mine, turning out products worth several million dollars a year, can be halted by the absence of ordinarily insignificant pieces of equipment. The unavailability of a small filter—worth $25—for equipment at Moa which pulverizes the ore into a fine powder can stop the operations of the whole nickel plant. The failure of small parts for the ventilators, or the overhead cable system which moves the copper around, can interfere with production at the Matahambre copper mine. There are thousands of such parts throughout the mines, factories, and electric power and telephone systems of Cuba.

Because the Moa plant was custom-built, the filter was made only by one company in the United States. Other parts for the various mines and factories were sold only by American companies or their Canadian subsidiaries—both subject to the American embargo. Even when parts were available in other capitalist countries, it took time to find them, and then order and get them.

The Moa filter and thousands of other parts had to be improvised. Technicians and workers used everything from baling wire to homemade pieces of delicate machinery to keep the mines and factories going. Workshops for the repair and production of parts were set up.

Workshops of the sugar mills, which had previously been idle a good part of the year, were pressed into service. And, when necessary, parts for one machine or piece of equipment were obtained by dismantling another.

Raw materials and component parts also gave trouble. One $4-million plant for the production of synthetic fiber, which was almost finished just as the Revolution came to power, could not be put into operation because it was not possible to get cellulose acetate of exactly the specifications required. The incubators produced in the old American Car and Foundry plant were designed to use thermostats produced in the United States; when I was in the plant the workers proudly showed me the substitute thermostat they had improvised.

Problems often arose even when it was possible to obtain the raw materials required in countries other than the United States. Russian wheat is apparently somewhat different from American wheat, and this required adjustments in Cuban processing equipment. The silica rock imported from Poland for the soap and detergent factories differed from that which had been previously used, and this created problems. The tire factories could be made to work on materials that did not have the precise specifications required, but at the expense of the quality of the product.

And yet with all the difficulties, the Revolutionary Government was able to handle the problem of industry management. Again the errors were innumerable. Machines were sometimes damaged by improvised parts which did not meet the required norms. Often, on the other hand, orders were blithely sent out for expensive new machinery from the socialist countries when it would have been better to try to repair or cannibalize the existing equipment. Sometimes the care of equipment was poor. There were interruptions of production in various factories and mines. But industrial production in 1960—despite the shock of the nationalizations—was somewhat higher than in 1959 and about 30 percent higher than in 1958 before the Revolution. It was in 1961, as the pre-existing inventories and last shipments of American spare parts and raw materials began to be used up, that serious difficulties erupted and total industrial production declined. The main problem was not management; it was the embargo.

As in agriculture, thinking about the future—about development—began immediately. Cuba has large reserves of laterite containing iron. However, there are technical problems to be solved: chrome is present in the ore and unless an economic method for separating it can be found, the finished iron will have an excessive chrome content; let's get technicians—including technicians from the socialist countries—to work on the problem and on the general prospects for an iron and steel industry. Cuba has large nickel reserves—perhaps the largest in the world; let's consider the possibility of having one of the socialist countries build us another nickel processing plant; nickel has an assured market, and we may in this way get additional exports of several tens of millions of dollars. Let's have teams of geologists from the socialist countries make a systematic survey of Cuba to see if they can find oil or other mineral deposits which the geologists of the foreign monopolies have accidentally or deliberately overlooked.

And again, as in agriculture, there was confusion, a driving impatience to make progress rapidly which resulted in unrealistically ambitious plans and a tendency to see things parochially—to look at industry without worrying about its interrelations with other sectors of the economy. Industrialization plans calling for the expenditure of hundreds of millions of dollars on new factories were elaborated without checking whether the foreign exchange required would be available. These plans would have entailed enormous expenditures of exchange to pay for some factories immediately, to meet the amortization and interest charges on the debts incurred to pay for others (these charges can mount to large sums very rapidly), and to pay for the raw and semi-fabricated materials with which the factories would operate. It was not until 1962, when a large balance of payments deficit appeared and forced consideration of the problem, that it began to be fully faced.

But still, as in agriculture, the ideas and plans pushed things forward. Many early ideas, like the one about developing nickel, turned out to be good; all were part of a process of groping and testing. This process began while the dust raised by the great shakeup of the Cuban economy was still flying and it was impossible to see clearly. Many questions simply could not have been answered in the early days; it was necessary to wait till things settled down a bit, to see how the many changes brought about by the Revolution worked themselves out in the economy. But the questions began to take shape—some posed in the industry plans themselves, others raised in reaction to them. What sort of new industries should Cuba set up? How fast should industrial development proceed? On what does this depend? How does industrial development tie in to the rest of the economy? To the standard of living? The development of agriculture? The balance of payments?

The successful takeover and operation of the Cuban economy depended greatly on how well its foreign trade was managed under the rapidly changing conditions produced by the elimination of the U.S. sugar quota, nationalization, the American embargo, and the need to reorient about 80 percent of Cuba's trade to the socialist countries. Cuba's dependence on foreign trade was very great.

Imports and exports were each equal to more than 25 percent of the gross domestic product. About $125-150 million worth of basic foodstuffs were imported, including wheat and flour, lard and other fats and oils, rice, beans, peas, onions, garlic, potatoes, and codfish. Some of these, like wheat, could not be produced at all in Cuba; others could not—at least within a short time—be produced in the required amounts. Tens of millions of dollars of medicines and drugs had to be imported; some—like insulin for diabetics—simply could not be allowed to run short; otherwise people would die. Industry needed over $250 million of imported parts and raw materials; even stretching improvisation to its limits, most parts and raw materials still had to be obtained by imports. How do you improvise $7 million of tinplate for a canning factory? The buses, railroads, telephone and electric power industries, television and radio stations, and water supply systems needed spare parts. Agriculture needed fertilizer, both imported and made in Cuba from imported raw materials; it needed imported fungicides and insecticides, animal feedstuffs, and tractor parts. And, finally, thousands of miscellaneous small articles were needed—razor blades, pencils, toothbrushes, screws, electric power plugs and switches, files for sharpening the machetes of the cane-cutters.

Before the Revolution, about 70 to 75 percent of Cuba's imports came from the United States. If the oil shipped to Cuba by the large oil companies operating in Venezuela is added, the figure comes to about 80 percent. Much of the remainder consisted of goods not produced in the United States—jute sacks for sugar from India or olive oil and traditional wines and foodstuffs from Spain. Cuba got 0.3 percent of its imports from the socialist countries in 1957 and 1958— things like Christmas tree bulbs from Czechoslovakia and some special earths and stones from Poland.

Like the other agencies set up by the Revolution, the *Banco Para el Comercio Exterior* (Bancec) was almost completely staffed with untrained, inexperienced personnel. Its executive head was an *administrador*—later to become Minister of Foreign Trade—about 27 years old. He had had some premedical training at the University, was a Major in the Rebel Army, and his father was a national hero, one of the martyrs who had been killed in an abortive attack on the Presidential Palace in 1957. The Deputy Administrator was an economist, but his experience had been in journalism rather than in working economics.

The remainder of the roughly one hundred people with whom the agency started was made up as follows: a young man of 23 who had worked for an export house for a few years and now was to be placed in charge of exports—several hundred million dollars' worth; another young man who had had about six months' experience as head of the department administering foreign exchange regulations at the National Bank, who was to be placed in charge of imports; numerous other people from the National Bank who had mostly worked as clerks in the administration of foreign exchange regulations or the preparation of letters of credit; four or five salesmen or

buyers from the old export and import houses; nine or ten accountants, four or five lawyers, a few people who had worked in warehouses, and a miscellany of stenographers and typists and graduate
students from the University of Havana.

Apart from one doctor who helped with the import of drugs for
Cuba's pharmaceutical houses, there were no technicians who understood the detailed characteristics of the replacement parts and raw materials required by Cuban industry. No one had participated before
the Revolution in the negotiation of trade and payments agreements.
No one had dealt with the socialist countries. There was one person
with long experience in the import of lard and other foodstuffs; he
was soft-spoken, competent, and did his job well for two years, having
general access to information and meetings—until it was discovered
that he was a CIA agent and he was arrested.

Bancec began its operations in July 1960, during the climax of the
crisis with the United States, and its first tasks stemmed from this
crisis. The United States was cutting off the sugar quota; the next
possible economic weapon was a general embargo on trade with Cuba.
During the early months of Bancec, problems of a general nature were
discussed in meetings that began at midnight so they would not interfere with the transaction of business during the day. At one of these
meetings, the administrator passed down the word from higher authorities that an embargo was to be expected and therefore Bancec
was to follow a policy of buying as rapidly as possible. Concern about
the dollar reserves was to be temporarily set aside; within reason,
problems of price and quality were not to be allowed to delay purchases. The important thing was to get as large a quantity of goods as
possible before the supply was cut off.

Only one person objected to this policy: the burly former National
Bank official who was to become head of the Import Division. To him
disrespectful handling of the dollar reserves was anathema, no matter
what the circumstances. He argued loudly, but was overruled. A few
weeks later he was in Miami broadcasting over the radio against the
Revolution.

Bancec had to work fast. Quickly a rudimentary organization was set up—Import and Export Divisions and a Financial Division to prepare the information required by the National Bank for opening up letters of credit. The Import Division was divided into nine purchasing sections: foodstuffs, drugs and medicines, raw materials, and so on. The Export Division was divided into similar sections: sugar, tobacco, minerals, minor exports. Each section was given a chief and told to go ahead.

Go ahead they did. The Export Division, which had only a few items to deal with, was relatively calm and orderly. But the Import Division quickly began to bustle with activity which continued till late into the night. In response to a request by Bancec in the newspapers, asking representatives of different parts of the internal economy to meet with Bancec officials to make known their import requirements, people came by the hundreds. Administrators of factories came to state the raw materials and parts they needed. Representatives of INRA and of People's Farms and cooperatives came with lists of tractor parts, insecticides, feedstuffs, and vitamins for chickens. Officials of the Ministry of Public Health came to make sure of medicines, and officials of the Ministry of Transport came about replacement parts for buses.

Foreign salesmen also presented themselves. Sharp-eyed operators from Miami offered bargains on automotive parts. Smoother-looking types from Canada probed to see whether they could get cut-rate sugar in exchange for replacement parts, pedigreed cattle, or anything else Cuba might need.

Besides all this, there were meetings with delegations from the socialist countries. Someone from each of the import sections was required at these meetings to make sure that no item that could possibly be obtained from one of these countries would be overlooked. Since the staffs of the sections were small and there was little division of labor, each section chief had to tear himself away from the people in his office, the telephone, and the people waiting outside to see him, to attend the meetings which usually lasted several days.

In the rush and bustle to buy quickly, few people kept systematic records of what they had bought, when it was likely to arrive, and to whom it was supposed to go. In most of the offices, there were no physical facilities—folders, books, or filing cabinets—for keeping records. There had been no time to work out clear-cut boundaries for the different sections; certain materials, for example, could be considered either drugs or chemicals, each imported by a different section. It was impossible to avoid different sections duplicating each others' purchases, each not knowing what the other had bought; or all of them failing to buy a certain item, each thinking the responsibility fell elsewhere.

The first, semi-organized undertaking of Bancec arose in connection with Major Guevara's mission to the socialist countries during November and December of 1960. The purpose of this mission was to make agreements with the socialist countries covering trade during the whole of the following year, and the mission could not accomplish this task by free-wheeling as Bancec had been doing. Statistics were needed giving the goods Cuba had available for export and those it needed to import during the year.

Because Cuban exports are dominated by a few main items—sugar, tobacco, minerals, coffee—the determination of export availabilities posed no problem. Two or three people working three or four days could do the job. They could check on the probable amount of sugar inventory at the end of 1960, the expected harvest during 1961, the amount required for home consumption, and then set up different possible distributions of the remainder between the world free market and the socialist countries and among the socialist countries. They could analyze the advantages and disadvantages of the various alternatives: for example, increasing the amount of sugar going to the free market meant more convertible currency which Cuba needed for the many purchases she had to make in the capitalist countries; increasing the amount going to the Soviet Union meant larger total foreign-exchange earnings because the Soviet Union was paying 4 cents per pound while the price in the free market was running at less than 3 cents. Similar distributions and analyses could be made for the main minerals—nickel, copper, chrome, and manganese. The possibility of selling some tobacco, coffee, and two or three less important products to one or another of the socialist countries could be raised. And the whole thing could be written up in a four- or five-page memorandum. The head of the Export Division and I jointly wrote such a memorandum and sent it to the administrator of Bancec and Major Guevara for their use.

But with imports the task was infinitely more difficult. The specific items that had to be imported numbered many thousands. Instead of a few clear, major alternatives to consider and pick from, there was a multitude of problems which touched all parts of the economy.

One of the first discoveries in attacking the job was the limited usefulness of many of the statisticians and much of the statistics. An embryonic Research and Statistics Division had been set up at Bancec. It was headed by a Professor of Statistics from the University of Havana who had gathered around him several other people from the University—a young lady with a doctor's degree in mathematical statistics, a few teachers of statistics, some graduate students. Between them these people could tell you about advanced probability theory and the finer points of sampling techniques. But somehow they could not seem to produce sensible estimates of how much wheat or petroleum Cuba would require in 1961, to say nothing of more difficult items. Their training seemed to imprison rather than help them, to make them slaves of their tools and techniques, too fastidious and inflexible for the dirty, rough-and-tumble world of practice. They were shunted aside and a new staff was improvised rapidly. It was headed by a person without much formal training who had learned practical statistics by helping his father in a small market research agency he owned and ran.

The latest year for which Cuban trade statistics were available was 1958 and conditions had changed greatly since then. The structure of the economy, the distribution of income, and the demand for many products were very different from what they had been before the Revolution. But even more important than such changes was the nature of the statistics themselves. They had not been set up to help with specific practical action and their descriptions and classifications were general and vague. *Parts and accessories for motors and mills* reads one category which accounted for imports of $4.5 million in 1958. But you don't order a miscellaneous assortment of parts and accessories; you have to say what parts and what accessories and how many of each; you have to be able to give specifications. Other typical categories were: *Parts and accessories for industrial machines*—$19.7 million; *Patent medicines*—$13.8 million; *Biological products*—$650 thousand; *Pills of all classes*—$160 thousand; *Other chemical products imported in bulk*—$6.5 million; *Other chemical products imported in small packages*—$1.2 million; *Plastics of all classes*—$1.5 million. The traditional statistics were of help with only a few simple items such as wheat. For the great majority of imported products, they provided only a hazy general perspective or no information at all.

To determine the import requirements for specific products and to get the concrete specifications required to describe these products to potential exporters, it was necessary to go to people working in different parts of the economy who might have such information or be able to get it: managers of sugar mills, factories, and pharmaceutical houses; officials of INRA and the Ministries of Public Health, Transport, and so on. Meetings with different groups of these people were set up and took place constantly.

There were difficulties. These were not people who had held their jobs for years, but officials appointed by the Revolution. And often even experienced people would have had trouble. Many U.S. firms had deliberately kept the personnel of their foreign subsidiaries in ignorance of the precise nature of the materials they were working with; ordering had been done by code numbers; for example, in many drug houses, Cuban employees would mix imported raw materials without anyone's knowing exactly what these materials were or what chemical processes were taking place. And aside from secrecy, much Cuban importing had been done from catalogues; the people ordering would select the part which the catalogue said was the right one for a given piece of equipment; but they could no more give the technical specifications of what they were ordering than an ordinary person buying, say, a motor for his Plymouth could provide a technical description of it.

Yet somehow thousands of different products had to be identified and described; the quantities required of these products had to be estimated; and the information had to be prepared for negotiations with representatives of the socialist countries who did not use the same nomenclature and spoke different languages. Thousands of errors were inevitable.

But the job had to be done. And it was done—in about two months, the statistical material required for Major Guevara's mission was ready.

But the difficulties in getting information and ordering imports were only the beginning. Difficulties also plagued the later stages of the import process—the reception of the merchandise at the ports and its distribution to the internal economy.

The whole port system of Cuba, from the design and equipment of the docks to the system of warehouses at the ports and in the interior, was adapted to a foreign commerce monopolized by the United States. Since Cuba was so close to the United States, almost any article needed could be obtained in three to five days through a simple telephone call. Shipments were frequent and small. Most goods came on the West Palm Beach Ferry or the Sea Train from New Orleans. Many goods arrived in freight or tank cars which rode on these ships from railroads in the United States and then rode off in Cuba and brought the goods directly to the factories in which they were to be used. Lard, for example, went in tank cars to the factory in which it was canned; raw materials for the Procter and Gamble plant went directly to its doorstep. The Ferry and Sea Train were small ships, and the other ships that arrived in Cuba rarely exceeded four or five thousand tons.

Cuban port installations were not well adapted to handling large transoceanic ships. Neither the depth of the water at the side of the docks nor the unloading equipment were, in general, appropriate to such ships. There was a minimum of warehouse space, both at the ports and in the interior of Cuba. It had not been necessary either to discharge large ships or to maintain large reserves; frequently eight or ten freight or tank cars parked outside a factory served as a warehouse, making unnecessary the construction of special buildings for this purpose. The arrangements for clearing goods from the docks and transporting them into the interior were also not geared to large ships; before the Revolution, goods could quickly be cleared off the docks by a few trucks.

But now goods were coming from the socialist and other far-away countries, such as Japan and Egypt, in large shipments on ocean-going vessels. One day news came that a ship from China was about to arrive with 5,000 tons of soy bean oil. A small crisis broke out. Where should all this oil be put? Shipments of fats and oil had never arrived in such large amounts before. Several people had to chase around for a week trying to find out if some of the tanks at the petroleum refinery could be cleaned out and used to store the oil, or if some tanks ordinarily used to store molasses were free.

The people in the Warehouse Section were confronted with hundreds of such problems. I often went out with them to the docks when I was working in early September on a memorandum recommending the construction of additional warehouses. A Japanese fishing boat arrived with a load of fresh fish which could not be discharged immediately because there were no refrigerated warehouses available; demurrage charges of $1,000 a day had to be paid while we rushed around looking for a suitable *frigorífico*. A load of onions arrived from Egypt and was placed in a warehouse unsuitable to receive onions that had gone through such a long voyage; a few days later three of us were at the warehouse inspecting sprouting onions; and then there followed a series of lightning meetings to decide how to get rid of the onions, if need be by giving them away.

Each problem aggravated others. The shortage of warehouse space made it desirable to identify goods and get them off the docks and out of the port area as quickly as possible. But many goods arrived and were unloaded without anyone's knowing at first to whom they should go. In part this was due to the failure to keep records during the hectic early days of Bancec. But there was also another important cause: as the United States proceeded with its efforts to isolate Cuba, the mail became slow and uncertain; shipping documents—bills of lading, packing lists, etc.—which used to arrive before the merchandise now often came afterwards or not at all.

As goods arrived and were unloaded, frantic telephone calls often had to be made to discover for whom they had been ordered. Generally the *destinatario* would be found; but there were also shipments which no one knew what to do with; and a shipment of caustic soda was somehow forgotten in Regla across the bay from Havana where, exposed to the sun and rain, it became unusable. Some imports came in large wooden boxes. Without packing lists, you often couldn't tell from the outside what these boxes contained. So they had to be opened on the docks; and sometimes—with drugs or chemicals, for example— it took an expert to know what he was looking at. Without the documents, it was often impossible to tell how much the imported goods had cost and what to charge the Cuban recipient for them. Goods had to be delivered without bills, with the question of payment reserved for later. A backlog of unpaid claims quickly built up and contributed to creating confusion in the financial operations of Bancec and a number of other organizations.

The docks often became clogged with goods. One dock caved in from being overloaded. Masses of volunteer workers, most of them accustomed only to office work, were mobilized to help clear the docks and worked many a Sunday, heaving sacks and shoving handcarts around.

But despite the innumerable errors and difficulties, Cuba was provided with the imported goods it needed to feed its people and keep its economy going. The cancellation of the sugar quota, the embargo, the pressure by the United States on Latin American and other countries to break relations with Cuba were weapons of great power. But Cuba, with the cooperation of the socialist countries and the resilience and strength that come from revolution, withstood them. Cuba's foreign trade was taken over by the Revolutionary Government and wheeled around 180 degrees without any major mishaps.

Revolutionary enthusiasm made up for much of the disorganization and confusion. The people at Bancec were eager to do whatever was necessary: they overlooked inconveniences, sat through endless meetings, took on the unfamiliar tasks, and didn't even complain much about extra, night-long jobs that resulted from the mistakes of the chiefs. As problems arose, they swarmed over them, dominating them by sheer numbers and effort.

Just eliminating the most glaring irrationalities in Cuba's foreign trade brought great immediate benefits. The Revolution stopped the import of luxuries and expanded the import of goods required for economic development. Counting only about 25 articles which are easy to separate statistically, the reduction in luxury imports saved Cuba $47 million in foreign exchange in 1960, and more in later years. Automobile imports sank from over $25 million in 1958 to $3.4 million in 1960; television sets from over $3 million to about $150,000.[4] If it were possible to disentangle all luxury goods from the jumble of statistics, the yearly total saved from 1960 on would come to at least $75 million.

And while the import of Cadillacs was going down, the import of tractors and other capital goods was going up. Table 1 shows figures for a few items.

From 1958 to 1961, the value of tractor imports went up more than threefold, trucks more than sixfold, and breeding cattle more than fivefold. In 1958, the amount spent for the import of breeding pigs was $2,000 and for breeding fowl $3,000; in 1961, more than $1 million went for each of these items. At first, the import of machinery rose even more rapidly than the other items, but it declined after 1959 as a result of the break in commercial relations with the United States.

The Revolutionary Government expanded trade not only with the socialist countries but with others as well. It dropped the old restrictive policy of selling only for dollars. Despite U.S. pressure and balance-of-payments problems, Japan bought large amounts of sugar from revolutionary Cuba; it now had more interest in trade with Cuba, because Cuba was willing to buy as well as sell, and Cuba's imports from Japan were rising. Before the Revolution, Cuba had virtually no trade

[4] "La Experiencia de Cuba en Comercio Exterior," *Comercio Exterior*, Revista Trimestral del Ministerio del Comercio Exterior de Cuba, No. 2 (abril-junio) 1964, p. 117.

Table I
Cuba: Selected Imports of Capital Goods, 1958-1961
(values in thousands of pesos equivalent to dollars)

	1958		1959		1960		1961	
	Quantity	Value	Quantity	Value	Quantity	Value	Quantity	Value
Tractors	2,408	5,507	1,724	9,744	3,081	8,208	5,614	16,915
Trucks	3,195	4,899*	2,603	6,190	1,158	3,982	11,766	33,568
Breeding cattle	2,533	427	53	19	5,429	2,083	7,341	2,203
Breeding pigs	23	2	—	—	5,479	570	34,736	1,372
Breeding fowl	9,144	3	415,716	135	4,324,415	1,928	1,660,957	1,012
Machinery for industry	—	27,444	—	45,857	—	30,200	—	29,987

* Includes spare parts.

Source: "La Experiencia de Cuba en Comercio Exterior," *Comercio Exterior,* Revista Trimestral del Ministerio del Comercio Exterior de Cuba, No. 2 (abril-junio), 1964, p. 118.

with Egypt; its exports in 1958 were $1,000 and its imports $18,000. But by 1962, Cuban exports to Egypt had risen to $9.9 million and its imports to $9.5 million. Cuba had imported almost nothing from Morocco; now it started taking increasing amounts of Moroccan goods and its exports to that country began to rise.

Cuba strove to increase its trade with Latin America. In 1961, trade with Chile increased; Chile needed sugar and could pay with onions and other products. Cuba bought rice from British Guiana. Transactions were carried out with Uruguay which for some time did not let itself be bullied by the United States on the subject of Cuba. There are many possibilities for trade between Cuba and the rest of Latin America, even given the one-crop economies and the channelling of the trade of the Latin American countries toward the United States rather than toward each other. Cuba could buy large amounts of lard from Argentina. Some day, Venezuela will be sending many million tons of petroleum to Cuba. But despite Cuba's efforts, its total trade with Latin America declined sharply after 1959. The pressure of the United States was too great; one after another the "republics" of Latin America—including all the holdouts but Mexico—broke relations with Cuba.

During the first few months, everyone at Bancec was so absorbed in buying, selling, attending meetings, doing rush statistical jobs, and clearing up problems at the ports that there was little time to try to think through questions of longer-run basic policy. But soon the wondering began.

The early decisions about sugar were strongly influenced by the sugar experts—the people who had worked for exporters or had been engaged in preparing statistics or writing articles on sugar. When these experts discussed sugar, they spoke with assurance. They announced in the fall of 1960 that with the United States increasing the demand for sugar in the world market by more than three million tons and with the socialist countries taking the Cuban sugar that had formerly gone to the United States—absorbing three to four million tons more than usual—the price of sugar would rise. "Let us not therefore be in a rush to sell." During the next six months the price of sugar fell from about 3.25 cents a pound to less than 2.5 cents. It became more and more clear in successive discussions that the understanding of the experts had a limited range: they could explain all the technical details of the specific operations they had worked on, or they were full of a kind of traditional sugar lore which they applied mechanically. But they did not know how to analyze and assess the world sugar market, especially under the changed conditions produced by the rupture of Cuba's trade with the United States. And so people in general began to wonder about the world sugar market. What sort of market is it, how does it work? About how much sugar can Cuba expect to sell in it? How fast is the world market likely to grow? What long-run prospects does it offer Cuba?

In the various meetings, there were also discussions of how to increase Cuban exports other than sugar: how to replace the U.S. market for Cuban tobacco, how to develop a market for Cuba's tropical fruits.

And then—haltingly at first—still more fundamental questions began to be raised. Cuba's foreign trade is far higher in relation to its gross product than that of any other socialist country. What is the significance of this? Does it mean Cuba will face new problems, somewhat different from those faced by the other socialist countries? What are the interrelations betwcen foreign trade, industry, and agriculture in Cuba? Between foreign trade and economic development?

4

Mounting Pressure Against Resources

During the first two years of the Revolution, its economic actions reflected an enthusiasm and audacity that recognized few limitations on what could be done. Both leaders and people were spurred by a driving impatience to right injustice, to improve the lot of *los humildes*, to get on with developing the economy and building a new Cuba, to show Latin America and the rest of the world what a revolution against imperialism could do. Attention was focused on what was necessary, what had to be done, not on what was possible, what the available resources would permit.

The financial precepts of the orthodox economists—such as Felipe Pazos and others like him at the National Bank and Treasury—were regarded with contempt. Both the precepts and those who intoned them had been part of a monetary system clearly designed to serve imperialism. Finances must be *sound*—the word is voiced with especial resonance by central bankers. But why do finances have to be sound and what are sound finances anyway? You don't have to search too hard to get at the answer: sound finances are necessary for a proper investment climate; unsound finances make foreign businessmen and investors unhappy because they can interfere with export markets and bring about controls which make it difficult to take out profits; and finances can be sound even though the unemployment rate is 25 percent and the economy is stagnating. The self-assured, orthodox economists became known to the revolutionaries as the *sesudos* (the brainy ones). The *sesudos* knew the rules and the jargon; if you needed people to write an application for a loan from the United States or from one of the American-dominated international financial agencies, they were the ones to do it. But for all the aura of profundity with which they surrounded themselves, the *sesudos* did

77

not have answers to Cuba's real economic problems. To succeed in wheedling a small favor from the United States was for them the supreme achievement. The sound currency which they worshipped above everything else could provide no land for the landless and no jobs for the unemployed. Here were the revolutionaries with visions of bringing education and medical care to everyone, of carrying out a true land reform, of eliminating unemployment, of getting economic development started; and there were the *sesudos* explaining all the things that could not be done because they might unbalance the budget. The orthodoxy of the old-line economists had to be disregarded; otherwise there would have been no revolution.

The revolutionaries surged ahead, guided by their own set of values. We cannot hold up the measures to bring education and medical care to the whole people while time-consuming studies of financing are carried out; somehow the money will have to be found. We have to give the land reform whatever financial backing it requires; there is no choice—you cannot make a successful land reform by operating like a commercial banker. We have to use the dollar reserves to stock up on goods before the American embargo is imposed. What good will the dollars do if the imperialists succeed in strangling our economy?

For many months, the economic and financial audacity of the Revolutionary Government brought great benefits and seemed to create no problems. The reduction of 50 percent in the rents of all who paid less than 100 pesos per month and of 30 or 40 percent for tenants in the higher brackets boosted the purchasing power of city dwellers. Reductions in electric power and telephone rates also helped raise purchasing power. The abolition of payments for the use of land meant a jump in income for tens of thousands of small farmers—the former tenant farmers and sharecroppers. As the state farms were set up on the old, lightly-manned cattle ranches, on formerly idle land, and on the large rice plantations, they began to create new jobs. The cane cooperatives strove to provide their members with work the whole year round, not just during the canecutting season. Many unemployed *campesinos* began to find work on the construction projects that were springing up around the countryside. In the cities, industrial output rose and commerce hummed.

The standard of living of most people, especially the poor, leaped upward. The *campesinos* began to eat meat and vegetables and buy shoes. The children of the lower-paid workers in Havana began to get milk. Everywhere bright-colored new construction shone in the sunlight.

True, the import of luxuries for the upper and middle classes had been shut off. But these people still had their cars, and there were no difficulties in getting spare parts. They had their apartments and household goods, their restaurants and night clubs. And for a surprisingly long time, the stores were able to meet the demand for many goods that were no longer being imported—Scotch whiskey, for example—from inventories.

Apart from the struggle with the United States and the disorganization inevitable in revolution, what were the problems? By the summer of 1960, there were signs of inflation, but nothing serious. The dollar reserves had been depleted during Batista's last years, but there was still a substantial amount of dollars left. Many specific errors were being made, but somehow they did not seem to have any discernible effects on the general working of the economy. It almost began to look as though the Revolution could do nothing wrong.

There arose a sort of exuberance about economics which intoxicated not only most Cubans, but many foreign economists as well. Everything seemed possible simultaneously and quickly.

Cuba would diversify and develop its agriculture, industrialize, bring education and medical care to everyone, build tens of thousands of new houses, improve the diet, and so on—all in record time. The upsurge in the economy since the Revolution took over had been easy, so everything else seemed easy. We ourselves can produce rice, beans, potatoes, and lard, instead of having to import them. Just by using more fertilizer and doing one or two other things, sugar yields can be raised 25 percent, or even more—this shouldn't be hard and it will free a large part of the sugar land for other uses. A flourishing cattle industry can be created in three or four years—think what this will mean! Freed of imperialism, we can quickly build a real industrial base—factories for producing shovels, pickaxes, refrigerators, tractors and trucks, perhaps also an iron and steel complex.

As usually happens when economists and statisticians are around, projections began to appear. If the Cuban economy grows by x percent each year, where—given the law of compound interest—will it be by 1965, 1970, and 1975? In the *Junta Central de Planificación* (*Juceplan* for short), people began to study the statistics on economic growth in Latin America, the socialist countries, and elsewhere, and became entranced with the march of the numbers. Analysis became a matter of mechanically comparing statistics instead of trying to understand how the Cuban economy worked and what concrete difficulties it might have to face as a result of the far-reaching changes and the U.S. embargo. One day I was having lunch with a friend who worked at the *Juceplan* and he told me of a meeting to discuss growth rate: the people at the meeting, he said, had divided into two groups, the optimists and the pessimists; the optimists argued that Cuba's annual growth rate should be projected at 14 percent, while the pessimists felt that the figure should be only 10 percent.

This sort of thing was not restricted to Cubans. The distinguished Polish economist, Michal Kalecki, prepared a "Hypothetical Outline of the Five-Year Plan, 1961-1965, for the Cuban Economy" which began to be circulated in December, 1960. The word "Plan" is used loosely in this title. The outline was not designed to serve as a basis for concrete planning and action; it was nothing more than a set of projections which might conceivably be realized, and also might not. Cuba's total output during 1961-1965 was projected to grow at an annual rate of 13 percent and consumption at 10 percent. Sugar exports were to go up over 60 percent. At the same time that this was happening, the output of other agricultural products would go up nearly 90 percent and industrial production over 140 percent. The obstacles that might interfere with the realization of these goals were not considered. That there might be difficulties in getting spare parts for machinery and equipment in industry, agriculture, and transport; that getting increases like 60 percent, 90 percent, 140 percent in five years involves more than putting down numbers on pieces of paper; that the Cuban economy was facing serious organizational problems; that industry and agriculture might be competing for the same scarce resources—for example, foreign exchange—none of this appears in the outline. The real basis for the high optimism of the projections was not given in the outline: it was simply the fact that the revolutionary economy had been surging upward till then.

One of the best comments on over-addiction to projections was made by Mark Twain. "In the space of one hundred and seventy-six years," he wrote, "the lower Mississippi has shortened itself two hundred and forty-two miles. That is an average of a trifle over one mile and a third per year. Therefore, any calm person, who is not blind or idiotic, can see that in the old Oölitic Silurian Period, just a million years ago next November, the Lower Mississippi River was upwards of one million three hundred thousand miles long, and stuck out over the Gulf of Mexico like a fishing rod. And by the same token any person can see that seven hundred and forty two years from now the Lower Mississippi will be only a mile and three quarters long, and Cairo and New Orleans will have joined their streets together, and be plodding comfortably along under a single mayor and a mutual board of aldermen. There is something fascinating about science. One gets such wholesale returns of conjecture out of such a trifling investment of fact."

While it was not fully clear at the end of 1960, the management of the Cuban economy during the first two years of the Revolution was made easier than usual by the existence of a large amount of reserves —using this word in the broad sense given to it by economists in the socialist countries. There were unutilized resources: idle land and labor and unutilized capacity in the manufacturing plants and the construction industry. There were some dollar holdings. There were over five million head of cattle.

Factories had stocks of spare parts and raw materials, and retail stores had stocks of finished goods. For example, retail stores had large supplies of hardware, parts for television and radio sets, lenses and frames for eyeglasses, and many items of clothing which lasted for many months after the importation of these goods from the United States had been cut off. I was able to buy several American-made Arrow shirts in a store in downtown Havana, more than a year after they had stopped coming in.

Cuba's foreign exchange controls—over imports, expenditures by Cubans for foreign travel, remittances to foreign countries—saved more than $100 million in foreign exchange, and until abolition of the sugar quota, this saving more than counterbalanced the losses in dollar earnings due to worsening relations with the United States. Nationalization provided the Revolutionary Government with a large additional source of revenues: the profits of the nationalized enterprises no longer went to private owners, but into the public purse.

Finally, there was the greatest reserve of all—the revolutionary enthusiasm of the people.

The rapid progress of the Cuban economy in the early years after the Revolution took power was made possible by the reserves. The very irrationality of the prerevolutionary economy served as a springboard for advance. By using the excess capacity of the construction industry and idle labor, you could produce schools, hospitals, and houses. By giving unemployed labor access to idle or under-utilized land, you could get quick increases in agricultural output. Because of the excess capacity, you could make industrial output go up more than 15 percent in the first year of the Revolution. You could cut out luxury foreign-exchange expenditures by a small part of the population and save tens of millions of dollars.

The reserves cushioned the Cuban economy against the consequences of error. How far wrong could you go so long as you were putting idle resources to work? You were perhaps not putting them to the best possible use, but you were clearly improving things over what they had been. The real cost to the economy of using resources that would otherwise be idle is zero—not the costs that appear in the conventional accounting ledgers.

When you raised the demands on resources to a level higher than the supply, the first consequences were not difficulties in the economy, but reductions in reserves. The demands by the economy for dollar imports might exceed dollar earnings; but this would first show up as a decline in the reserves, rather than as a difficulty in the working of the economy that had to be faced immediately. And the statistics on dollar reserves—inherently simple—were kept in a needlessly complicated form at the central bank and watched and understood by only a few specialists. The same thing applied to other parts of the economy. You could sustain an over-high level of meat consumption for a while, if you were willing to accept a reduction in the cattle population. And there were no simple, clear statistics on what was happening to the cattle population.

As the Revolution developed and its economic measures took hold, the demands on resources grew. The increase in agricultural output was absorbed like rain after a drought. The internal demand for coffee began to shoot up, cutting into the amount available for export. The jump in the demand for the goods produced by Cuban factories increased the requirements for the imported raw materials that went into them. Matters were further complicated by the elimination of luxury imports: this was a good measure, an unavoidable measure; but it let loose a large amount of purchasing power which had formerly been absorbed by the luxuries, and this further increased the demand for everything else.

Then American imperialism began to employ its heaviest economic weapons against Cuba. The abolition of the sugar quota, the embargo on U.S. exports to Cuba, the pressure by the United States on other countries not to trade or have any communications with Cuba—measures such as these were bound to cause difficulties.

The unutilized resources were reduced, one after the other, until the economy began to press against the limits. Difficulties began to crop up.

Among the first places where pressure on resources appeared was dollar imports.

In November 1960, Major Guevara's economic assistant at the central bank and I carried out a review of the dollar-exchange situation. The dollar expenditures were running three times as high as the dollar earnings; if the deficit continued, it would wipe out the dollar reserves in about four months. The policy of rapid buying which had gotten under way in July had of course been justified. But this policy had now been in effect four months; many goods were in the pipeline. The rapid buying could not be continued indefinitely. Many goods of secondary importance were being bought for dollars that would be sorely missed if the reserves were allowed to evaporate. A country in a situation like Cuba's needed some reserves for possible emergencies. A system of controlling dollar expenditures had to be introduced rapidly.

Both Major Guevara, the President of the National Bank, and Major Mora, the Administrator of Bancec, were abroad and not due back for two months. There was no time to wait for their return. Meetings were set up with the Vice President of the National Bank and the Deputy Administrator of Bancec; their approval for action was obtained and a rapidly improvised system of controls was instituted.

The system was simple. We made an estimate of what Cuba's dollar receipts would be in 1961, based mainly on how much sugar had been reserved for sale in the free market against dollars, on expected tobacco sales for dollars, and on the dollar payments that would be made by the Soviet Union and China in accordance with their payments agreements with Cuba. The estimate was subject to uncertainties: although the sugar price we had assumed was modest, the actual average price during the year might turn out to be still lower; we had included an estimate for dollar earnings from tobacco sales to the United States which could be stopped at any time. So from the initial estimate of dollar earnings, we deducted an allowance against errors and unforeseen contingencies. The remainder, divided by twelve, gave the amount of dollars that Bancec (and in a few months the Ministry of Foreign Trade which replaced it) could spend each month. This amount was divided up each month among the nine import sections of Bancec, except for 10 percent which was held by the Administrator of Bancec or his Deputy. The distribution of the "monthly expenditure quotas" to the sections was in the charge of a "Controller of Dollar Expenditures"—a job which I held for about nine months, after which it was transferred to the vice minister of imports.

Every month each section would submit a "quota request," giving the amount of dollars it thought it would need to spend in the following month and the items it proposed to buy with these dollars. For the first three or four months, the sum of these requests came to two or three times the amount available, and severe cutting was necessary. This process began with a series of meetings between the "Controller" and the chiefs and other key officials of each section. The section people were asked what would happen if they received only a fifth or a fourth the quota they had requested, which of the items they had proposed buying they would not buy, how this would affect the internal supply of these items, how much of a reduction *they* thought should be made, and the like. Then the "Controller" drew up a tentative set of quotas and a general meeting was held with the key people of all the sections to amend or ratify these quotas. Any section head could object to the quota for his section, and it would be increased if there were general agreement that this should be done. But the people at the meetings could not make any increases in quotas unless they simultaneously agreed to compensating reductions, so that the overall amount available for expenditure would not be exceeded.

The 10 percent held by the Administrator of Bancec was a reserve —to be used to cover large, special import requirements, to meet urgent requests for imports that cropped up during the month after the quotas had been fixed, to pay for last-minute increases in the prices of the goods being bought. When the section chiefs felt they were faced with an emergency which called for expenditures beyond their quotas, they could appeal to the Administrator of Bancec (later the Minister of Foreign Trade).

At first, there was great uneasiness and uncertainty among the section people about the controls. It was easier to order everything that an official of INRA, the Ministry of Public Health, or some factory

requested than to have to look into the requests and make decisions
postponing or rejecting the import of one item in favor of another.
The section people were understandably worried that if some factory
had to shut down or some foodstuff ran short as a result of the controls, they would be held responsible.

And it took several months for understanding of the controls to
spread among officials of other agencies of the government. Previously,
all requests for imports had been honored without question. Now officials were often told that before spending dollars on the import of a
certain item, an investigation would have to be made to see if it could
not be obtained from a socialist country; many requests for dollar
imports were reduced and some were rejected. So officials began to
stream into Bancec to find out what happened to their requests, to
argue, to object. A red-bearded young guerrilla fighter strode in to
find out about the air-conditioning system for a textile factory whose
construction he was supervising; the head of a coffee-packaging plant
came in about cellophane for wrappers; people came in from the telephone company, the Ministry of Transport, INRA, and so on.

Sometimes officials tried to back their requests by invoking high
rank. The Minister of Public Health, we were told for example, is
personally worried about the possibility of a shortage of medicines
and would like to see these requests fulfilled quickly. We were also
worried that a shortage of medicines might result from the controls.
So we arranged a meeting with the Minister of Public Health and
other high officials of his Ministry. We explained the dollar problem
and the rationale behind the controls. We too, we said, do not want
a shortage of medicines. But dollars cannot be handled as though they
came from a *pozo sin fondo* (a bottomless well); they are scarce. If
everyone were to spend dollars as he pleased, the reserves would soon
disappear and the Ministry of Public Health would be much worse
off than with an orderly system of priorities. Precisely because medicines have such a high priority, it is in the interest of the Ministry of
Public Health to support controls. But even though medicines are of
the highest importance, they too can be bought in excess. There is
such a thing as over-insurance, and tying up a few million dollars in

excessive stocks of medicines could mean a shortage of parts or raw materials for some factory. Except for one or two people, we at Bancec are laymen as regards medicines. We would like the help of Public Health people in cutting the import requests, so that this can be done intelligently and the chances of error minimized. Almost as soon as we began to present our arguments, the Minister's face took on a friendly smile. He had not been aware of the dollar problem, he said. But now that he had heard about it he was in agreement with us about the need for controlling expenditures. He had gotten the feeling, he said, that the import requests of his Ministry would be treated with a sense of responsibility at Bancec. For his part, he would take personal charge of reducing the dollar import requests of his Ministry. And he kept his word.

Three chiefs of import sections at Bancec did not cooperate to make the controls work. They would, for example, spend their whole quota during the first week of the month and then use the remaining three weeks to create emergencies—to bring up additional requirements "that just have to be met." Two of these chiefs left shortly for Miami. The other stayed on for a while. He seemed like an enthusiastic revolutionary. He organized the filing system for his section and then called on everyone, from the Administrator down, to come see the model improvements he had brought about. During meetings, he would go into strident denunciations of American imperialism, and it was sometimes difficult to get down to business. Somehow he arranged a transaction which called for him to take a trip to Canada and for a $150,000 letter of credit to be opened up in favor of a Canadian dealer. A few weeks after he left for Canada, word came that he had disappeared: the letter of credit had been written in such a way as to permit payment of the $150,000 upon presentation of shipping documents for some junk, and the Canadian dealer had been an accomplice.

Nevertheless, the controls worked. In the first month they were applied (December 1960) dollar expenditures were reduced by more than half and the total quota was exceeded by only about $2 million. In January 1961, the excess over the quota was reduced to a still smaller amount and from February on expenditures were held within the pre-fixed limits. No significant shortage or difficulty in the internal economy was ever traced to the controls.

The controls prevented the depletion of the dollar reserves and much waste in expenditures. Just as writers whose space is limited have to make each word tell, so buyers who are held to a budget have to make each dollar count. The major luxuries had been cut out of Cuba's imports in 1959. But Bancec had nevertheless been spending a large amount of dollars on less obviously nonessential goods—such as patent medicines, gadgets, toys—which now were also eliminated. When different agencies could simply order dollar imports as they liked, without even being aware of the problem of the dollars to pay for them, they tended to overestimate their requirements, sometimes grossly. Often internal inventory management was poor. One factory might have a large stock of a given material, while another was short. Some hospitals had large stocks of certain medicines of which others were running low. It was easier to get additional goods through imports than to try to rationalize their internal distribution. Now the central controls over dollar expenditures forced improvements in the estimates of requirements and exerted pressure for better internal distribution of goods.

The controls also brought out much useful information about the Cuban economy. Take paper, for example. Cuba was spending over $20 million in foreign exchange, a good part in dollars, to import pulp, paper, and paper products, and then—reflecting habits formed when it was a colony of the richest country in the world—wasting paper on a prodigious scale. Almost all retail purchases were given an impressive paper wrapping: a two-cent piece of candy, a pencil, a paperback book would all be put into large bags. Stinginess with foreign exchange could bring about big savings. The imported cellophane on the outside of cigarette packages could be eliminated; a domestically produced substitute could be found for the filter paper used in manufacturing cigarettes; the combined saving per year came to more than half a million dollars in hard currency. The magazine *INRA* did not have to be made with super-fancy imported chrome paper which cost over $300,000 a year.

Jute is another example. Each year Cuba spends from $15 million to $25 million in hard currency for jute sacks in which to transport sugar. This is always a large sum; but it was one thing when Cuba's dollar earnings were running over $700 million per year, and it is another now that about 80 percent of Cuba's trade is with the socialist countries and its dollar earnings are only a fraction of what they used to be. On top of the real need for large expenditures on jute, the functionaries at the General Administration of the Sugar Centrals were ordering jute in excessive amounts in 1960. They could be held responsible for a shortage of jute sacks and were nervous about it, whereas a possible shortage of dollars was someone else's responsibility and did not worry them. The over-insurance would not have mattered much if the excess jute sacks were all carried over from one year to the next. But this did not happen. Some of them somehow rotted in the warehouses. And others were always being commandeered to hold potatoes or something else that could just as easily have been put in cotton or paper sacks, not nearly so costly in foreign exchange. The controls not only saved dollars by deflating the estimates of jute sack requirements and causing people to stop misusing the sacks. By focusing attention on the large amount of dollars required for jute, they also helped show the importance of mechanizing the handling of sugar and shipping it in bulk.

One day a request came in from the Petroleum Institute for the import of $500,000 worth of tetraethyl lead, which at that time was available only for dollars. This being a large sum of money, the head of the raw materials section and I decided to ask some questions. The lead, we were told, was needed to get the desired octane rating in the gasoline turned out by the Institute. Domestically produced alcohol could also be used, but its local currency cost was higher than that of the tetraethyl lead and this would mean a large reduction in the Petroleum Institute's profits. Some of the technicians of the Petroleum Institute felt that the use of the alcohol might cause the gasoline to damage rubber parts in fuel systems, but others held that this was unlikely or at least that they could somehow fix the gasoline so it would not happen. Most of the alcohol would remain unsold if it were not used for the gasoline. We at Bancec decided to press for the use of the alcohol. The saving of so many scarce dollars was more important than the profits of the Petroleum Institute. The difference in profits was fictitious anyway—if the alcohol were not sold, the use of tetraethyl lead would raise the profits of the Petroleum Institute at the expense of lowering them for the economy as a whole. A meeting was arranged at which the Administrators of Bancec and the Petroleum Institute were present and the problem was argued back and forth. Finally, the Petroleum Institute withdrew its request for the import of tetraethyl lead.

After a few months, people got used to the controls. The flow of visitors to Bancec with arguments and objections subsided. And the tone of the arguments and objections changed. At the beginning, people usually came with the certainty that the import they were requesting should be approved because it was necessary. Being necessary was enough. Now they recognized that other things might be even more necessary.

The controls on dollar expenditures marked the beginning of a transition to a new phase in the revolutionary economy. As pressure on resources increased, exuberance had to be tempered by calculation. It was not possible to do everything simultaneously; the Cuban economy had to adjust to its resources; priorities had to be fixed, choices made.

The first shortages came in the spring of 1961. People began to notice that a few goods such as toothpaste, soft drinks, and beer were not always available at the retail stores. But the shortages seemed to be limited and sporadic. One store would not have toothpaste, another would. You would ask for a soft drink or a beer and be told there were none; then a week or two later, they were again to be had. The shortages were not serious, and everyone understood that difficulties were to be expected as a result of the break in commerce with the United States.

Then, in early summer, shortages of basic foodstuffs suddenly appeared. Chicken, meat, vegetables, lard, and *viandas*,[1] which had previously been easy to obtain, began to vanish from the stores. This was the first eruption of serious economic difficulty, and it came as a shock. Nobody seemed to have a clear, systematic understanding of what was happening and why these shortages were suddenly appearing. So the Revolutionary Government jointly with the National Direction of the Integrated Revolutionary Organizations (ORI)—the embryo Communist Party that was being formed from the old revolutionary movements—called a "National Production Conference" to determine the causes of the shortages and what was being done about them, and to report to the people.

The conference, which took place on August 26 and 27, 1961, was attended by 3,500 people from the government and the leading economic and revolutionary organizations—all the Ministers of the Revolutionary Government; the national, provincial, and municipal officials of the ORI; officials of INRA and other government agencies having to do with production, transport, and supplies; administrators of industrial enterprises, People's Farms, and cooperatives; representatives of the trade unions, the Association of Small Farmers, the Federation of Cuban Women, the Association of Rebel Youth, and the more than 100,000 Committees for the Defense of the Revolution. The proceedings were held in the large Chaplin Theater in Havana and were broadcast by radio and television throughout the country.

The method of the conference was simple. Officials in charge of different sectors of the economy, such as Ministers and the heads of key departments, gave long reports in which they projected future economic growth, analyzed difficulties, told of the measures being taken to meet them, and presented criticisms and self-criticisms. After each report, the official answered questions submitted by people throughout the theater. Sometimes officials would disagree with each other and a small debate would develop. Fidel made the introductory remarks and the final summation.

[1] There is no English equivalent for *viandas*; they consist of tubers such as malanga, boniato, and yucca, the pumpkin-like *calabaza*, and green bananas. *Viandas* have always been a very important source of carbohydrate in the Cuban diet.

The conference, Fidel said in his introduction, was a "profoundly revolutionary and democratic act."[2] Its first purpose was to inform the people, so that they would know "what are the difficulties and what are the possibilities"; and so that they could participate in running the economy, because "absolutely nothing can be achieved without the participation of the masses—the people."

Fidel went on to place the economic problems and difficulties in perspective. "We have problems of supply," he said. "They are fundamentally due to the fact that the purchasing power of our people is $500 million per year higher than before the triumph of the Revolution. . . . The problem to resolve is how, with the resources at our disposal, to satisfy the fundamental demands of the people."

We have also made errors, said Fidel. "There are goods that perhaps would not be lacking if we had had a little more foresight. Sometimes we became involved in a great agricultural purpose, for example, the supply of fats, the supply of rice, or the production of cotton, and great results were achieved. . . . Nevertheless *malanga* was forgotten, despite the many times we have said that if there is nothing else to eat we will eat *malanga*. There has been no *malanga* anywhere and this naturally created immediate pressure on *boniato*. And then when both were scarce, the consumer went in search of potatoes, and the stock of 10,000 quintals daily, calculated for normal situations, turned out to be insufficient."

Then there are the aggressions of the imperialists. "They have not just attacked us militarily, but have tried to wound us mortally through the economy." They have abolished our sugar quota; they have embargoed the export of spare parts to us, knowing that our machinery comes from the United States; they have embargoed the export of raw materials for our factories; they try by all means to prevent us from obtaining foreign exchange. "The imperialists thought that the masses would turn against the Revolution when there was a lack of lard or any of the other articles that have become scarce. . . . But once again they have been mistaken. . . ."

---

[2] Obra Revolucionaria, *Primera Reunión Nacional de Producción*, Agosto 26-27, La Habana, Imprenta Nacional de Cuba, 1961. All following quotations from this source unless otherwise noted.

"Still," said Fidel, "it should not be enough for us that the masses have a revolutionary spirit, that they will stick firmly by the Revolution, no matter what the circumstances. . . . We must exhaust the last atom of our energy . . . to give the masses the maximum of welfare, even in the midst of this stage of struggle against imperialism, even in the midst of these first years which are the most difficult ones."

The first report was made by Regino Boti, the Minister of Economy and head of the *Juceplan*. Boti said a few words about shortages and difficulties. "Before the triumph of the Revolution, a very high proportion of the rural population did not consume its own products. Before 1959 many *campesinos* consumed almost no meat, eggs, or milk, and were unacquainted with butter. The Land Reform has so raised the standard of living of the rural masses that the consumption of food products has grown extraordinarily. The increase in consumption in the countryside has at times resulted in an inadequate supply for the cities. [Also] the shortage of work hands that—for the first time in thirty years—appeared in the Cuban countryside during the last (1961) sugar *zafra*, interfered with the harvesting of certain products."

But most of Boti's remarks concerned economic planning and future growth. "A socialist economy has to be a planned economy. . . . Planning is not the result of the speculation of a few technicians who make calculations and determine coefficients. . . . Every one of the laborers of Cuba, every *campesino*, every worker in a factory, in construction, in transport, every employee, every technician has the right and the duty to contribute to the planning of the national economy."

On growth Boti said: "The total material production of Cuba will grow in the years 1962-1965 at a rate of not less than 10 percent (per year) and probably not more than 15.5 percent." As a result of this growth, the standard of living would soar. "In relation to 1958 the increase in consumption per capita will be more than 60 percent. . . . The per capita consumption of cloth will be almost 60 square meters, which is superior to that of Sweden, Norway, and Belgium, and similar to that of France, Australia, and Czechoslovakia." Cuba will be producing 5,000 tractors per year. And so on.

Many of the reports on specific sectors of the economy contained projections for very rapid growth similar to those of the *Juceplan*.

But while at that time the *Juceplan* had no practical responsibilities, the other Ministries and organizations did. They were not just making projections and writing memoranda. They were running things; they had to face concrete practical problems; they were far closer than the *Juceplan* to the workings of the economy. And so, while many of their reports spoke of great plans that would soon be carried out, they also reflected something else—the hard struggle with a mulish reality.

Eduardo Santos Ríos, Chief of Production of INRA, began his report by citing some accomplishments of the Land Reform and INRA. Sixty thousand *caballerías* of additional land had been brought under cultivation. (This is a large amount of land; the total amount of land under sugar cane during the years 1958-1960 was 105,000 *caballerías*, and even though the sugar land is of much higher quality, the addition is very significant.) The people had taken over Cuban agriculture: a former canecutter was in charge of all cane on the lands taken from the United Fruit Company. The value of total agricultural output in 1961 would be 996 million pesos as compared to 850 million in 1960—an increase of 18 percent.

But soon the problems appeared. "Everyone is aware of the impetuous growth of the purchasing power of our people. . . . But in meat this has gone to violent extremes." The per capita consumption of beef was 37.73 pounds in 1959, 49.77 pounds in 1960, and 55.49 pounds in 1961. We did not have good data on the inventory of cattle. So we strained ourselves to the utmost and quickly carried through a cattle count. We have approximately 5.5 million head of cattle, of which 30 percent, 1,650,000, are breeding cows. Taking the birth rate at 60 percent, the infant mortality rate at 10 percent, and allowing for the retirement of old cows, rejections, and the like, we can estimate the number of head of cattle that we dispose of for consumption. "We have 781,000 head available for consumption, and consumption is one million. If the consumption of cattle is a million, while we dispose of no more than 781,000, we can march toward ruin in seven or eight years—or in less, because every day the people are eating more—we can finish off our cattle population.

"It is exactly the same with hogs, which the population threatened to eat up. Fidel called us and said: not a single sow is to be killed; we have to buy all the females in the cooperatives and the People's Farms and fence them in."

It was a similar story with milk. The production of milk for Havana had gone up to 470,000 liters daily from 400,000 the year before. "One day we hit 500,000 liters." But the demand had been rising even faster. The cafes bought their milk in bulk and paid 16 cents a liter for it; ordinary consumers paid 20 cents. The ordinary consumers kept taking more and more milk and it started disappearing from the cafes.

Practical management of agriculture is not easy. "Fowl is being imported, but if we do not synchronize the imports with the quantity of breeding fowl, with the installation of incubators, with the men who are going to handle these millions of fowl which have cost our people millions of pesos or dollars, then come the difficulties. Then come the epidemics, which wipe out 50 percent of the fowl, because we have had them crowded together, because we did not have sheds for them; and many times, trying to fulfill a goal for a certain quantity of breeding fowl, we get crowding and the loss of 50 percent." This is what happens when we try to carry out a plan "without taking into account all the keys of the piano, which start with the sowing of grasses, with the grains and plants for producing feedstuffs, with the sheds for the fowl . . . and so we fall into the net of our own errors."

There are also difficulties with hogs: "There are devoted comrades who at three in the afternoon on Sundays are in the pigpens struggling to do their job; but on the People's Farms, there isn't the high level that these technicians have; and the hogs that were nurtured with four pounds of feedstuffs daily, that were bred and acclimated by us with sufficient water, do not have water. The trough of feedstuffs has not yet been prepared. The *pangola* has not yet been sown; the quarters have not yet been prepared. And we have to return and say that we cannot yet send hogs to these farms."

And there are fungi and insects that attack the crops. "The insecticides and fungicides have to be on time, because neither the *fogata*, nor the *picudo*, nor any of the insects that cost millions and millions of pesos [wait]. . . . I just want to say that the borer is an insect that perforates the stalk of the cane and its damages are estimated to be 43 million pesos annually."

And then there is always the rain. You are going to plant cotton. If you wait too long and the heavy rains come, you will not be able to plant. If you plant too soon and the rains do not come, you will have planted for nothing. "Instructions are sent out by telegram and radio to the chiefs of provinces, to the technicians, to the administrators of the farms to give orders immediately to plant while it is still dry." But a lot of people are worried that it will not rain soon; and so only about 80 percent of the desired planting is carried out.

But Santos Ríos did not let the problems weaken his optimism about future goals. "The goal set is for a thousand pigpens. Each one of these thousand pigpens with 500 sows, to arrive within two years at a final supply to our people of 5 million hogs of 200 pounds. Note what this quantity means: 500,000 sows and ten sucklings per head gives 5 million hogs. It is as though to each one of us—because we are almost 7 million and the hogs are 5—as though to each one of us there corresponded a hog of 200 pounds. We would have to eat a lot of meat in a year to eat all that and we hope that it will not be all eaten and that we will be able to export meat."

Chickens are another example. Chicken production was running at about a million a month at the time. "But we are fighting to achieve 4 million by December and 7 million by next March."

The tone of many other reports at the conference was similar to that of Santos Ríos. They told of problems, difficulties, and errors—and they exuded optimism about quick results in the future. The other reports on agriculture gave further concrete information on the causes of the shortages and the problems of managing the economy, of which a few examples are worth giving.

Although the overcrowding and epidemics reported by Santos Ríos had been costly, the main reason for the shortage of chickens was something else. "Normally here in Cuba," explained an official of the National Administration of the People's Farms, "all the chickens that were fattened, that is all the chickens that went to the markets, were imported from the United States. Normal imports were 1,200,000— sometimes 1,500,000—chickens monthly. When economic relations were broken . . . we saw this quantity go down to zero."

The agrarian reform was bringing about many changes in the distribution pattern between country and city. The small farmers, relieved of the payments they had formerly had to make as tenants and sharecroppers, were themselves consuming more, the head of the National Association of Small Farmers pointed out. But in addition, many of the goods that they had formerly supplied to the cities were now going to the members of the People's Farms and the cooperatives and their families. Again, the increase in purchasing power. The purchasing power of the people on the collective farms had risen far more than the current output of these farms because a great deal of the initial work had gone into investment—setting the farms up and adding to existing installations or building new ones.

There were also shifts in the regional distribution of goods. The green bananas consumed in Havana had always come from the province of Oriente. Now they were not to be seen in Havana and people wondered why. Had production failed? Production had not failed. With the increase in their purchasing power, the people in Oriente were consuming more, and so the green bananas no longer got as far as Havana.

There were problems with the distribution of fertilizer. The use of fertilizer had almost doubled between 1960 and 1961. But this put a strain on the transport system. Fertilizer has to be available at the specific time it is needed. Since there is a shortage of storage facilities on the farms, the transport of large amounts of fertilizer has to be carried out in a very short time. And the time when the fertilizer is needed conflicts with other demands on the transport system. Sometimes the little open cane wagons of the sugar centrals—called "cages"— have had to be used for the fertilizer. And sometimes, because of this and because of the lack of storage capacity, the fertilizer has been exposed to the elements, to the rain, for more than a month. The losses have been less than three percent of the total. But still. . . .

A last example: problems with equipment. "The difficulties," said an official of the cane cooperatives, "start with the fact, known to everybody, that all our agricultural equipment was of American manufacture, and in the majority of cases was in the worst possible condition. American imperialism not only cut off the supply of equipment, but even more important, the supply of replacement parts. This is constantly causing the paralysis of equipment, in some cases for good.

"The effort which the socialist countries have made, sacrificing their own needs to supply us with tractors, is something that the members of the cooperatives will always remember. We are constantly receiving equipment from the socialist countries, but never in the quantities we need." Also, "we have tractors and we don't have plows and we have plows and don't have tractors."

Enrique Cabré, the head of the Department of Agricultural Machinery of INRA, explained why there were difficulties with plows. "The implements which existed all came from the United States. . . . Several of our technical comrades undertook the task of designing and constructing plows for the tractors which the socialist countries are sending us. We have built 2,163 plows. . . . To make plows, coordination is necessary because we in Cuba are not yet in a position to produce some of the parts which plows need, such as disks and roller bearings, which are important. . . . There are large quantities of finished plows in the Anglo Cuban Company and the American Steel Company awaiting roller bearings . . . in recent weeks we have received some disks. This information has been passed to the comrades at the Bank of Foreign Trade."

Several reports had stressed the need for better care of equipment, and Cabré put it strongly: "It is time to take severe measures, to apply penalties to those who do not take care of agricultural equipment." He told of the machine shops being set up and complained that sometimes the mechanics were pirated away by other departments of the government which offered higher pay. And he also told of what was being done to train people in the use and maintenance of tractors: operators were being given instruction on the farms, and provincial tractor schools were being set up.

The head of INRA's Department of Fishing told a story similar to those about agriculture. Like many other economic pursuits, fishing had not been developed in Cuba. Although Cuba is an island, it did not have a strong maritime tradition like Britain or Japan. And Cuban education had avoided ships and fishing. "Do you know that there does not exist in Cuba a single naval architect?" If you had asked Cuban university students whether they wanted to be fishermen, how many would have said yes? None. Because they considered fishermen to be something pretty low; fishermen were practically declassed people. Fishermen constituted one of the most illiterate groups in the population, the hardest to teach to read; "very few knew how to navigate; fewer were naval mechanics. . . ." Now the Revolution was sending the sons of fishermen to school, teaching them navigation, naval mechanics, and modern methods of fishing.

"Everyone knows of the war to the death between the fishermen of Manzanillo who use cast nets and those of Santa Cruz who use dragnets. . . . Using cast nets is a very rudimentary way of catching shrimp. . . . A man spends entire nights on the poop of his little boat throwing the net and then rowing rapidly ahead . . . all to catch 40, 50, or 100 pounds of shrimp. . . . The dragnet is the correct way, used in all the highly industrialized countries, and allows one to catch far more. Nevertheless, when we attended the meeting of the comrades in Manzanillo they almost threw us into the water for maintaining this method was better."

Modern fishing requires technique. "The yellow-finned tuna, for example, likes to be in water of 28 degrees [centigrade]. . . . If instead of taking this into account, you depend on luck and throw out the line, you can be there a year without catching anything. The Japanese, who are a little sharper than we are in this, first investigate where the tuna is in general to be found. Then they try to see how much tuna there is in specific zones. They drop the thermometer to 200 fathoms, for example, and encounter a temperature of 28 degrees. Nobody on board has seen the fish, but they immediately begin to drop the lines, the floaters and weights are put on, and the hemp rope with the bait is placed. That is to say: the hemp rope hangs with its bait in the latitude where the temperature is 28 degrees. Every 24 hours a boat fishing for tuna can take in 10 to 15 tons. What it takes one of our ships two weeks to catch, a Japanese ship gets in one day."

To develop a modern fishing industry would take a little time. "How were boats formerly made? How many boats were formerly made? . . . Now the total number of boats under construction in the different ports is 184."

"We planned the best we knew how. . . . Nevertheless, from Camagüey to here, with nine shipyards and 135 boats under construction, we have not yet been able to launch even one. There are problems of supply. Many times the material takes too long to get to the shipyard. There are problems of transport which the comrades directing the Ministry of Transport know about; and there are problems of supply in some of the parts essential to a boat. We need, for example, 200 foghorns, 200 rudders, 200 propellers. . . . It is necessary to bear in mind that a boat is a complex thing. Many things are necessary to make it go. . . . And although we have tried to make as much as we can here to save foreign exchange . . . 85 percent of the investment is made abroad. Even the navigation maps, the compasses, the T-squares, the motors, the screws—all these things have to be bought abroad, and so it is to be expected that they will not all arrive at the right time."

And there is something else. "Every little movement imperialism makes—the first thing it affects are the ports. . . . During the first 25 days of this month, the port of Casilda has been closed 14 days; Caibarién 11; Cienfuegos 4; without counting the rest of the island . . . and in Isabela de Sagua one cannot enter after 6 in the afternoon or leave before 8 in the morning. . . . In Casilda, 10 boats have been taken over by the militia and this disrupts production. . . . There are 350 militiamen who are out in their boats. And the comrades cannot produce because . . . well, there have already been fatalities among the fishermen who go out; a militiaman yells halt at them, and maybe they don't hear."

At this point, Fidel interrupted to say: "In many cases it is not the government that gives this kind of order. I am happy that you are bringing out this problem here, because it is incompetent chiefs who are giving these orders." The speaker replied that this encouraged him because "often we felt somewhat impotent, not knowing where these orders were coming from."

And finally, with seafood as with everything else, the increase in purchasing power and the new social system had changed the pattern of distribution. "Before the triumph of the Revolution, 95 percent of the production came to Havana, to the *Mercado Unico* [the central market], because in a capitalist system, the market with the highest price was where the intermediary wanted to sell his product; the socialist system tries to make a better distribution, so that everyone eats equally well."

But the redistribution in favor of the interior can also be overdone. "We want to make the self-criticism that sometimes we have allowed our administrators of cooperatives to get enthusiastic about giving the fish to the towns of the interior. We are not against the comrades of the interior eating fish, but the reality is that Havana is a market of more than a million inhabitants. Corralillo, Cifuentes, or Florida can remain without fish and there is no problem, but when there are no fish in Havana, the problem is delicate. This is aggravated by the fact that there is an almost complete absence of chicken. The people chase after meat and when the meat is finished, they go looking for fish. There is another factor: the people don't get to see fish because when it arrives at the reception center here in Havana, we immediately have the schools of dramatic art, the militias, the hospitals, asking us for 1,000, 2,000, 3,000 pounds; and if there are 40 or 50 thousand pounds of fish, all these organizations carry them away to those whom it is also necessary to feed, and so fish does not appear on the street."

Yet there is some good news. "November of this year the first of the Polish boats . . . will arrive along with six Polish fishermen to teach us how to handle them." And the Ministry of Foreign Commerce has approved our request for the purchase of five Japanese boats, and negotiations are now going on in Japan to get these boats by the middle of next year. And soon the boats we ourselves are constructing will begin to come off the ways."

Major Guevara gave the report on industry. He began by emphasizing the need to point out errors. "It may be that some errors are justifiable; however, the important thing is not to justify errors, but to keep them from being repeated." Then he turned to his Ministry:

"Like all the recently created Ministries, the Ministry of Industry was constructed on the basis of enthusiasm, of technical aid, of a certain veneer of knowledge possessed by some of the comrades. . . . Nevertheless, it has constantly been necessary to change directors, to substitute administrators, to send some away to improve their cultural and technical capacity, others to improve their political position; and in the midst of the process of production, it has been necessary to work also toward the creation of leading cadres for the very technical, very complex industries that Cuba will have in the future."

The Ministry of Industry has been trying to plan the operations of industry. "For the Ministry, planning is something fundamental, and here it is necessary to make one of our severest criticisms. The plan never was anything more than a very nebulous scheme within the Ministry of Industry; we were not capable of working with well-elaborated hypotheses. . . . At the beginning, the Office of Planning set up production goals that would have been logical if one assumed an idyllic situation in which there was no struggle going on in relation to the markets that supply the country, especially the American market. Practice demonstrated that the plan lacked reality . . . it was based on production possibilities calculated on the assumption that everything that was supposed to arrive would arrive. . . . You will therefore see that absolutely none of the production goals has been met. Perhaps one or two of the goals of the 40 enterprises have been met; all the rest have been below what we had hoped for, although in some cases—in a good many cases—there has been a considerable increase with respect to last year. . . . The lack of raw materials and some spare parts has imposed, in addition to stoppages, a slower rhythm of production. . . .

"It is on the problem of spare parts that we made our first really effective contact with the mass of workers . . . and the results have been really marvellous. We set up spare parts committees at the base, and in this way, with the emulation of everyone and with the work of all the workers of all the factories of the country, innumerable problems have been solved. Now there arrive at the Superior Committee of Spare Parts—at the Ministerial level—only those problems which cannot be solved at the other levels; and this committee can determine whether there is still a possibility of finding a solution within the country or whether it is necessary to go looking outside. At this moment we are studying a second emulation campaign . . . which would have as its name: 'Construct your own machine.' "

As to specific stoppages and scarcities Major Guevara said: "There is at present a scarcity of toothpaste. It is necessary to explain in detail why. Since about four months ago there has been a paralysis in production; there was, however, a large stock. The measures urgently required were not taken, precisely because there was a very large reserve. Afterwards the reserves began to decline and the raw material did not arrive; that was the moment to get going full speed and ask for things. When the raw material—bicalcium sulfate—did arrive, it did not meet the specifications for making toothpaste. The technical comrades of the enterprises got to work and made a toothpaste. And I'll say this to all the hoarders: it is a toothpaste as good as the old one, it cleans equally well, but after a month it becomes hard. Don't applaud; they didn't do it on purpose; it just came out that way. They did the best they could, but I am advising people not to hoard toothpaste and then come around after four months with the protest that they have a stone in the tube. . . .

"There has been a considerable decline in the production of soft drinks because of insuperable errors in getting raw materials, and there have also been serious problems with beer. Here is where we can see how an error can result in a series of problems. We have been facing a shortage of bottles; this shortage has made itself felt in soft drinks, in medicines, in beer, and even sometimes in milk. That is to say, a whole series of industries have been feeling the shortage of adequate containers. The glass factory very probably remained shut down because of a lack of technical ability. Some workers accused the technician of sabotage. We cannot be so harsh about a person who did not have sufficient experience. But it is true that this person, besides having reactionary political ideas, stopped the reconstruction of a furnace and the utilization of Cuban raw materials. A Czech technician in the plant thought that much time was being lost, that it was necessary to use Cuban raw material, that possibly the glass wouldn't come out exactly the same but it would still be good enough. We had a meeting in which I participated personally several months ago; a delay was granted, because at that time the Ministry of Foreign Commerce announced that a cargo of raw material was arriving from abroad. Afterwards in the dizziness of continuous work, I lost sight of the enterprise, and after a while I found out that it was still in the same state: the raw material had not come in from abroad and the technician still declined to use the Cuban one. All this has now been overcome. The furnace is running well, Cuban raw materials are being used, and the bottle is being turned out . . . it has been said that the bottle is caramel in color to keep out the light; but the truth is it just came out this way. It isn't so good, but anyway it's a bottle. . . .

"Coca Cola," Major Guevara went on, "was one of the most popular drinks in Cuba, but today it tastes like cough syrup. It has seven, eight, or nine—I don't remember how many—ingredients, some of which are secret. This was one of those secrets held by the American factories: ingredients arrive with the label 'xz-29' and all the Cuban technician has to know is that he must put a certain amount into the mechanism in which the components are mixed, and out comes ordinary Coca Cola with the taste we all know. It was necessary to do much investigation and a substitute has been found, but sometimes we have to eliminate an ingredient that we can't get and can't make. It is necessary to work harder because we have to make sure of a quality product in quantities sufficient for the whole people to consume. . . . Soft drinks in Cuba are almost a necessity, given the climate."

Like Fidel in his opening remarks, Major Guevara placed the problems and difficulties in a revolutionary perspective. There was no fear of difficulties. "There has never been any question of fear even in things as fundamental as the atomic threats of the American warmongers. Why should we think that a people that has this attitude will not be clear politically, will not be capable of the greatest sacrifices, in order to reach the goal that we all know and all desire?"

Then came more problems. "The Antillana de Acero—an iron and steel factory—had to shut down for some days because of a shortage of raw materials, but we were able to tie this in with its normal stoppage for repairs. The Pheldrake, which produces copper cable, had to stop because of a lack of raw material. It was nobody's fault, the raw material is on the way, but sometimes it gets delayed a little—from China to here the normal trip is two months. . . . We have to try to accumulate reserves of all the fundamental articles, of the fundamental raw materials."

About matches: "Matches are one of the worst disgraces we have at the Ministry of Industry. . . . Evidently, there is almost no one in Cuba who doesn't remember the Ministry of Industry several times a day when he strikes a match. We can unload some of the blame for this—the major part—on imperialism and the lack of raw materials; but we are also at fault. We are now working to improve a national glue factory, but the production is small, the demand is large, and the glue doesn't dry well; and afterwards come the problems you all know. . . . We are going to make an effort to solve the problem with domestic products, without having to bring anything from the dollar area, bringing some products from the countries with which we have bilateral agreements [so that dollars are not required]; but we are going to look for some means whereby the people of Cuba won't have to fall back on flint and steel in order to light a cigarette."

The production of the Consolidated Rubber Enterprise, which turns out tires, tubes, and a few other rubber products such as sneakers, was down 29.6 percent compared to 1960. The factories were paralyzed for periods of two to four months because "they used up all the materials that came from the dollar area; and just now it has been necessary to reduce production because of a shortage of wire for the beads of the tires. The last shipment to arrive was wasted because the material was not exactly what had been requested by the company."

The production of paints was about 13 percent lower than in 1960 because of a shortage of materials. Purchase orders had been placed toward the end of 1960 and in February 1961, but the materials did not arrive on time. The materials formerly came from the dollar area; now formulas were being adopted which would permit the use of substitutes.

"The amount of wheat milled was lower than had been planned because wheat and bromate [for bleaching] were short and because the wheat received was a soft one that reduces the amount of flour that can be extracted from it. In addition there were shortages of additives such as pyrophosphate, calcium phosphate, etc., necessary for bakery products. We here have made some errors . . . and there has been a lack of coordination with our suppliers who sent us a type of wheat with which our mills do not work well."

It seemed to me as I listened to Major Guevara that his voice took on a tone of special warmth for his subject when he got to drugs and medicines; he was speaking as the former physician, who had taken up medicine for itself, not for money-making, who did not view medicine as a narrow specialty but as part of society as a whole.

"The major difficulties are: managing the import of certain items; the shortage of containers—this has caused, for example, a decline in the production of a simple thing like serums; and the great variety of brands. There has been much talk in Cuba of the lack of this or that medicine. One way that has been used to make counter-revolution—very simple and in some cases pretty efficacious—is for a doctor to tell you, take this product because it is good and if they give you some other, say no because this is the only good one. The doctor prescribes something by Abbott or Lilly or some other American brand, and when a substitute is given, people don't want it because the doctor said that the only thing that will cure them is this other thing. The formula is the same or similar. Not so many things have been discovered in medicine. There are four, five, or ten products which are used daily, and then there are some hundred fundamental products, or perhaps five hundred, but not more—certainly not the thousands of brands that there are on the market in the capitalist countries. Each company produces its own brand. . . . They are all about equal; one company may be a little more serious than some other; but in the end the difference is very small. Yet each company has doctors who prescribe its products. All this has ended in Cuba, but it is worth pointing out that in some capitalist countries the relations between the sales houses and the doctors is such as to require police action. . . . Here a formulary is being worked out . . . by Public Health. This formulary, with five hundred or six hundred formulas, will have all the remedies necessary for the country, in a simplified form, without all the fanfare that serves only commercial purposes. . . .

"There will not be any great difficulties in meeting necessities during the rest of 1961. . . . The products which the socialist countries have committed themselves to giving us are arriving regularly in ships, or rather in all forms of transport, some things in airplanes, and we can assert that our pharmaceutical industry will in general be operating at an adequate level."

Despite all the problems, there were many industries in which production was as high as or higher than in 1960. With the sugar harvest at the second highest level ever reached, the production of crude sugar was 15.4 percent higher. And this of course also increased the production of by-products. Molasses was 11.4 percent higher; wax 57 percent; alcohol 16 percent.

Cement production was 4.7 percent higher than in 1960. Ceramics production was much higher: firebrick 50 percent, bathtub basins 64 percent, tiles 89 percent, washbasins 264 percent higher. Apart from wire and cable, the production of non-ferrous metals had gone up strongly; for example, the output of structural aluminum was over six times as great as in 1960. The production of nickel was 6.8 percent higher, despite a shortage of containers and difficulties with spare parts. And iron and steel production was 120 percent higher.

Electric power production was about the same as in 1960. It had been expected that the demand would increase, but this had not occurred. "Cuba was a country in which electricity was used to supply light to the most aristocratic neighborhoods of the city, to supply light for advertising, and for other unnecessary uses." The decline in demand for these uses compensated for the increase in other types of demand. There had been some stoppages for repairs, but these had not caused any great inconvenience. "The main difficulties have been acts of sabotage; there have been political problems in the Cuban Electric Company; the flight of technicians continues; some spare parts are short; and the organization was bad at first, but little by little has been getting better."

The Consolidated Petroleum Enterprise had had difficulties with specialized equipment that the socialist countries were not able to supply on time, and with some types of special oils. Here, too, there had been a swindle—this time for $500,000. The swindle was "well-executed by an individual who instead of delivering what he was supposed to, sent some worthless tubing and then rapidly collected on the letter of credit—and the loss hurts all the more because the stolen money was dollars." But the output of the petroleum industry in 1961 was only one percent lower than in 1960.

The production of shoes was much higher than in 1960. Consumption had gone up "enormously." But a major problem could be foreseen. Even when the slaughter of cattle was uncontrolled, there had been difficulty in obtaining enough hides for leather with which to meet the demand for shoes. Now cattle slaughter was being controlled and the number of cattle slaughtered had recently been reduced.

Major Guevara also touched on something which people were beginning to notice and wonder about: a deterioration in the quality of goods. People saw that many products were simply not as well made as they had been. Often it was obvious that the problem lay in the inability to obtain the right raw materials. But sometimes the shoddiness seemed clearly to be due to the workmanship—the seams on an article of clothing were not quite right, or the two shoes sold as a pair did not match exactly.

"There are enterprises and comrades in the Ministry who . . . identify quality with counter-revolution, who feel that quality is a capitalist vice and that one does not have to trouble oneself about it under socialism. If the paper band on a cigar comes out bad . . . if the drawing is ugly, if the tobacco mixture isn't made in exactly the right way, if—to take something else—cloth is not of good quality, if the print is poor . . . these things often do not seem to interest our comrades. Quality is constantly being sacrificed in many sectors of our industry to assure savings, to assure production. We have had discussions with the directors of enterprises and have insisted on something fundamental. . . . The development of socialism is not undertaken in the interest of some abstract philosophical entity, but in the interest of man. . . . The Revolution has no quarrel with beauty. To turn out an article of common use that is ugly when it could be pretty is truly an error. And it is an error that we often fall into in our country . . . because some of our comrades think that you can give anything to the people . . . and if the people protest, they are counter-revolutionary. But that is false, completely false."

It is doubtful that any of the people listening to Major Guevara, aside from the technicians from the other socialist countries, realized that the problem of quality was not something special to Cuba, but one that all the socialist countries have had to grapple with. This knowledge was to come later as we got deeper into the practical problems of running a planned economy, and many people began to read up on and discuss the experiences of the other socialist countries.

Major Guevara ended his report with a number of criticisms of the Ministry of Industry and other government agencies. First his own Ministry. "There still exists a large dose of bureaucracy in our Ministry. . . . There is also a continuing lack of contact with the masses; a lack of contact which reflects itself in the relations between the leadership of the trade unions and our Ministry. . . . There is no vision of the problems as a whole. . . . There is a lack of coordination with other state organizations. . . ."

Then other agencies. "To the Ministry of the Armed Forces: Militiamen have been taken away from their jobs, and kept away for a long time, without any consideration being given to their importance in industry. In addition, vital equipment has sometimes also been taken. . . . Equipment of all types, construction equipment, maintenance equipment, above all vehicles, have been taken—in periods of crisis, every little lieutenant and every little captain thinks he has the right to seize everything that passes his way, even when it is not really needed for defense. It is necessary to be clear: when the moment for defending the country arrives we have to think of nothing but defense. But there are people who seem to be lying in ambush in every situation to get hold of an automobile and then hold it until it is taken away from them."

The Ministry of Foreign Trade: "There has been a lack of foresight in the requests, a lack of an order of priorities, a narrowness of vision on the part of lower-ranking functionaries. . . . But the work of the Ministry of Foreign Trade has been improving."

Major Guevara was especially severe with the Ministry of Internal Commerce. This Ministry "has had the grave defect of overestimating its capacity. It took an existing and functioning distribution setup and changed and deformed it completely, creating some serious foul-ups." The takeover of Havana's central market is an example of what Major Guevara was referring to. One day the newspapers carried a statement by the Ministry listing all the things that had been wrong with the market and the great accomplishments that could be expected now that it was being nationalized. But only after the old market organization was abolished did the Ministry begin to work on a new one to replace it.

Finally, came a criticism of the Ministry of Public Works. This Ministry, said Major Guevara, had been suffering from "chronic slowness" for a long time. And what happened when it did try to speed things up, when it undertook an emulation campaign? It delivered this little park for the 26th of July, and then another little park, and then four little houses. But what about the factories? They are left for later.

"We have had one or two absurd cases in which the construction of factories stopped because the cement was taken away for works of this type—works of social benefit. These works are not being undertaken just for the sake of doing something: houses are necessary, social clubs are necessary, all these things are necessary, but we have to fix orders of priority."

When Major Guevara finished, Fidel took the floor, explaining that several people on the platform had asked him to say something so that it would not look as though the errors committed by some units of the armed forces were typical of them all. "Errors of this type," said Fidel, "can just as easily be committed by one sector of the Revolution as by another. There have been cases of waste, in which more supplies than are necessary have been asked for, in which meat or milk have been squandered. But this cannot be considered typical.

"All of us," Fidel went on, "have had to live through two moments: the moment in which we are completely enthused about production and it hurts us to see even the wheel of a truck withdrawn for something else such as military defense. . . . And the moment in which we are in the presence of the danger of invasion, or invasion itself, and realize that all the tractors, the plows, the trucks, the cultivated fields, mean nothing if we do not repulse the enemy. And then we almost lament that we have not devoted more resources, more vehicles, and more men to the defense of the Revolution. We always live in the midst of the danger of invasion and cannot ignore it. This is why it is so important that we bear in mind the importance of satisfying both needs—the one and the other—without prejudice to either one.

"Every time there was a mobilization it was necessary to use the transport of almost every organization. So transport was requested from Public Works, from INRA, from Communications, from the Ministry of Transport, and from the highway transport enterprises. . . . When the hour arrived, it was necessary to mobilize tens and tens of thousands of men in all the provinces, and there was no other solution except to use these trucks. Naturally this type of operation often brings with it the destruction of a large number of vehicles which are not in good shape. And, of course, there are many people who don't know how to drive, who use the vehicles to excess, who don't take proper care of them, who sometimes drag trucks around with jeeps. . . . Military operations always cause a great deal of disorder in transport and other things. . . . And when one of these mobilizations has passed, the organizations that borrowed the vehicles take their time about returning them and then give them back half-destroyed. . . . This is all due to the chaos which always accompanies things that have to be improvised, and . . . to the lack of discipline that still exists, the lack of organization, the lack of responsibility, the lack of training. . . .

"We have been speaking of goals, of increases in production, and of deficits in the production of some items. We have almost—almost—forgotten that we have had to be mobilized three times in less than a year, sometimes for weeks, pulling some of the most competent people out of the factories, using their equipment. . . .

"It should be said that there have been big changes in the Rebel Army, that it is not the same as in those early days when it was invaded by a good number of bums and loafers, people who had never done anything either in their own lives or in the Revolution, but who got themselves into a barracks. There has been a great advance in solving these initial problems, a great educational and cultural advance in the army. . . . Now there remain in the army those comrades who have truly advanced themselves, those comrades who are truly revolutionaries, truly workers. And the army is now fulfilling important functions, social and military. It suffices, for example, to know that there are 6,000 soldiers constructing the Camilo Cienfuegos School City near the Sierra Maestra. . . . The spirit of the Revolution, of the revolutionary leadership, is to inculcate in the Army as well as in the Militia a great spirit of sacrifice and a great discipline. And we shall not rest until this discipline is inculcated.

"There are people who have not yet advanced to a revolutionary consciousness. And if we think revolution is simply to say revolution and that socialism is simply to say socialism . . . we are completely mistaken. We don't accomplish anything by proclaiming we are socialists and running a truck at sixty-five miles an hour down the highway, and crashing and destroying it."

The destruction of vehicles "is due to two things: one, the lack of a clear revolutionary consciousness, of a sense of responsibility for the things that belong to the country; and two, a lack of technical capacity in the handling of these vehicles. . . . How are we going to solve the problem? Well, we are simply going to set up schools and we are going to make people really pass through these schools. But if we apply this to military organizations, we must also apply it to civilian organizations. . . .

"We must begin by understanding that we all still have much to learn, and that we have more people who want to be revolutionary than who are truly revolutionary. But we have to learn to be revolutionary; it is not enough to want to be so. A revolution is a process of education. A revolution doesn't presuppose that everyone is prepared and trained for it. What it presupposes is that as it goes on people will be training and preparing for it, and that the great mass of the people will be educating themselves more and more."

The reports by the people in charge of specific sectors of the economy resumed. Alfredo Menéndez, the head of the General Administration of the Sugar Centrals, predicted that the shortage of labor for cutting and loading sugar cane, which had begun to be felt in the middle of the 1961 harvest, would become more acute in 1962. There should be no illusions about mechanization, he argued. It is being worked on; we have asked for technical assistance from the socialist countries; we are confident that the problem of mechanizing the cutting and loading of cane can be solved. But many changes in the machines still have to be worked out. The machines cannot yet be produced in quantity and will be of very little help in the next harvest. So we must begin immediately to organize the labor supply for it.

Major Alberto Mora, the Minister of Foreign Trade, told of some of the problems in this sector of the economy and what was being done about them. For example: "It is not enough to have an estimate of the *annual* requirements for a given product and then buy the amount indicated by this estimate, or even somewhat more to provide a margin of safety; the deliveries throughout the year must be scheduled and controlled"—the goods must be in Cuba when needed and yet cannot arrive in quantities so large that there is no storage space in which to put them. At first there was little of such scheduling and control. "But now a system of control cards is being worked out: they will tell, for each product, the amount required for the year, the amount already purchased, the amount remaining to be purchased, the amounts shipped, the actual or expected arrival dates, and the like. And to make this problem more manageable in the future, additional warehouse space must be constructed and reserves built up."

To provide assurance of future supplies, Major Mora presented data on some of the goods scheduled to arrive during the remainder of

1961. He began with basic foodstuffs—vegetable oils, potatoes, wheat, corn, beans, peas, and lentils.

The data on vegetable oils were received with special interest. Cuba had been a heavy consumer of lard; per capita consumption was so high that Cuba was one of the world's largest importers of lard even though it is a small country. In 1960, the value of the lard imports exceeded $25 million. Cuba had traditionally obtained lard from the United States, where it is turned out as a by-product of pork and ham. But a few weeks before the production conference, the ferry from the United States had stopped running. At the Ministry the people responsible for food imports had been investigating other possible sources of supply such as Argentina and Holland. They had made an interesting discovery: there just wasn't that much lard to be had outside the United States; and for various reasons—the greater cost of transportation, the shortness of the supply—prices were higher. So it was not possible to replace the American lard; and even if it had been possible, Cuba could not have afforded the additional dollar outlays required. The only thing to do was to place lard under ration and increase the import of other fats and oils as rapidly as possible.

After foodstuffs, Major Mora turned to a different type of goods. "Bicycles purchased: 81,567, still to arrive: 61,532; Czech motor scooters purchased: 3,527, still to arrive: 1,510; motorcycles purchased: 3,929, still to arrive: 2,649; ball point pens purchased: 12 million, still to arrive: 8 million." There were also radio and television sets, electric fans, electric irons, and toys. These were—at least in good part—nonessential goods, but this point was overlooked in the presentation. The emphasis was on the demands of the Cuban market, not the resources—the foreign exchange—available to meet them.

And so on through the other sectors of the economy. The Minister of Internal Commerce explained why there were mix-ups in the lard rationing—he and the other people in his Ministry had simply had no experience with this sort of thing and had made errors. But he hoped things would get straightened out in a few weeks.

The Minister of Transport likewise faced many problems. There were about two thousand busses serving the Havana metropolitan area. Many of these were American-made—General Motors—and depended on American parts. Breakdowns were running at an average of about 280 daily, i.e., over 7,000 per month. Over 400 busses were out of action with serious defects. But the problems were being worked on. Many of the breakdowns were due to motor trouble; now the possibility of using Soviet motors in the old busses was being tested. New busses had been ordered from the Soviet Union and Czechoslovakia. And since the skill of the drivers was a problem here also, a school for bus drivers had been created.

A great number of pilots and other technicians in the Cuban airlines had deserted, often paid by the Americans to do so. An aviation school was therefore also necessary.

Many enterprises receiving materials by railway did not rush to unload them, and often used the railroad cars as warehouses, holding them for 30 days or more. This immobilization of freight cars could not be allowed to continue, and the unloading time would have to be reduced.

The operation of the ports would have to be rationalized. Studies of the mechanization of the ports were under way. Meanwhile, the Ministry of Transport was going to set up a special trucking company with one job: transporting goods from the docks when the ships came in, so that the docks would not get clogged.

Vilma Espín spoke for the Federation of Cuban Women. She told how the Federation was preparing a pamphlet of menus for a month, with recipes that required little lard or oil, and that suggested different ways of using the canned meat and other foodstuffs that were being received from the socialist countries. She discussed the production of powdered milk for babies, the distribution of canned baby food, the shortage of diapers. And she asked why the shoe enterprise did not produce the cheap slippers which women were accustomed to wearing in the summer; besides saving a great deal of leather these slippers were more comfortable than ordinary shoes.

Osmani Cienfuegos, the Minister of Public Works, is a younger brother of Camilo, the hero of the revolutionary war who died in a plane crash in 1959. He now proceeded, with what I thought was great dignity, to defend himself against Major Guevara's charge that his Ministry was constructing parks at the expense of factories. He admitted at the outset that Public Works suffered from a large number of faults: slowness in getting things done, high costs, bureaucracy, poor organization, lack of coordination with other Ministries. He said he was working to improve the organization; he offered to work more closely with the other Ministers to improve the coordination. But his Ministry *was* giving priority to industrial projects. It was true that a little park had been finished in time for the 26th of July, but so had been seventeen industrial and agricultural projects. Two industrial projects could not be finished because the Ministry of Industry had not sent certain supplies on time.

Major Guevara had doubts about some of the data and came up to the rostrum to question Cienfuegos about them. Confusion had arisen because some projects which the Ministry of Public Works had classified as industrial were for factories to be run by INRA rather than the Ministry of Industry. So the two disputed for a few minutes which projects were industrial projects and which had really been completed. But they ended agreeing on the need for priorities and coordination.

Carlos Rafael Rodríguez spoke for the ORI (Integrated Revolutionary Organizations). Early in his talk, he referred to goals for economic growth. "The Cuban Revolution is setting for itself minimum goals of 10 to 15 percent cumulative annual growth." Then he turned to his main theme—the need for organization, planning, and husbanding of resources. He told a story from the Mexican Revolution about the free-wheeling revolutionary who resigned his government job when the revolution began to organize itself. This revolution, said the revolutionary in disgust, is degenerating into a government. "But," said Rodríguez, "we don't complain that the Revolution is degenerating when we begin to organize it. We know that the Revolution is growing and that it will maintain its rhythm and its romantic character with organization."

The fundamental point brought out by the conference, said Rodríguez, is "the total character of the economy. An economy is not an aggregate of isolated organizations . . . but an organic whole. . . .

The economy has to be planned and planning means that we have to realize that we are not alone in the world, that other sectors of the economy also have their needs, that resources have their limits."

Fidel gave the summary speech. He also talked about resources. "In the first year of the Revolution, there was an excess of everything because nothing was being done. The warehouses of the cement factories were full. One of the problems we had was what to do with this cement. . . . It was necessary to put people to work. . . . So an infinity of projects were got under way; streets started being paved left and right. . . . No matter how many new projects were suggested, there was always enough wood and cement to carry them out, and enough people anxious to work. . . . But now it is not the same; there are an enormous number of projects, and the available cement, wood, and construction equipment are not enough to go around. There is simply no alternative to calculating what we have and what can be done, and then giving priority to certain things over others. . . . Priority will have to be given to factories and to other centers of production. . . . After factories come other things . . . schools, hospitals, aqueducts. . . . I know that INIT is being held to the construction material it already has. Why? Because other things are more important than recreation centers. . . . We could produce 100,000 houses. How nice it would be . . . to give houses to all who request them, to construct houses in the country, to construct houses everywhere. This would be very nice, but we cannot do it because then we would remain without factories and without schools. . . . The only thing we would have would be houses. And then what would we bring into the houses, what would we eat in the houses?"

Fidel talked strongly of the need for planning. "I have confessed here that I was one of the leading promoters of uncoordinated projects. . . . But now I propose to be one of the great defenders of planning."

He reviewed the shortages; some would take time to resolve. When the consumption of milk in Havana goes up by 18 percent from one August to the next, it is "not so easy" for production to keep up with it. Some increase in the production of milk can be achieved fairly quickly by improving pastures, by milking twice a day instead of once. But to increase the number of milk cows, time is required.

He proposed belt-tightening. "We are going to launch the slogan that hogs are to be fattened to 350 pounds; that little pigs are not to be eaten." These little pigs, which are eaten by four or five people, could be giving us 100 pounds of lard, could be providing a family with fat for almost a year. "What are we going to do Christmas Eve and New Year's? Every year we of course eat roast suckling pig on those days and if we don't eat roast suckling pig it seems to us not to be a holiday. But we are going to pass one Christmas and New Year's without roast pig. We are going to make a sacrifice this year in order to increase production."

The same was true for cattle. Slaughter must be controlled; females of productive age are not to be killed. This means a reduction in slaughter from over a million head per year to about 700,000. We will be consuming less beef than recently, but beef consumption will still be higher per capita than before the Revolution.

Fidel was optimistic about some shortages. The shortage of *viandas*, he said, is due to the error of not having planted enough to take care of both the great increase in consumption in the interior and the traditional demand. "What has been done this year? The figures on the amount of land to be planted to these crops have been deliberately made higher than is necessary. With *malanga* there is a special problem: during May, June, and July there is no harvest except from irrigated land. . . . The necessary number of *caballerías* of irrigated land will be planted so there is no shortage even during these months." On top of this, a thousand *caballerías* will be sown in Camagüey as a reserve. And all the People's Farms that are close to the cities should also maintain a reserve. Nothing can be lost by doing this since *yucca* and *boniato* are useful in the feeding of pigs and whatever the people don't consume can be invested in the animals. There is no excuse for the shortage of *viandas*; and we can commit ourselves that they will never again be scarce.

As for beans, Fidel said: "Last year we calculated and calculated: we would have a surplus of beans. . . . But beans have been short and we have had to import them. So we have fixed another goal for this year: to sow 15 thousand *caballerías* of beans. . . . Beans will be in surplus. If they are, we will hold them for the next year and reduce the production somewhat."

On chickens: "In March, we will be producing seven and one half million. That is to say between now and February, the production of chickens will go up sevenfold. This will help us greatly to solve the problem of meat."

Fish: Fidel called Salvador Pérez, head of the Department of Fishing, to the rostrum to see whether a "normal supply" of fish could be achieved by June, 1962. Pérez would not commit himself on canned fish, but "as regards fresh fish, we feel we will be able to supply the local markets throughout the island by June."

Fats and oils: By the end of 1962, said Fidel, we will be producing enough hogs to provide us with 60 percent of the animal fat we need. "And the other 40 percent? What will it be? Vegetable oils—which we will produce here, here in Cuba. . . . We are going to produce cotton seed oil; we already have 2,500 *caballerías* under cotton and will perhaps increase it to 4,000. . . . We will even get fat from tobacco seed . . . and from *palmiche* [the fruit of a palm tree]. . . . But we will get the bulk of the vegetable oils from peanuts and soy beans. . . . Peanuts give magnificent oil . . . and next year we will have 12,000 *caballerías* sown to peanuts."

Fidel finished his summary by talking about industry. He listed the new factories that had already been constructed by the Revolution: a nonferrous-metal pressure smelting plant, several cotton mills, a spinning mill, several plants for canning tomatoes, a plant for making stuffed dolls, a pencil factory—ten in all.

Then he listed the more than twenty factories which were under construction. There was the large INPUD[3] plant in Santa Clara with an annual production capacity of 45,000 stoves, 40,000 refrigerators, 100,000 pressure cookers, and 40,000 kitchen sinks; this plant would employ over 1,400 workers. And there were also a steel foundry and

[3] *Industria Nacional de Producción de Utensilios Domésticos* (National Industry for the Production of Household Equipment).

plants for producing picks and shovels, barbed wire, locks, knives and forks, brushes, kenaf sacks, plastics, animal feeds, antibiotics, salt, cocoa, and more canned tomatoes.

This is not all, said Fidel. We have plans for other factories—many more will be coming. And "notice the distribution of these factories and how fair it is; they are being distributed throughout the whole national territory. . . . Their location is not determined by the convenience of a private owner who lives in the capital and wants the factory there. . . . The Revolution is putting up factories in the most outlying little towns, which formerly kept asking for factories but never got them. . . . We are distributing the factories rationally to get a rational distribution of the national income between the capital and the rest of the island."

From what has been given here of the conference, the reader can judge for himself whether it was, as Fidel said at the outset, "a profoundly revolutionary and democratic act." One point is worth adding, however: Think of what the conference tells of the principles and qualities of the leaders of the Revolution. Take, for example, the frankness with which Fidel and Che discussed certain failings of the Rebel Army and the Militia. They did not do this because of public pressure. Most people were unaware of the problems. I was. You could go from one end of Havana to the other and through the provinces—and the only thing that would strike you about the soldiers and *milicianos* was their courtesy and good behavior.

The production conference was part of the transition from unrestrained exuberance and euphoria to organization and planning. It reflected both these phases of the revolutionary economy—the one coming to an end, the other getting started.

The leaders of the Revolution and the others at the conference were confident that the Cuban economy would continue to surge ahead as rapidly as it had during the first two years of the Revolution. The *Juceplan* had concocted the figures for rates of growth of 10 to 15 percent, and it had fallen to Regino Boti as head of the *Juceplan* to present these figures. But the optimistic spirit that lay back of them was not confined to the *Juceplan*; it was general. The figures were accepted and used by others. The same Carlos Rafael Rodríguez who insisted that resources have their limits talked about growth goals of 10 to 15 percent per year. Major Guevara and Fidel had both used the figures in speeches.

The spirit that produced the confidence in the growth rates also affected the assessment of the shortages and other difficulties. Most of them were regarded as temporary growing pains which could be brought under control fairly quickly. Within a few months the shortage of *viandas* would be eliminated, beans would be in surplus, chicken production would go up first fourfold, then sevenfold; by next June there would be enough fresh fish, and by the end of next year Cuba's requirements of fats and oils would be met by domestic production of lard and vegetable oils. Beef and milk would take more time. But with large supplies of chicken, fish, and other foodstuffs, there would be no serious problems, and by June 1963 there would be a surplus of proteins.

This assessment was based on old habit—not on a realistic attempt to digest the lessons of experience and integrate them into the plans, the goals, and the theories. The conference itself threw up a profusion of examples of the orneriness of practice—chickens are subject to epidemics, there seems to be a bug or fungus for every plant, the rain doesn't always come when you want it to. The factors outside of control must always be taken into account. When plans for industrial production are based on unrealistic assumptions about the arrival of raw materials from abroad, they are not met. A plan for the production of chickens is not just a matter of the arithmetic of reproduction rates. The inexperience of the farmers, the possibility of diseases, the problem of providing food, must also be taken into account. At some stage in the construction of every economic plan one must ask oneself: What things can make this plan go wrong? What can reality do that will cause the desired results not to be attained? The equivalent of failing to do this would be for a military commander to make a plan based only on what *he* wants to achieve, and leave out of account what the enemy might do. Yet although the conference contained many eloquent accounts of the problems of practice and reality, they were in the past tense; their lessons were not applied to the future; somehow future plans and goals were immune to such things as chicken epidemics, errors, and unrealistic assumptions.

But alongside the optimism about shortages and difficulties, ran the other main theme of the conference: resources have their limits, priorities must be fixed; the economy must be organized by an over-all economic plan. Realism and calculation were beginning to merge with revolutionary enthusiasm and impetus.

The new theme was still weak, however, because it was understood more in the abstract than in the concrete. Everyone could understand in general terms that resources are limited and must be handled accordingly. And a number of specific shortages had arisen whose significance was also clear. There were difficulties with cement, for example. Several different speakers making the point that resources are limited all used the same example—cement. But there were many other cases to which the point could have been applied and was not.

Foreign exchange is a resource, an important one. But when Major Mora listed a number of nonessential imports such as motor scooters and motorcycles, nobody objected or even raised questions. Everyone knew that dollars were scarce and had to be spent according to priorities, but it was not yet felt that the principle of limited resources applied to purchases from the socialist countries.

Nobody thought much about it when Fidel began to tick off the amounts of land that would be devoted to *viandas*, beans, peanuts, soy beans, cotton—irrigated land to produce *malanga* in May, June, and July; more land to *viandas* "than is necessary" and besides this a centralized reserve of over 1,100 *caballerías* in Camagüey and other reserves in the People's Farms around the cities; 15,000 *caballerías* for beans; 12,000 for peanuts; more land for soya; 4,000 *caballerías* for cotton. But land is also not a limitless resource. Everyone understood in the abstract that the economy must be seen as an organic whole. But nobody asked where this additional land was coming from; whether it would have to be withdrawn from other uses; and if so, what the over-all economic consequences might be.

Fidel pointed out that the planting of reserves in the People's Farms could often be accomplished without additional workers by mobilizing the enthusiasm of those who were already there. But in the main these crops would require additional labor, large amounts of it. The question where this labor would come from was not raised. The warning by the head of the General Administration of the Sugar Centrals that the shortage of field workers for the sugar harvest would become more acute in 1962 was not discussed by anyone else at the conference. Neither Carlos Rafael Rodríguez nor Fidel dealt with the problem of sugar workers in their summary speeches.

And the problem of financial discipline was completely ignored. Finances also have to do with the distribution of resources. At the beginning, a Revolution cannot be finicky about finances, any more than it can be about most other things; and with a large amount of resources unutilized, it doesn't have to be. But after a while, with finances as with everything else, order and discipline must be established. Otherwise, monetary demand will rise so fast—so much faster than the supply of goods and services can possibly rise—that the distribution mechanism of the economy will be disrupted; it will become increasingly difficult to distribute anything—goods, services, resources—in an orderly way. Or as Fidel was to put it at a later date: Everything will float around in a sea of money.

"The two methods which we Communists should employ in carrying out any task are, first, the linking of the general with the specific, and second, the linking of the leadership with the masses."[4] At the production conference the general was only beginning to be linked with the specific, and the leadership was only beginning to be linked with the masses in the management of the economy.

Almost everyone in Cuba understood in the abstract the need for "contact with the masses." It had been mentioned in many a speech. Politically, the Cuban leaders are exceptionally talented in communing with the masses. When you have watched the Revolution surge forward, passing through crisis after crisis, with the leaders and masses pulsing as one, you realize how strong this communion is. When you

[4] Mao Tse-tung, "On Leadership," *Selected Works*, New York, International Publishers, 1956, Vol. 4, p. 111.

have heard Fidel speak at mass demonstrations, when you have heard him talk the accents and language of the *campesinos* on television, when you have seen him wandering through the streets of Havana talking to the people of all classes, occupations, and ages—on even terms with all of them—you get some idea of his genius for identifying himself with the people and their aspirations.

But in the concrete the concept "contact with the masses" has a thousand facets. When you are dealing with an economic problem, what does "masses" mean, which "masses" do you turn to? For some problems, masses may mean all the people; for others it may mean the collective farm workers or the small farmers; for still others, factory workers, transport workers, government employees, and so on. When you want to get behind the official reports to the workings of, say, the Ministry of Foreign Trade, whom should you talk to—the higher officials or the lower officials, those engaged in planning or those engaged in operations? There is no pat answer; it depends on the problem; and an ability to sense the right people to talk to about different problems is very important. Often people will tell you important things of their own accord; but still more often the value of the information you get depends on the questions you ask. The ability to ask the right questions is one of the high arts. And the information you get must be evaluated, integrated with other information, generalized, used to formulate policy and decide action. There are no simple formulas for integrating the opinions of the masses into policy. Sometimes, the masses may be recalcitrant fishermen wedded to obsolete methods of work; sometimes they will understand more than their leaders about certain aspects of the problems.

Although several speakers at the conference stressed the need for contact with the masses, judgments were made which glaringly reflected a lack of such contact. What, for example, was the central weakness of the overoptimistic growth figures prepared by the *Juceplan*? It was lack of contact with the masses. These figures were prepared in offices by people who were not getting smeared with oil and grease from the Cuban economic machine. They were based on extrapolations of past growth, on studies of international statistics of economic growth, especially those of the socialist countries, on everything except a hard look at how the Cuban economy was actually working. They did not take into account People's Farm workers who still had to learn how to care for chickens and hogs, fishermen who had to learn how to fish, factories having trouble getting raw materials and spare parts, and broken-down tractors and busses. The conference was in itself a kind of contact with the masses—it was throwing up some of their problems. But it was still too soon for the implications to be fully drawn and absorbed, and the optimism about the growth figures was not dampened.

Here, a word of caution: I have faithfully listed criticisms because they are important to understanding. But I am writing with hindsight. And I am no longer engaged in practical economic administration, but in writing a book. I am now master of my time and priorities in a way in which no one bearing practical responsibility ever is. I can sit back and spend more time calmly pondering the production conference than the conference itself actually took.

To understand fully the judgments made at the conference you must try to imagine the situation as it was then. Suppose you had been sitting in the Chaplin Theater; imagine yourself holding any position you like, high or low. Now how much of an over-all understanding of the Cuban economy would you have brought to the conference? How could you have gotten a real—not a formal—over-all understanding? An endless flow of practical problems would have had a high priority on your time and pre-empted most of it. You would have been occupied handling the area of responsibility assigned to you: organizing and running agriculture, industry, foreign trade, transport; having almost daily to face problems that could not be set aside and make decisions that could not be postponed. Now suppose, because your job required it, or simply out of general interest, you had wanted to get a picture of parts of the Cuban economy other than the one you were working in. Would this have been easy? How would you have gone about it? You couldn't simply turn to standard reports and statistics; there were very few standard, easily available reports and statistics, and almost nothing on current developments. The Revolution had disrupted the old flow, and a new one had not yet been started. The main way to get information on other parts of the economy was to talk to people at other agencies, hold meetings with them, and this would take time. Usually the people at the other agencies would not immediately have the precise information and statistics required for the problem in which you were interested; they would have to prepare them, and this would mean more meetings and more time. Some questions could be answered in a few days, but others might require weeks or months. And when the information was in, it would answer one question or set of questions, but to get a true over-all understanding of the economy many such questions—hundreds, thousands—would have to be asked and answered by many people. So the chances are that if you had been at the conference your understanding would have corresponded to that of the other people present. You would have been informed about some things and not about others. You might have disagreed with some of the judgments put forth and not noticed others. But it is unlikely that you would have seen the failings and their ramifications as clearly as is possible now—looking backward.

For all its failings, the conference was a long step forward. It brought together for the first time a mass of information about all the major sectors of the revolutionary economy. This information was only partly digested; fundamentals were often buried in details; there were inconsistencies; the information was far from being an integrated whole. But it helped everyone—leaders and others alike—to break away from parochialism, to look beyond their own immediate tasks to other parts of the economy and other problems, to the working of the economy as a whole.

Even partial recognition of the principle that resources are limited constituted great progress. This principle was not just being discussed by a few officials and technicians; it was being taught to the whole conference, to the whole country. The conference was like a gigantic economics seminar which was helping to change the style of work of the whole Revolution—adapting it to organization and planning.

With time, the understanding of the principle would grow; it would be applied to more and more resources. The interrelations between different sectors of the economy would become clearer; it would be seen, for example, that limits on manpower can affect the sugar crop, foreign exchange earnings, and the balance of payments; and that limits on foreign exchange can affect the standard of living and agricultural and industrial growth.

With time would also come a more realistic and balanced understanding of the problems and prospects of economic growth. Earlier, everyone's mind had been full of the immense cost of imperialism to the Cuban economy—with its irrationality, its drainage of profits and wealth, its simple thievery. Just breaking free of imperialism would mean tremendous progress. And it did; the Cuban people achieved freedom and dignity, and the economy surged forward. But then other things began to become clear also. Transformation creates problems. Imperialism fights back and creates problems. And apart from the initial upsurge, the elimination of imperialism does not produce economic growth automatically—it simply clears the way for it. With time, it would become clear that henceforth economic growth would depend on increasing productivity, on expanding the capacity of agriculture and industry.

Most of the goals announced at the conference were not met: the goals for over-all annual economic growth of 10 to 15 percent, for the production of tractors, for the elimination of the shortages. There was no fourfold increase in the supply of chickens by November 1961; fish was still short by the next June; and fats and oils were still short by the end of the year. The same buoyancy and drive which enabled the Cuban leaders to attack the Batista dictatorship with twelve men led them to errors of judgment about economic goals. Yet though the errors must be recognized, their proportions and significance should be gauged with care. Over the longer run, there *will* be mammoth increases in the production of chickens, eggs, *viandas*, beans, fats and oils, pork and beef, and other foodstuffs. There *will* be factory after factory and Cuba *will* achieve a balanced, rational industrialization. The standard of living *will* rise much more than the 60 percent per capita projected by Regino Boti. It is now a matter of time. And the time will be a minute compared to the hundreds of years during which the people of Cuba suffered under slavery and imperialism. The Cuban leaders were wrong about how quickly everything could be done, and this has its importance. But—and this has far more importance—their basic vision is true.

For a while after the production conference, the food supply became a little more plentiful, although shortages of different items erupted sporadically. Then in the early spring of 1962, the shortages became more general and more severe. Rainfall in the last months of 1961 was less than usual; Cuba was in a drought, one that turned out to be very severe. The supply of milk which goes down even in ordinary dry seasons proved inadequate to meet the increased demand. *Viandas* and vegetables suffered. Cattle became thin and bony, further reducing the meat supply. Along with problems in agriculture, Cuba was having technical difficulties with its first over-all economic plan, scheduled to be put into effect at the beginning of 1962. This caused delays in the signing of import contracts with the other socialist countries, and so a slowdown in the arrival of foodstuffs from abroad was added to the other factors producing shortages. When the people found they could not get one item, they increased their demand for others, and the strain spread to the whole food supply. It became necessary in March to introduce general food rationing.

Under the ration, children under seven years of age were entitled to a liter of fresh milk per day. Everyone above this age was entitled to a fifth of a liter. Each person was allowed ¾ pound of beef per week; 8 eggs per month; about 5 pounds of beans per month (¼ pound a week of each of five different varieties); 6 pounds of rice per month; 3½ pounds of *viandas* per week, with 2 additional pounds for children under seven. Lard and oils had been rationed since the early summer of 1961 at one pound per person per week.

These figures should not be taken too literally. Sometimes, especially in the first weeks after rationing was instituted, one or another of the items called for in the ration books was not available at the stores. At other times, extra supplies of various foods were distributed —fruit and vegetables when a harvest came in, or canned beef or pork from the Soviet Union, Bulgaria, or China when a shipment arrived. Many of those living and working on farms consumed more of certain foodstuffs than the rations received by those in the cities and towns. Many tens of thousands of students at public boarding schools received a diet that exceeded the ration. At first, there was little food to be had in the restaurants; food was deliberately withheld from them to make sure that the amounts called for by the ration books could be met at the retail stores. But after a few weeks, restaurants began to receive allotments of food; and the little outdoor stands began once again to sell meat sandwiches, oyster and shrimp cocktails, and the like.

It would be futile to try to work out precise statistics on food consumption in Cuba during this period. But some general judgments can be made. There is no comparison between the diet of the Cuban agricultural worker and small farmer before and after the Revolution, even with rationing. A large number of city dwellers also were eating better, though not by as wide a margin. Now everyone got milk, and hundreds of thousands of small children who would never have had milk without the Revolution were getting a liter per day. Several million people who had almost never eaten meat or eggs were now getting a regular ration. For the middle and upper classes and the better-paid workers in the cities, the ration provided less food than they had been used to. It was a discomfort, but they could often supplement their food supplies and mitigate their discomfort by going to restaurants.

From time to time, other things besides foodstuffs became scarce. For a while, it became almost impossible to obtain shoes and certain articles of clothing, such as men's shirts and women's underpants. Rationing was extended to soap, detergents, toothpaste, and shoes and clothing.

But the pressure on resources was still spreading through the economy. The shortage of field workers became more acute during the 1962 sugar harvest than it had been in 1961, even though the amount of cane to be harvested was much smaller—the 1961 harvest had been a near record 6.7 million metric tons, while the 1962 harvest was only 4.8 million tons. The labor shortage had a double aspect: it reflected a great achievement, the virtual elimination of the immemorial unemployment of the countryside; but it also portended further problems in running the economy.

Volunteer labor to help with the harvest was mobilized on an even larger scale than in 1961. My wife went out many times as a volunteer; I went out two or three times. I had done volunteer work at the docks; once I had engaged in a friendly competition in sack lifting with a Russian volunteer worker and held my own. Cane-cutting was harder work—the tropical sun is very strong.

Finally, there appeared in 1962 a large balance-of-payments deficit. Many factors combined to produce this deficit and it reflected the shortage of resources of the whole economy in a general form.

Table 2

Cuba: Exports and Imports
and Commercial Surplus or Deficit, 1960-1962
(in millions of dollars)

	Exports	Imports	Surplus (+) or Deficit (−)
1960	618.2	579.9	+ 38.3
1961	624.9	638.7	− 13.8
1962	520.6	690.2	−169.6

Source: "La Experiencia de Cuba en Comercio Exterior," *Comercio Exterior,* Revista Trimestral del Ministerio del Comercio Exterior de Cuba, No. 2 (abril-junio) 1964, p. 110.

With exports and imports of over $600 million each, the deficit of $13.8 million in 1961 was not significant except insofar as it foreshadowed a larger deficit in the future. But the deficit of $169.6 million in 1962 was serious; imports were over 30 percent higher than exports.

The deficit resulted both from decreases in exports and increases in imports. Export earnings declined by $104 million between 1961 and 1962. Most of this decline was accounted for by the reduction in sugar output. The 1962 crop was almost two million tons below that of 1961. Sugar exports, however, declined by only 1.4 million tons because there was a large carry-over from the 1961 crop which was exported in 1962. The value of each million tons of sugar depends of course on the price; at the price of four cents a pound which the Soviet Union was then paying for Cuban sugar, every million metric tons was worth about $88 million, and 1.4 million tons was worth about $123 million. But the average price received by Cuba from all its sugar sales, including those in the world market, was somewhat higher in 1962 than in 1961, and this partly compensated for the decline in physical volume. The decline in export earnings from sugar and its products between 1961 and 1962 was about $93 million.[5]

Tobacco (primarily cigars and cigar tobacco) accounted for the rest of the decline in exports. Out of total tobacco exports of $50 million in 1958, $30 million had gone to the United States, where the presence of a large wealthy class and tastes developed over many years created a big market for Cuban cigars. Cuban tobacco is a very special product: the finest in the world, according to many experts, and expensive. It goes to special markets. Spain took over $7 million: here again the market is historical. The markets in other countries are small. In 1958 Holland took $1.4 million; the United Kingdom $1.3 million; West Germany $970 thousand; France $879 thousand; Italy none—all together less than $5 million.[6] Ordinary tobacco is subject to very high customs duties by these countries, or its entry is controlled by a state tobacco monopoly. But these countries do not prevent the entry of Cuban tobacco because it goes to the limited markets for good cigars and does not compete with low-cost, mass-market tobacco from the

[5] "La Experiencia de Cuba en Comercio Exterior," p. 10.
[6] *Comercio Exterior, 1957-1958*, Ministerio de Hacienda, República de Cuba, La Habana, 1959, pp. 606, 610.

sources they favor and protect. It is difficult to expand the market for the high-grade, expensive tobacco and if Cuba were to try to sell a low-cost type, it would come up against the customs and other barriers which restrict the entry of ordinary tobacco. When the United States cut off the $30 million American market early in 1962, it was impossible to replace it, at least within a short time. Tobacco exports in 1961 were already $10 million below 1958. They fell a further $14 million in 1962.

On the other side of the ledger, imports had been rising since 1960. Between 1958 and 1960, they had dropped $200 million as a result of the elimination of luxury imports by the Revolutionary Government and the American embargo on trade with Cuba. But then, even without the luxuries, they started to rise again. Soaring purchasing power increased the demand not only for domestic goods but imports as well. As the supply of meat was put under control to prevent depletion of the cattle population and as shortages of other local foodstuffs broke out, requirements for imported foodstuffs rose. For example, the requirements for imported wheat and flour shot up by several million dollars worth. Raw material requirements for Cuba's factories were also high: inventory reserves had to be built up to prevent periodic work stoppages. And the impetus to economic development set off by the Revolution swelled the requirements for capital goods: trucks, tractors, bulldozers, cranes, ships, electric power generating equipment, and machinery for factories, old and new. Imports, which had risen by $59 million in 1961, rose by a further $52 million in 1962.

It was already known in the late summer of 1961, when the first versions of the economic plan for 1962 were completed, that there would be a large payments deficit in 1962. If countermeasures such as the pruning of requests for imports had not been undertaken, the deficit would have been larger than the $170 million it actually reached. The earliest analyses of the deficit made at the Ministry of Foreign Commerce already showed that it was not a one- or two-year phenomenon which would disappear in 1963 or 1964, but one that would last for some years to come.

The balance-of-payments deficit became Cuba's central economic problem; it reflected and accentuated the key difficulties of the whole economy. Cuba had a deficit because it was short of resources, and it had to stay short of many specific resources because it had a deficit. Many internal shortages and difficulties could be eliminated by importing more—by increasing the imports of foodstuffs, household goods, busses, shoes, clothing, and soap. But a payments deficit means going into debt, and importing more means increasing the deficit and the debt. The debt could quickly become very large and a serious burden on the future. Entering into debt is a form of disinvestment; it could counterbalance much of the internal investment and development that were taking place. The accumulation of debt could not be allowed to run a simple, natural course of least resistance; it had to be controlled according to a policy which analyzed and weighed the different factors and considerations involved.

As analysis and discussion proceeded, it was seen that the problem of the deficit would affect all aspects of Cuba's economic development. Deficit and debt limit the amount of capital goods that can be bought; they limit possible imports of raw materials for new factories, additional fertilizer for agriculture, and the increased petroleum that economic development makes necessary. Development plans would now have to be reviewed to see what was possible and what was not. And for several years one of the main tasks to be accomplished by development would be to control and eliminate the deficit; one of the most important considerations in determining the specific forms for development to take would be the deficit. The deficit had implications for the proper balance between sugar and other products in agriculture; the relations between agricultural and industrial development; the speed with which industrialization could take place; the types of industries to be built; and the rate at which the standard of living could rise.

The balance-of-payments deficit culminated the process by which the Cuban economy began to press against the limits of its resources. First it became clear that choices would have to be made and priorities fixed for a few specific resources such as dollar exchange and cement. Rationing began with lard and meat and spread to other foodstuffs as well as shoes and clothing, soap and toothpaste. But now the need for fixing priorities was making itself felt on the scale of the whole economy. Choices would have to be made between alternative lines of development—choices that would determine the structure of the economy for years ahead.

5

The Introduction of Planning

The increasing tightness of resources in 1961 provided important arguments in favor of organization and planning. However, the need for organization and planning was recognized long before resources began to be tight, for it was broader than the problem of resources.

During my first assignment in Cuba at the National Bank, I worked in the office of Major Guevara's economic assistant, which adjoined that of Major Guevara. Sometimes, late at night, Major Guevara would come in through the side door, his eyes smiling, and sit down; his guard and others would come in also and there would be a bull session. Many things were talked about, including the Cuban economy. I don't remember any exact words, but it was clear that already at that time—May and June 1960—Major Guevara was concerned with the problem of organization and was looking ahead to the day when the Cuban economy would be socialist and operated by planning. It was about that time that he launched the slogan *Producir, Ahorrar, Organizar*—Produce, Save, Organize.

The method of work and administration that prevailed during the first years of the Revolution was known to the Cubans as *por la libre*. It is not easy to give the full flavor of this much-used Cuban term in English. It means "freely, without restraints." When an official does something without bothering to get instructions from above or to co-ordinate with other officials who might be interested, he is said to be acting *por la libre*—on his own. When the whole economic administration operates with little attention to the need for rules, organization, coordination, and systematic plans, the term *por la libre* is also applied to it. The general method of administration is *el por la libre*—free wheeling.[1]

[1] When an extra supply of eggs arrives at the stores and they are to be sold unrationed in any amount the customer wants, the sign says "Eggs—*por la libre*."

Both individuals and organizations wheeled freely, held back by only minimal, sporadic restraints. This was especially true of the new, revolutionary agencies. When a task or problem presented itself at INRA or Bancec, people scrambled to get at it, unhampered by the official duties of their own job or formal lines of organization. Take, for example, the problem at the docks that confronted Bancec: almost everyone who wanted to—the Chief Accountant, the Legal Advisor, the Chief of Finances, the heads of an Import Section, and three or four members of the Warehouse Section—could join the group working on the problem, whether their own jobs had anything to do with it or not. A person could keep himself constantly busy by attaching himself to four or five such groups among which he could flit back and forth as he saw fit; often, this kept him "overloaded," providing a fine excuse for shortcomings in the fulfillment of his own job. This method of work invaded parts of the older agencies, although there were stretches of encrusted bureaucracy, mostly simple routine jobs, that remained immune.

Cooperatives, People's Stores, factories, and other economic units were often run like private firms, little restrained by outside guidance or controls. For example, months after Bancec had been placed in charge of exports, the head of an agricultural cooperative could go to Canada to arrange for the sale of its tomato crop and then put the money into a personal bank account to be used for the import of agricultural equipment and breeding bulls for the cooperative. Many enterprises, such as the electric power and telephone companies, would contract long-term debts in foreign exchange and place the contracts into their own files without informing anyone else; later, it was a difficult job for the central bank to round them all up and obtain an over-all view of the debt and payment obligations that had been incurred. Individual enterprises could obtain large amounts of bank credit on their own. They enjoyed wide discretion in purchasing raw materials and equipment, undertaking large capital projects, and fixing levels of output. Though there is a similarity in all this to the operations of private firms, there is also a difference: Cuban enterprises and the Cuban economy were no longer subject to the controls and discipline of the market and the profit system. The distribution of foreign exchange, credit, raw materials, and capital equipment was no longer being controlled by the market. The drive for profits was no longer exerting pressure to keep down costs, to avoid waste and inefficiency. There were neither the discipline and controls of the market nor those of a planned economy.

In practice most enterprises and other economic units were operated from day to day, without systematic programs for months, quarters, or longer periods. When the bus company found it needed parts, it ordered them through Bancec; a few weeks later the company found it needed more—in a hurry; so it sent in another order, a rush order. This was the general method for buying materials and equipment, obtaining railroad or truck transport, or distributing and selling a crop that had been harvested.

The Ministries were also run like separate economic fiefs. Each confined its attention almost exclusively to its own tasks and aims, entering into relations with others only as particular needs or problems required it to do so. INRA fixed its own financial and credit policies, unrestrained by guidance or control from the Treasury or National Bank. Bancec set new internal prices for many imported goods without guidance from a general price policy or outside review of its actions. There was no systematic review of the different Ministries— their organization, their methods of work, their accomplishments, their projects for the future.

Various Ministries prepared ambitious plans: INRA for great increases in the production of crops and livestock, the Department of Industrialization for many new industries, Education for thousands of new schools and millions of new textbooks, Public Health for new hospitals and vastly improved health services, INAV for tens of thousands of new houses and apartments, INIT for new hotels, motels, and other tourist facilities, and Public Works for new parks, roads, highways, and bridges. But the different Ministries did not try to coordinate their plans with each other. Nobody checked whether there would be enough land, labor power, construction materials, equipment, foreign exchange, and financial resources to carry out all the projects.

There were scattered attempts at collaboration and coordination.

Representatives of the different Ministries joined in innumerable *ad hoc* meetings to deal with specific problems. The National Bank and Bancec tried to collaborate in the control of dollar expenditures. A joint Industry-Bancec committee was set up to handle emergency requests for industrial raw materials that were running short. But of the total administrative apparatus, only a few parts were touched by this improvised joint effort.

There was no systematic economic leadership above the level of the Ministries, no individual or group effectively holding responsibility for the management of the economy as a whole, no over-all unity of economic and political leadership.

The top leaders of the Revolution themselves held responsibilities for specific ministries. Fidel, in effect, ran INRA; Major Guevara was head of the National Bank and the Department of Industrialization. The *Juceplan*, which was supposed to be concerned with the economy as a whole, had little to do with its practical workings. Fidel and the other leaders held potential authority and responsibility over the whole economy, but over large parts of it the authority was not systematically exercised—there were only sporadic decisions on specific problems. And the over-all responsibility was not effectively accepted; there were economic sectors and problems with which the leaders felt themselves little concerned.

Some agencies—INRA, Education, Public Health, Public Works—had revolutionary projects to carry out. They had no responsibilities for the financial stability of the economy. Other agencies—the National Bank and Treasury—had responsibilities for watching over financial stability. But their financial responsibilities were not matched by real authority over the revolutionary agencies and their projects. There was no higher authority effectively holding both sets of responsibilities, trying to balance the benefits of the projects against their financial consequences.

There was no point at the top at which all the lines of authority and responsibility—political as well as economic—joined. In politics, Fidel and the other leaders provided clear, comprehensive, over-all leadership. There was nothing comparable in the management of the economy, and there was no one systematically balancing political and economic considerations against each other. In late 1960, for example, the question arose at Bancec of accepting an offer from Japan of toys for Christmas at a cost of $1 million. Politically, there were benefits in having the toys; but $1 million is a large amount of foreign exchange. The high authority to whom the problem was referred was sensitive to political considerations, but felt little responsibility for the exchange reserves; he decided without information on the prospective exchange situation that the toys should be purchased.

A subtle form of opportunism appeared: definite, immediate political benefits were given greater consideration than less clear, longer-run economic costs, even though economic problems might later result and entail political disadvantages greater than those being avoided in the first place.

Although many questionable economic decisions were being taken everywhere, the main problem was not individual decisions—it was the need to change the general style of work, to introduce organization, to operate the economy not as an agglomeration of separate little domains, but as an integrated whole, according to an over-all plan. For many months, it was impossible to begin a comprehensive attack on the problem, to try to introduce economic planning. Although the leaders of the Revolution were looking ahead, their attention and energy were engaged by the daily moves and countermoves of the struggle with the United States. Till the fall of 1960 when the major nationalizations were completed, most of the economy was still under private control; and for some time after the nationalizations, free wheeling was inevitable—it was necessary to keep things going. A large part of the state apparatus still had the prerevolutionary organizational structure and was unsuited to the operation of a planned, socialist economy.

But it began to be clear by mid-1960 that the time was rapidly approaching when *por la libre* would have to be eliminated. The nationalizations placed the strategic parts of the economy in the hands of the state. The elimination of the sugar quota and the U.S. embargo forced Cuba to reorient more than three fourths of its trade to the socialist countries. These changes created the main prerequisites for planning and at the same time made planning necessary. The Revolutionary Government now had the control of the economy without which real planning is impossible; it could plan because it had the power of practical decision formerly held by the foreign monopolies or the local private owners. Except by planning, Cuba could not manage the nationalized sector of its economy, defend itself against economic warfare by the United States, and reorient its trade.

In foreign trade, the need for planning imposed itself immediately. With the breaking off of trade with the United States, Cuba had to ensure the sale of its sugar and other export products and the importation of the goods necessary to keep its economy going. It could not rely for this on trade with Europe and other parts of the capitalist world. But to do so with the socialist countries meant planning. With their planned economies, these countries could not work with sporadic offers and requests scattered throughout the year; they required annual agreements. The data prepared for Major Guevara's trade mission to the socialist countries in November and December of 1960 constituted, however imperfectly, a plan. In the economic sectors other than foreign trade, the need for planning did not impose itself so sharply. But the delay in introducing planning could not be too extended.

After the nationalizations and the break in trade with the United States, there remained the problem of the state apparatus. Toward the end of 1960, a committee headed by President Dorticós was already well along in the preparation of legislation reorganizing the government. The purpose of this reorganization was to complete the task of rebuilding the state apparatus, to give it the structure required to operate a socialist, planned economy.

The reorganization had to be comprehensive. Previously, the Revolutionary Government had created new agencies to meet specific needs as they arose in the course of the Revolution—INRA to carry out the land reform, the Department of Industrialization to administer factories taken over from Batista's henchmen, Bancec to administer foreign trade when the United States eliminated the sugar quota. But now the revolutionary process had culminated in a change in the nature of the whole economy. It had become socialist. The whole apparatus for administering the economy had to be remolded. Those old agencies which have no function in a socialist economy had to be abolished. The remaining old agencies had to be given new functions and reorganized. New agencies had to be created to administer the nationalized sectors of the economy. The whole apparatus had to be given the structure required to create and execute over-all economic plans.

I was for a short time a member of the committee working on the new laws and attended three or four of its meetings. For one of them I was asked by the Administrator of Bancec, who was unable to attend himself, to present the Bancec position that customs duties, except on goods brought in by travelers, should be abolished. I had to argue against one of my favorite people in Cuba, the unpretentious, straightforward naval officer who was serving as Treasury Minister. We at Bancec felt that with the creation of a Ministry of Foreign Commerce, which under the organic law being prepared for it would hold a monopoly of foreign trade, customs duties on imports would no longer make sense. Such duties can have as their purpose discouraging the import of certain goods, providing revenues, or both. But what point would there be in having one agency of the government applying a duty to discourage the import of something which another agency, charged with the responsibility for imports, has decided to bring in? And with a state trading agency, customs duties are no longer necessary to obtain revenue; now not just the duty, but the whole of the import profit—the whole of the difference between the internal sale price and the cost, less administrative expenses—would automatically accrue to the Treasury. The Ministry of Foreign Commerce could replace the former customs revenues, or provide more, simply by fixing prices at the appropriate level. The old system with its several hundred customs officials, its complicated administrative rigmarole, and the delays it imposed on the movement of goods would be a wasteful anachronism. The Treasury Minister agreed with these points but was reluctant to see the duties wiped out until he could be absolutely sure that the revenues they had provided would still be forthcoming. The commission agreed with Bancec; it decided to abolish the duties on goods to be imported by the Ministry of Foreign Commerce and to restrict the Customs Bureau to the task of applying the customs and foreign exchange regulations to travelers. It also decided to transfer the Customs Bureau to the Ministry of Foreign Commerce where new jobs in the administration of the docks could be found for those officials whose old tasks had been eliminated.

The new legislation also abolished the Department of Commerce. This agency was another hangover of capitalism; its main function had been to provide information and assistance to businessmen; it was not adapted to the task of running anything, of taking over the administration of the commercial sector of the economy.

Two old agencies—the National Bank and the Treasury—received new organic laws to adapt them to a socialist economy. Both had been geared to serve an economy in which everything of importance was private, and their activities were peripheral. Private commercial banks supplied the economy with credit; the National Bank did not control these banks, but could only try to exert influence on the volume of credit they granted. Private enterprises ran industry, agriculture, commerce, transport, electric power, and communications; profits and investment in these areas were private. The Treasury received only a small part of the investment funds produced by the economy, and public investments were limited to roads, public buildings, schools, and the like.

Now all this was changed. The banks were all public. The profits of the nationalized enterprises belonged to the people. Investment—and the development of the economy—was a central responsibility of the state. The National Bank and Treasury would be required to do much more than try occasionally to exert a little influence on the economy; they had to be central parts of the apparatus which would actually run it; they had to be geared to planning.

Under its new organic law, the National Bank became the whole banking system. With the nationalization of the banks, there was no need for a multiplicity of separate institutions performing the same functions. The National Bank would perform all banking functions in Cuba, operating a network of branches throughout the country. It would take over all the other banks and constitute, in the words of the preamble to the law, "a single, centralized, state banking system."[2]

The new National Bank would exercise the usual functions of central banks, such as the emission of money. Just as central banks often do even in capitalist countries, it would serve as the custodian of foreign exchange and the agency through which all foreign exchange transactions are carried out. It would enter into payments agreements with foreign banks.

But beyond this came functions appropriate to a central bank in a socialist economy. The National Bank would "effectuate all the short-term credit operations of the national economy, no matter what activities or sectors are involved." It would hold all bank deposits—"of the state and official organizations, of state enterprises and cooperatives, of private enterprises, and of the people, no matter what the nature and term of the deposits." It would "organize and carry through payments between different organizations and enterprises." All funds provided for capital investment by the state budget, either as loans or grants, would be turned over to the National Bank for distribution. In short, the National Bank would have a monopoly of short-term credit, of payments and clearing operations, of the distribution of all capital investment funds; and it would have custody of the working funds of all organizations and enterprises and the savings of the people.

To complete the credit monopoly of the National Bank, the granting of credit by other organizations and enterprises to each other was prohibited. Goods could not be sold on credit. An enterprise selling goods to another could not accept payment in 60 or 90 days from delivery; it would have to be paid on delivery. If the enterprise purchasing the goods needed credit, it would have to turn, not to the seller,

[2] Law 930, February 23, 1961, *Leyes del Gobierno Provisional de la Revolución*, xxx, 1-28 February 1961. La Habana, Editorial Lex, March 1961, p. 15.

but to the National Bank. Consumer credit was excepted from the prohibition on the sale of goods on credit; but it could be granted only under regulations to be agreed upon by the Ministry of Internal Commerce—yet to be created—and the National Bank.

The new National Bank would be very different from central banks in capitalist countries. Its control over the volume of credit would be direct. It would not have to try to influence the lending of other banks by varying the rate at which they could borrow money from it, or the reserves they had to keep. It would itself *decide*. When the National Bank felt that credit should be decreased, it could decrease it—or vice versa. And—to use the jargon of the capitalist central banks—its control over credit would not only be *quantitative*, but *qualitative*. The central banks in the capitalist countries content themselves with trying to control the *volume* of credit; the *specific purposes* for which loans are granted are decided by the private, commercial banks that make them. But now with the National Bank itself granting the credit to the economy, it would be deciding on both the total volume of credit and the specific purposes for which it would be used.

Finally, the National Bank would work with economic plans. It would prepare Credit Plans—both short- and long-term—and a Foreign Exchange Plan for receipts and payments from noncommercial operations with foreign countries (operations other than exports and imports, the plans for which would be made by the Ministry of Foreign Commerce). It would distribute long-term funds according to the Investment Plan of the state and grant long-term credits according to the directives of the *Juceplan*. And it would "carry out monetary review and control of the fulfillment of plans . . . by public bodies, state enterprises, and cooperatives."

Some time would have to pass before the National Bank and the new monetary arrangements could work as they should. The new organic law provided, not for the immediate, but the "gradual and progressive introduction of the principles of planning credit and monetary circulation." The swirl of revolutionary measures had left widespread confusion in record-keeping and accounting which could not be eliminated overnight. It would take time for orderly financial procedures and systematic accounting to be installed in the farms, newly organized government agencies, and in many of the industrial and commercial enterprises—and for people to be taught how to work with them. Until this could be done, the "monetary review and control of the fulfillment of plans" would remain a clause in a law rather than an effective reality. But no matter how difficult they were, the problems would be solved with time. The new National Bank with its centralization of monetary resources, its power of direct decision over credit, and its integration into a broader planning mechanism would give Cuba a powerful instrument of monetary planning and control.

The Ministry of the Treasury underwent analogous changes. It would "prepare the proposed Global Budget of the Public Sector to be submitted annually to the Council of Ministers for its approval."[3] But now this budget would be the financial plan, not of a capitalist government, but of the whole economy: the public sector would include the most important economic enterprises of the country. Budget revenues would no longer consist almost exclusively of taxes. They would now include the profits and depreciation funds of the state economic enterprises; and the policy of the Revolutionary Government would be to decrease direct taxes on the people, to get an increasing proportion of revenues "from the sources of production, through profits."[4] The budget would now be the main source of investment funds for agriculture, industry, and commerce—the main provider of the means for economic development. Again there would be centralization: the budget would bring together the formerly dispersed profits of the separate economic enterprises, providing a central fund from which money for investment would be allocated to different parts of the economy.

The changes in the scope of the budget required changes in the Treasury's policy interests. Taxes would no longer be the main means of varying budget revenues; this could also be done by altering prices or wages in the economic enterprises of the state. The Treasury would

[3] Law 937, February 28, 1961, *ibid.*, p. 76.
[4] Speech by the Minister of the Treasury, *Revolución*, March, 1961, p. 3.

have to concern itself, not just with tax policy, but with price and wage policy as well.

And changing revenue has a far greater significance in a socialist than in a capitalist state budget. The socialist budget is the main source of investment funds; it determines the proportion between consumption and investment in the whole economy. Prices, wages, and taxes would have to be seen as a set of means by which the state would centrally control the allocation of resources between consumption and investment. The Treasury would now have a direct interest in the efficiency of economic enterprises since the profits of these enterprises would constitute a large part of total budget revenues.

Some of the additions to the policy interests of the Treasury were reflected in the functions given to it (or to its subdivisions) in the new organic law. Among those functions were:

"To study price policy in coordination with the *Juceplan* and the appropriate offices in the Ministry of Internal Commerce.

"To study the effects of variations in wages in the enterprises of the state.

"To analyze the costs and goals of the organizations included in the budget."

Finally, like the National Bank, the Treasury would be tied to the over-all planning apparatus. Its first objective would be "to assure the development of the national economic plans, providing the financial means for them."

The new legislation created three new Ministries—Industry, Foreign Commerce, and Internal Commerce. These Ministries had become necessary to administer the nationalized enterprises and activities and to help develop and carry out over-all economic plans.

The Ministry of Industry would "govern, direct, supervise, and carry out the policy of industrial development of the nation and administer the industrial enterprises of the state in accordance with the directives and plans of the Revolutionary Government."[5] Several organizations formerly controlled from INRA, such as the Petroleum Institute, the Cuban Mining Institute, and the Department for the General Administration of the Sugar Centrals were incorporated into

[5] Law 932, February 23, 1961, *op. cit.*

the new Ministry of Industry. Besides administering the state's enterprises, the Ministry would also "orient the private sector of industry."

The Department of Industrialization of INRA had been outgrown. An organization with the rank and size of a ministry was required. The state no longer held a handful of factories taken over from fleeing *Batistianos*. It held hundreds of industrial establishments, including 161 sugar mills, three oil refineries, electric power and telephone plants, and tobacco, metallurgical, textile, drug, paint, soap, and food factories. The book value of the American industrial enterprises alone that were nationalized in July, 1960, was $800 million.[6] And the process of nationalization was still continuing.

The organic law for the Ministry of Foreign Commerce gave it a monopoly of foreign trade. When Bancec began operations in July, 1960, it had been too early for a state monopoly of foreign trade. The big waves of nationalization were just getting started and the export and import of many goods was still being carried out by private companies. But by the end of the year, the basic export industry—sugar—was nationalized. Most imports of industrial raw materials, replacement parts, and machinery were going to nationalized industries. Most imports for agriculture were going to state farms and cooperatives. The bulk of foreign trade had fallen to Bancec. The best way to bring order and centralized planning and control into the management of Cuba's foreign commerce was to place the new Ministry in charge of all of it.

The organic law laid down the major plans which the new Ministry would have to prepare and work with.

"The Ministry of Foreign Commerce will prepare annually:

a) The draft Export and Import Plan. . . .

b) The draft Foreign Exchange Plan—the receipts and payments of foreign exchange resulting from commercial operations with foreign countries;

c) The draft Financial Plan for Foreign Commerce, which will evaluate the incidence of this commerce on the State Budget and on the Credit Plans of the National Bank of Cuba; . . .

[6] Dudley Seers, ed., *Cuba, The Economic and Social Revolution.* Chapel Hill, University of North Carolina Press, 1964, p. 296.

"In addition to the annual plans . . . the Ministry of Foreign Commerce will prepare Long-range Export and Import, Foreign Exchange, and Financial Plans in conformity with the periods and objectives contemplated in the Global Plans of the *Junta Central de Planificación* [*Juceplan*]."[7]

Finally, the organic law also touched on how the Ministry of Foreign Commerce was to be organized. "The commercial operations of exporting and importing will be in the charge of special Foreign Trade Enterprises or Houses, with independent juridical personality and their own administration and property." This form of organization responded to a legal need to limit the liability of the organizations engaged in foreign trade. It did not affect the centralized control of that trade. The Foreign Trade Enterprises were to be created by the Ministry and subject to its instructions.

The Ministry of Internal Commerce would be responsible for the internal distribution system. There was need for a new agency not only to run the state's stores and warehouses, but to plan and administer the distribution system as a whole.

The organic law, besides placing the new Ministry in charge of the state's commercial enterprises, also stated that it would:

"Distribute the articles produced by state enterprises, as well as those imported, and supervise distribution when it was being carried out by the private sector. . . .

"Inform the Ministry of Foreign Commerce, with the necessary anticipation, of the requirements for the importation of consumer goods. . . .

"Adopt the measures necessary to guarantee the national supplies by means of the adequate storing of consumer goods."[8]

Finally, there was a new organic law for the *Junta Central de Planificación* which provided for its complete reorganization. The old organic law of March, 1960, was full of high-sounding generalities:[9] the *Juceplan* would "lend advice to organisms carrying out plans . . .

[7] Law 932, February 23, 1961, *op. cit.*
[8] Law 933, February 23, 1961, *op. cit.*
[9] Law 757, March 1960, *op. cit.*

orient the foreign trade policy of Cuba . . . mobilize the factors of production so as to utilize the productive capacity of the country to the maximum in the benefit of society." You could read this law several times and still not know—concretely—what the *Juceplan* was supposed to do. The law had been promulgated at a time when the conditions for real planning were not yet present in Cuba.

The new law was less than half as long as the old one; it was stripped for action.[10] There were no more phrases about lending advice. "The plans which the *Juceplan* formulates will be submitted to the consideration of the Council of Ministers and once approved will have the force of law." The new *Juceplan* would not be engaged like the old one in preparing academic studies which were unrelated to the practical work of running the economy, in making vague general recommendations which were not binding on anybody. It would now be in charge of the plans according to which the economy would actually be run.

The organization of the *Juceplan* was outlined clearly and specifically:

It would consist of a Plenum, an Executive Committee, and six Offices [*Direcciones*].

The Plenum would not be a working body, but one for exercising broad review and control. The Prime Minister would act as its president; all Cabinet Ministers concerned with economic matters would be included, and meetings would be held only once every three months.

The Executive Committee would be closer to day-to-day operations, but would still concern itself mainly with policy. It would meet not less than once a week to review and approve "draft political-economic directives for the elaboration of plans . . . . draft plans and budgets . . . . drafts of measures to be taken by Ministries and other organisms in connection with the fulfillment of plans . . . . proposals to improve the organization and functioning of the state apparatus."

The daily work of the six offices—the working staff of the *Juceplan*

[10] Law 935, February 25, 1961, *op. cit.*

—would be in the charge of the Executive Secretary of the Plenum who would also have the rank and title of Minister of Economics. The six Offices would be as follows:

(1) Central, (2) Agriculture, (3) Industry, (4) Internal Commerce, Public Works, and Transport, (5) Balances, (6) Statistics.

The Central Office would coordinate the work of the others and prescribe norms for organization and planning throughout the state apparatus. It would also prepare plans that were of general interest— for example, the plan for the coordination of scientific and technical investigation, the plan for supplying the economy with basic products, and the over-all foreign commerce plans.

The next three Offices would, in coordination with the appropriate Ministries, prepare plans for particular sectors of the economy. The Office of Agriculture, working with INRA, would prepare the plans for agriculture; the others would do the same for industry, internal commerce, public works, and transport.

The Office of Balances would be concerned with distributing resources among different uses, balancing the requirements for resources against their availability. It would "be in charge of the fundamental balances for the allocation of productive forces among the various sectors and the division of the national product between consumption and investment."

The Office of Statistics would be in charge of the statistics required for the formulation of plans.

Finally, the law did not limit itself to the organization of the *Juceplan*. It also stated that there should be "Sectoral Planning Offices in all the Ministries directly tied to the functioning of the national economy, which should in their turn create . . . planning offices in the economic units dependent on them." In other words, the law called for a chain of planning offices throughout the economy.

These laws for the reorganization of the government were socialist laws. They were drawn up with the advice of technicians from socialist countries, and the reorganized and newly created agencies were modeled after similar bodies in these countries. Everything was geared to an economy in which the important powers of decision—over bank credit, profits, investment, production, exports, imports, prices, etc.—were no longer held by private enterprises, but by the state.

On February 13, 1961, it was announced that 1962 would be the Year of Planning—the year in which the economy would for the first time be operated by a single, comprehensive, economic plan. And in the last week of February, the laws reorganizing the government were promulgated.

The dates have a significance beyond the timing of the steps toward planning. They bear on the question of when the leaders of the Cuban Revolution began to consider it a socialist revolution. The official announcement that the Revolution was socialist did not come until mid-April, at the time of the Bay of Pigs invasion. But already in February laws for a socialist reorganization of the government were coming out in the *Gaceta Oficial*. These laws were not drafted the night before their promulgation. I myself had attended one or two meetings on the Ministry of Foreign Commerce law in November, 1960, and a friend of mine had begun working on the whole law project a number of months earlier.

The organic laws of February, 1961, were a key advance in the adaptation of the Cuban state apparatus to running a socialist economy. But much remained to be done. Though the organic law for the *Juceplan* outlined its organization in detail, the organizational forms for other agencies—for example, the Ministries of Industry and Foreign Commerce—were still to be thrashed out. A chain of planning offices throughout the economy had to be set up. And, most important of all, the laws and the organizational forms had to be transformed from paper into living realities that would work as they were intended.

Toward the end of 1960, a Czech economic delegation arrived to provide technical assistance on socialist organization and planning. About the time the laws for the reorganization of the government were being promulgated, this delegation began to hold a series of lectures and discussions, attended by representatives of the various economic agencies of the government. Along with three or four others, I attended for the Ministry of Foreign Commerce. I was fascinated by the prospect of obtaining a close view of how socialist planning is carried on.

The lectures and discussions reminded me of the gunnery school in Texas I attended during the war. The Czech technicians explained organization and planning from manuals in the same way as the army instructors had taught the mechanism of guns. Different government and economic organizations were defined and their functions listed—1,2,3,4. The interrelations between the organizations were described as though everything worked with the rigidity and precision of the breech block of an anti-tank gun. The *how* of things was given in overwhelming detail; the *why* was hardly touched upon.

One lecturer read through the whole organization chart of a central planning office. Another handed out mimeographed sheets on the planning of industry and then read the sheets to us. For industrial enterprises there were:

The production plan, giving the goods to be produced, the quantities, the production schedule;

The labor and wage plan, giving the number of workers, the target for increased productivity, the amount of wages to be paid;

The material supply plan, giving the requirements for raw materials, fuel, electric power, equipment;

The capital construction plan, giving the volume of construction to be done, requirements for labor, materials, and equipment, the target dates for completion;

The financial plan, giving the outlays for everything and the income; and so on.

We were deluged with models used for planning in Czechoslovakia, some of which were read to us line by line. One speaker, for example, went through every item in the model for the Foreign Exchange Plan: receipts and payments from exports, imports, insurance, interest charges, and so on.

Different balances for allocating resources were explained to us. There were three broad classes of balances and many individual kinds:

Materials balances, for example, of raw materials, metals, fuels, machine tools, construction equipment, articles of consumption;

Manpower balances, giving the requirements of different branches of the economy, and the availability by different levels of education and types of skill;

Value balances, for example, the cash income and expenditure of the population, the state budget, the national accounts showing the distribution of resources between consumption and investment.

There was no discussion of why the different organizations were set up the way they were, what alternative forms were possible, and what advantages or disadvantages they might have. The planning models used in Czechoslovakia were presented as immutable and fully applicable everywhere.

The Czech organizational forms required a large number of trained people—economists, statisticians, experts in prices, finance, the balance of payments, and many others. Hardly 10 percent of the required technicians existed in Cuba. But the absence of trained people was ignored. There was no discussion of what might happen if one insisted on following the organization charts, on setting up large offices with people who could not do their jobs, and no attempt to work out organizational forms which took the number of trained people realistically into account.

The Czech planning models required detailed and precise statistics. In the model for the Foreign Exchange Plan, there was a line calling for expected earnings from shipping. The statistics and financial accounts of the Cuban shipping company were then in a semi-chaotic state; and the earnings from shipping were piddling in relation to the other items in the balance of payments. But the line had to be filled with numbers even if they had to be dreamed up. The models were not to be tampered with; they were rather to be cluttered up with meaningless figures which made the few important ones all the harder to see.

In one discussion, an economist from our Ministry asked some of the Czech planners whether they thought the Ministry of Foreign Commerce should operate a system of warehouses at the ports, whether this would not make it easier to handle the confusion and congestion at the docks. Well, ran the answer, the Ministry of Foreign Commerce in Czechoslovakia does not have any warehouses. As those of us who had struggled with the problem thought a bit, we realized that this answer did not help: Czechoslovakia is not an island, and trains and trucks bringing goods from foreign countries can carry them inland close to the points of use. But our efforts to draw the Czech technicians into a discussion of Cuban circumstances did not succeed.

Placing all the emphasis on the formal methods of planning, the visiting technicians made no attempt to isolate and grapple with Cuba's concrete economic problems. No one discussed the special importance of agriculture, sugar, and foreign trade in the Cuban economy. No one touched on the problem of tailoring programs and goals to resources. The lectures, translated into Spanish for Cubans, could, with minor changes, have been translated into Persian for Iranians.

In the mimeographed sheets on planning handed out by the Czechs, and in the other manuals from the socialist countries that we were eagerly reading at the time, there recurs a quotation from Lenin: "Stereotyped forms and a uniformity imposed from above have nothing in common with democratic and socialist centralism. The unity of essentials, of fundamentals, of the substance, is not disturbed but ensured by *variety* in details, in specific local features, in methods of *approach*, in *methods* of exercising control."[11] There also recurs, in different paraphrases and variants, Lenin's emphasis on the importance of grasping the "main links of the chain" to control a situation. *"Singling out the leading economic links is one of the most important principles of socialist economic planning."*[12] But despite the omnipresence of the quotations, these are exactly the principles that were violated in the approach of the Czech technicians to economic planning in Cuba.

The people attending the lectures and discussions had mixed reactions. The subject, socialist organization and planning, was inherently fascinating. The underlying logic of the socialist forms and methods was impressive. It was useful to have the Czech models, even if the mechanical way in which they were explained often made listening

[11] For instance, in I. Yevenko, *Planning in the U.S.S.R.*, Moscow, Foreign Languages Publishing House, p. 12. Also, for just the second sentence, P. Nikitin, *Fundamentals of Political Economy, Popular Course*, Moscow, Foreign Languages Publishing House, p. 241. Emphasis in original.
[12] Nikitin, *ibid.*, p. 252. Emphasis in original.

tedious. Some people also sensed that the lectures and discussions were not getting at the real workings of the Cuban economy, but their uneasiness was allayed by the belief that the socialist planning methodology would somehow automatically solve the problems, even those which the people engaged in planning did not themselves understand.

As soon as the organic laws were promulgated in late February, a great wave of activity got under way. Specific organizational forms had to be worked out for many agencies, both those covered by the new organic laws and others as well. It was not just the government but the whole economy that needed an organization suitable for socialist administration and planning; the nationalized enterprises had to be reorganized. The newly-created organizations had to be staffed with personnel. Everything had to be done quickly because work on the 1962 plan would begin within days. For many months, a large number of different tasks would have to be carried out simultaneously.

The principles underlying the organization to be set up were simple. There would be *operating* units to administer, to execute, to do the work. Alongside the operating units, there would be *staff* units to plan, to advise, to gather and give out information. And, as stated in the new organic law for the *Juceplan,* planning offices would be set up, not just in the Ministries, but in the economic units dependent on them, down to farms, factories, large stores, and often down further to individual departments of such units—forming a hierarchy which linked the *Juceplan* to the whole economy.

In April, the basic organization of the Ministry of Foreign Commerce was set up; the Ministry was divided into four major parts, called *Subsecretarías* (later Vice Ministries): Exports, Imports, Commercial Policy, and Economy.

The Vice Ministries of Exports and Imports would be operating units. They would supervise the two enterprises engaged in exporting and importing, the Cuban Export Enterprise and the Cuban Import Enterprise.[13]

---

[13] Later the Cuban Export and Import Enterprises were subdivided into a number of smaller units responsible for specific commodities.

The Vice Ministry of Commercial Policy would have both staff and operating functions covering policy and action by countries and regions. It would formulate commercial policy toward different countries, supervise Cuba's commercial attachés abroad, carry out trade negotiations with other countries, and represent Cuba at international trade meetings.

The Vice Ministry of Economy would be a staff unit. It would supervise the preparation of plans by different parts of the Ministry, integrate the partial plans into over-all Ministry plans, and coordinate the Ministry plans with other government agencies, in particular *Juceplan*. It would also prepare analyses of prices and markets and formulate general foreign trade policy.

In the foreign trade enterprises, along with the subdivisions doing the exporting and importing, there would be planning and policy units to prepare the first versions of the enterprise plan, to analyze commodity prices, to study markets, to prepare data on plan fulfillment. These units would work partly under the supervision of the Vice Ministry of Economy, linking it to the operating enterprises.

The Ministry of Industry was also divided into four *Subsecretarías* (likewise called Vice Ministries later): Basic Industry, Light Industry, Industrial Construction, and Economy. The first three would be operating units, the last a staff unit.

The Vice Ministries of Basic and Light Industry would administer the state's industrial enterprises. They would "collaborate with the [Vice Ministry] of Economy in the preparation of the Ministry Plan" and supervise its fulfillment by the enterprises.[14]

The Vice Ministry of Industrial Construction would be responsible for the growth of industrial capacity. It would "prepare the over-all Investment Plan of the Ministry" and "elaborate and carry out the individual projects."

The Vice Ministry of Economy would, as always, be the planning and policy unit. It would "direct the preparation and control of the plan for industry." And it would "advise on wage policy . . . check

---

[14] Reglamento Orgánico del Ministerio de Industrias, *Gaceta Oficial*, November 13, 1961.

and control the application of price policy . . . [and] attend to the rational organization of the activities of the Ministry."[15]

And so it went through the various Ministries. Each adapted the basic organizational principles to its own particular tasks. Take the Ministry of Transport as a last example. It set up *Subsecretarías* (Vice Ministries) of Sea and Air Transport, Land Transport, and Economy.

The organization of the government economic agencies could not be worked out in calm isolation from the daily turmoil of running the economy. It had to be done *sobre la marcha*, as the Cubans would say —while on the go. The Ministers and their assistants had to wrestle with such problems as spare parts for factories or equipment in the afternoon, and the organization charts for their Ministries in the evening.

While they were organizing themselves, moreover, the Ministries had to organize the economic units under them. For example, before the by-laws outlining its own organization had been issued, the Ministry of Industry was issuing the by-laws for the Consolidated Enterprises (*Consolidados*) into which factories turning out similar products were to be formed: there were, for example, the Consolidated Electricity Enterprise, the Consolidated Petroleum Enterprise, and so on, through nickel, cement, paper, textiles, and the other industrial products. For a while, the Ministry of Internal Commerce was spouting decrees creating Consolidated Enterprises in its sector of the economy —the Consolidated Food Store Enterprise, the Consolidated Barber Shop and Beauty Parlor Enterprise, the Consolidated Gas and Service Station Enterprise, the Consolidated Drugstore Enterprise.

Each Consolidated Enterprise would be headed by a director assisted by a council. It would be subdivided into departments according to the nature of its activities. Industrial *Consolidados* would have a Production Department, while Transport Enterprises would have Traf-

---

[15] In May, 1963, the number of Vice Ministries was increased to six, by adding a First Vice Ministry (a kind of office of deputy to the Minister) and a Vice Ministry of Technical Development. Reglamento Orgánico del Ministerio de Industrias, *Leyes del Gobierno Revolucionario de Cuba*, No. 47, marzo, abril, mayo de 1963.

fic Departments. But all the Consolidated Enterprises would have an Economics Department to plan. And these Economics Departments would link the enterprises to the Vice Ministries of Economics in their Ministries and through them to the *Juceplan*.

The establishment of the new organizational forms was pushed ahead rapidly. Resolutions and decrees giving organic by-laws for Ministries, setting up Vice Ministries, and reorganizing enterprises appeared one after the other in the *Gaceta Oficial*. By the second half of 1961, the new organization of the government and the economy had begun to take shape. But it was many months before even the formal reorganization could be said to be complete.

Work on the 1962 plan began toward the end of March, 1961. Then, just after it had gotten under way, it was interrupted by the Bay of Pigs invasion. I remember walking into the office of our Minister the morning of the attack. One of the new Vice Ministers was fooling with a transistor radio; others present were discussing the nature of the terrain around the point of invasion, at what other points landings might be expected, what the enemy strategy was likely to be; the Minister as a Major in the Rebel Army was expecting a possible call to a military station. For about ten days, work on planning was dropped. Then it was resumed again with an increased sense of urgency: preliminary versions of the plan were needed by September to serve as the basis for trade negotiations with the other socialist countries.

Everywhere there were many tasks to be done. As soon as the new planning units were officially created, and sometimes before, they would have to be staffed—to be converted from organization charts on paper to living bodies that could undertake the necessary work. Hundreds of planning forms would have to be discussed, designed, printed, filled out: forms for production plans, construction plans, credit plans, financial plans, export and import plans, foreign exchange plans, forms for the many different types of balances required. To fill out the forms, thousands of estimates would have to be made: estimates of the food, raw materials, and equipment required; of production to be expected; of the amounts of various goods that would be available for export; of the amount that would have to be supplied by imports; of the probable prices of the exports and imports, and so on through a long list. The plans produced by parts of Ministries would have to be integrated into Ministry plans, the Ministry plans would have to be integrated into over-all plans, financial plans would have to be fitted into physical plans—everything would have to be dovetailed together to form a single, economic plan. There would have to be meetings and discussions by people at the farms, the factories, the transport lines, the Ministries, between different offices of the same Ministry, between different Ministries, and with the *Juceplan*.

In staffing the new planning units, only one principle could be followed: that of the old Spanish proverb which says, *Hay que arar con los bueyes que hay*—You've got to plow with the oxen you have. So those who could run calculating machines became statisticians, and bookkeepers became experts on finances and the balance of payments. And cadre schools, university courses, and education programs in the other socialist countries were quickly set up to provide trained personnel for the future.

While there was no alternative to using untrained people, it was sometimes carried to extremes. Take, for example, the Price and Market Division at the Ministry of Foreign Commerce. This Division was in the Vice Ministry of Economy, part of the Office of Foreign Exchange and Finance which I headed during the first six months of its life. When the time came for staffing the Division, the Vice Minister, the head of the Division, and I found that while the organization chart called for about twenty people with training and experience in the analysis of prices and commodity markets, we had two who, if you stretched things a little, could be considered qualified. We decided that it would be best not to staff the whole division but to begin with two or three and then expand as we found people who could really do the job. We felt that while some types of jobs simply had to be filled, whether with qualified people or not, this was not true of the jobs in this Division: price and market analyses, unless they are good, are better dispensed with, since they clutter up desks with use-less paper. The Vice Minister and I argued strongly at the Minister's Council, but three or four others, including the Czech and Soviet technical advisors, disagreed, and we were overruled. The jobs were all filled; as it happened, with personally very attractive people, a lit-tle intimidated by their new responsibilities. About three months later, the first set of market analyses came in; one, on the lard mar-ket, was fairly good but the rest did not even approach being usable and had to be filed away within the Division. The Division functioned on paper, not in reality. This happened in many other places throughout the government, swelling the bureaucracy, creating problems of its own.

In the design of the planning forms, the manual and models of Czechoslovakia—and sometimes also those of the Soviet Union—were used for guidance. The models helped immeasurably. It would have taken years for the Cubans, without experience in planning, to design a comprehensive set of such forms on their own.

But the spirit of rigidity about the forms that had first become no-ticeable during the lectures and discussions of the Czech technicians had now spread almost everywhere. Most people working on the plan, knowing the limitations of their technical knowledge, were wary of taking the responsibility for tampering with the forms—especially since the Czech technicians discouraged such action. And so, as was foreseeable from the first lectures and discussions, the forms came out adapted more closely to Czechoslovakia than to Cuba; they asked for accounting information from economic units in which accounting sys-tems had not yet been installed, for statistics where none existed, for thousands of little estimates and projections which could not be made meaningful no matter how many telephone calls were made or meet-ings held, which could only tangle and confuse everything.

A spirit of formalism began to spread. Just as organization charts have to be filled with people whether they can do the job or not, so the planning forms have to be followed whether they mean anything or not. One day our Office, which was in charge of the Financial Plan of the Ministry, received a set of forms for this plan from the *Juce-*

plan. On studying the forms for the Export and Import Enterprises, we noticed that they simply did not apply. They had been designed for enterprises engaged in production, not in foreign trade. For example, they requested a detailed breakdown of *cost of production,* but the foreign trade enterprises did not have any costs of production: they only bought and sold. On the other hand, the main element in the finances of our enterprises—the differences between the prices at which they bought and those at which they sold, and the surpluses or deficits arising from these differences—were not brought out clearly.

We arranged a meeting with the head of the Finance Division of the *Juceplan* to propose more appropriate forms, and several of us from the Office went. We did not get far. Our host struck me as conscientious and able, but without real knowledge of financial problems; he knew what was in the manuals and forms, but not the principles. Yes, I see your point and agree, he told us, but there is nothing I can do. The forms have been agreed upon and I can't take the responsibility for changing them. He shone with determination to make good in his new job, to fulfill his assignments. And fulfilling his assignment meant getting his forms to his boss on time, not raising questions about them. Handing in his forms on time would be counted as getting the job done, even if the contents were useless. Many people were handing in useless statistics—this would not be held against him. But questioning the forms would mean discussions, meetings, delays, and perhaps failure to meet the deadlines. So our group went back and raised the problem with our Vice Minister of Economy. It was not easy to know what to do—there were hundreds of problems like this. Eventually our Office had to fill the senseless forms with numbers, which were later accepted by the *Juceplan* without a word.

In filling out the forms, the measure of achievement became the quantity of statistics prepared, not their accuracy. At each stage in the hierarchy, the chiefs would check whether those below were fulfilling their assignments, and the closer the deadlines, the heavier the pressure to get out the numbers—any old numbers. The formalistic attitude was accentuated when, as was often the case, the statistics for a particular form had to be collected from other Divisions, Offices, or

Ministries. Then the person in charge of the form could place the responsibility for the statistics on the organization from which they had been obtained, or claim that he could not work the statistics into a sensible whole because only these organizations had authority to change them.

The style of work became bureaucratic. Under the old *por la libre*, the criterion had been *resolver*—run the economy somehow, solve problems as they came up. But this had been done inefficiently, wastefully, without organization and planning. Now organization and planning came in with a vengeance. People worked so hard at these tasks that they forgot what they were for; they lost all concern with *resolver*. All the emphasis was placed on rules of procedure and method, on when each Ministry submits certain papers to the *Juceplan*, on who signs what; the real economy and its problems became something remote.

Everybody was flooded with papers, and for many people the papers became the end-all of the work. Since everything now had to be coordinated, the meetings became almost endless, developing a momentum of their own. And many—usually those who had gloried the most in the indiscipline of *por la libre*—quickly learned how to maneuver within the bureaucracy, how to shift and escape responsibility, how to avoid making simple, clear decisions.

Everyone noticed the growth of bureaucracy and sometimes grumbled about it. The leaders of the Revolution were troubled by it. One evening Fidel gave a long speech castigating bureaucracy at the National Bank. Among other stupidities, the Bank had been trying to apply overnight the letter of the law about credit monopoly, and abruptly cut off even the traditional credit at grocery stores. But it was hard to know what to do about the problem in general—how to have organization and planning and still avoid bureaucracy.

Among the key elements in the plan were the goals: goals for the construction of houses, roads, factories, farm installations, schools, and hospitals; for the production of sugar, tobacco, nickel, copper, coffee, textiles, canned pineapple; for the amount of such goods that would be available for export; for exports to various countries; and for foreign-exchange earnings, both in convertible and nonconvertible currencies.

Most goals were fixed at impossibly high levels. This partly reflected revolutionary exuberance and partly deliberate policy. Many seemed to think that high goals were necessary to stimulate people to their greatest efforts.

In the Vice Ministry of Economy at Foreign Commerce, we first noticed the general overoptimism in the figures on the amount of goods available for export. The goals for a large number of goods were far out of line, it seemed to some of us, with past figures on production and exports. When the first export goals were sent in from the Cuban Export Enterprises, we felt that the overoptimism was being compounded: not just the amount of goods that would be available for export, but the ease of selling many of the goods in capitalist markets was being grossly overestimated.

Since the Office I headed was responsible for foreign exchange, we were greatly concerned about overestimation of future export earnings, especially those in convertible currency. We felt that it could lead to over-high import plans, and then to deficit and a shortage of exchange. And if you have to make large reductions in import plans during the year, you may find you have committed a large amount of money to secondary items and are short of it for more important ones.

The Vice Minister of Economy and I raised these problems several times at the meetings of the Ministry Council, proposing that the goals and estimates be reduced. There were many discussions and debates. One person quoted the manuals on the latent reserves in the economy and the need for goals that would mobilize them fully. Another pointed out that the manuals also said that goals should be realistic. A third argued that excessively high goals, just as much as low goals, can result in failure to mobilize, for people stop taking them seriously as it becomes clear that none of the goals will be met; and also in a modern economy with its manifold dovetailing, failure to meet a goal in one item or area can affect many others and cause confusion and waste. The head of the tobacco export section assured the Council that his people would find ways of selling more tobacco in Western Europe and Latin America and meeting their high goals. The person in charge of the Export Plan argued that he had no authority to question the production and export availability figures submitted by INRA and the Ministry of Industry. In the end, the goals and estimates of export earnings were not reduced.

Related to the over-high goals was the failure to set up adequate reserves in the plans. Several of us at Foreign Commerce argued that even if the goal for earnings of convertible currency were left high to stimulate people, the total planned imports for such currency should deliberately be fixed at a lower level—the difference would constitute a reserve against failure to meet the earnings goal and other unfavorable developments that might occur. Again no luck.

It was the same at the other Ministries: the plans were set up without allowing margins for error and unforeseeable contingencies. It was, in effect, assumed that things would work with perfect precision and smoothness, that every last little drop could be squeezed out of the available resources. Agriculture undertook commitments to provide goods for industry, export, or the local market whose fulfillment could easily be prevented by bad weather. Industry undertook commitments whose fulfillment could be prevented by the failure of agriculture or the Ministry of Foreign Commerce to provide the necessary raw materials. In spite of growing shortages of cement and other materials, the goals for construction were set very high—making no allowance for possible shortfalls in the production of materials, and tacitly assuming that they would be perfectly distributed among the different construction projects around the country.

The "first variant" of the Plan for 1962 was completed by September and appeared in fat volumes of machine-prepared statistical sheets. The Trade Mission to the socialist countries was able to leave on time. But so many things were clearly wrong with the "first variant" that work began immediately on a "second variant," and soon a new set of orange-colored volumes was floating around. Eventually, at least seven such variants were made. Sometimes it was hard for those working on different parts of the plan to tell whether they were using the latest variant or not.

Ordinarily, trade negotiations among socialist countries are completed some weeks before the end of each year. This makes it possible to work up the final plan and pass it into law in time for the beginning of the new year in which it is to apply. But the 1961 negotiations with most of the socialist countries stretched out beyond the scheduled time, and were uncompleted by the end of the year. It was therefore not possible to begin the new year's operations with a final, approved plan.

This caused uncertainty and confusion. It delayed the conclusion of many import contracts, including some for foodstuffs. The operating people throughout the economy had no firm basis on which to act. The people in the planning units who should have been engaged in checking and controlling the execution of the plan could not do so. Much of their time was still taken up with preparing different variants; there was no clear plan to check and control. The last variant of the plan did not come till about May.

The first several variants of the plan underestimated requirements for the import of foodstuffs. The estimates of how much domestic agriculture would supply had been based on optimistic assumptions—and then came the severe drought. On top of this, the delay in signing import contracts caused a decline in deliveries from abroad. It became necessary not only to impose rationing, but to arrange rapidly for the import of additional foodstuffs.

The problem was now too important to be left to lower-level technicians. There was no time for lengthy meetings, approvals by different parts of the bureaucratic apparatus, and the like. The highest political authorities decided on a rapid increase in food imports, and President Dorticós took charge of determining what and how much, and having the arrangements made. It was not possible to coordinate the increases in food imports with the plan, in any of its variants. They were made on the basis of fresh, rough-and-ready estimates of requirements, without too much worry about what the plan said, or how the increased purchases would affect its different parts.

Innumerable others problems arose in addition to that of foodstuffs. As time went on, it became increasingly clear that a large number of goals would not be met. Except for sugar and a few other major items whose output was relatively easy to estimate, production goals were not being met. Partly because of shortfalls in production and in the amounts of goods made available for export, and partly because of overoptimism about market possibilities, many of the goals for dollar exports were not achieved. Except for the tobacco goal, most of the goals that were missed by wide margins were for secondary items. Still it became necessary to restrict dollar expenditures.

In construction, the goals were simply impossible to fulfill. An article published later by Regino Boti, the Executive Secretary of *Juceplan*, showed that the total planned construction exceeded by a large percentage the materials available for carrying it out.

The 1962 Plan did not control the Cuban economy. Until action was taken to assure an adequate supply of foodstuffs, the economy floundered. The Plan could not be given the force of law—this would have been to legislate unreality and error, to force people into doing what was clearly wrong just because the plan told them to. Whenever people saw that the Plan offered no answers, or clearly erroneous answers to the problems confronting them, they disregarded it; they took whatever action the problems seemed to call for. A large gap developed between the Plan and the practical work of running the economy. The Plan became a ritual which people performed with respect —they held meetings on the Plan, worked up new variants, and later even made a few attempts to check on plan fulfillment. But the real work of running the economy was still being done *por la libre*.

Why did Cuba's first plan fail? Mainly because it is hard in a country without a long tradition of organization, without a large number of trained and experienced people, to convert an anarchic economy into a planned economy overnight. Even with the tradition and trained personnel, the setting up of a large organization to perform new and unfamiliar tasks is much more difficult than many realize. I worked for the United States War Production Board in 1942. It, too, suffered from confusion and disorganization.

But the 1962 Plan also failed because of the manner and method with which planning and organization were introduced in Cuba. For all its faults, *por la libre* had had one virtue—it looked to the external world and to people. And for all their potential virtues, organization and planning as they were introduced in Cuba had a basic defect— they almost forgot about the external world and people.

Disdain for the world of people and problems showed itself at all stages of the introduction of organization and planning. When the Czech technician read an organization chart, he was presenting the "scientific" way to organize something. The chart guaranteed that the real organization would function "correctly." But the men and women who would work the chart? They didn't seem to matter much. If somehow the real organization did not work well, the chart was not at fault, but something else. And this problem was not for the trained technician, but for others to solve. His job was to present the "science," not to struggle with the lesser task of making things work.

The elementary distinction between the objective and the subjective was forgotten many times in preparing the 1962 Plan. Planning means establishing the right proportions between things—the right amount of fertilizers, raw materials, foodstuffs, equipment, labor power, and so on, all properly related to one another. And whether proportions are right depends on the external world; plans can be mistaken. A plan may call for insufficient oil—and then there will not be enough for the trucks, tractors, and machinery to run on. Stalin stressed this in his *Economic Problems of the U.S.S.R.*[16] "Our yearly and five-year plans," he wrote, "must not be confused with the objective economic law of balanced, proportionate development of the national economy. . . . The law of balanced development makes it *possible* for our planning bodies to plan correctly. But *possibility* must not be confused with *actuality*. They are two different things. In order to turn the possibility into actuality, it is necessary to study this law, to master it, to learn to apply it with full understanding, and to compile such plans as fully reflect the requirements of this law." The same thought is repeated in the Soviet manual, *Fundamentals of Marxism-Leninism*.

[16] New York, International Publishers, 1952, p. 11.

And yet more than once at the meetings of the Council of the Ministry of Foreign Commerce, I heard the Soviet technical adviser talk as though he had never heard that plans are not automatically right, that whether they are right or wrong depends on objective criteria. When we discussed goals and estimates, he would often assert impatiently: The important thing is to decide, put everything into the Plan, and then give it the force of law. What the Plan says is right.

In the effort to convince everyone of the need to end *por la libre*, planning was made into a fetish: people would not have to struggle with problems any more; the Plan would automatically solve the problems and run the economy. Under planning, said different Cuban officials, the economy will run like a clock.[17] When, at the production conference in the summer of 1961, Osmani Cienfuegos, the Minister of Public Works, invited Major Guevara to "coordinate" with him, he was chided by Carlos Rafael Rodríguez of the Integrated Revolutionary Organizations: You have four months left for this type of coordination; after the Plan begins, coordination between Ministers ends; the Plan will do the coordination.[18]

But it is not plans which solve problems and run the economy; it is people. People have to make the plans and carry them out.

In making plans, the people can receive guidance from the models and methods worked out in the socialist countries. But as the Minister of Foreign Commerce once put it: The models and methods solve about 15 percent of our problem; the other 85 percent is up to us. Models can help with analysis where circumstances and problems are similar, but even then the analysis has to be completed by people. Where problems and circumstances are not similar, the models can also cause difficulties. And models don't exercise judgment; they can't make policy; they can't force people to face hard problems and make the right decisions. You can work a prudent foreign-exchange policy into the models or a rash one, a sensible allocation of construction re-

[17] Fidel, whose thinking is never mechanistic, seemed not to hold this clock view of planning; but in those days he did not play a big role in planning, saying that he did not claim to understand it.

[18] *Obra Revolucionaria*, "Primera Reunión de Producción, Agosto 26-27," La Habana, Imprenta Nacional de Cuba, 1961, p. 207.

sources or one which causes confusion and waste. Problems have to be understood and solved by people; the solutions contained in plans are those that people have put into them. But when people are taught planning mechanistically, when it is presented to them as a fetish, they are not encouraged to grapple with problems but rather to look away from them.

The failure to build reserves into the 1962 Plan stemmed from the clock conception of planning. If plans worked with absolute precision, there would be no need for reserves. Reserves are a cushion against error and unforeseen contingencies. But no economic plan works with absolute precision. There are always errors. And in the real world, the unforeseen is always happening and affecting plans. There are droughts, hurricanes, and plant and animal diseases; delays in the completion of construction projects; zigzags in world market prices; failures by foreign suppliers to meet their commitments on time; changes in trade and political relations with other countries; and embargoes, crises, and wars. Soviet writers on planning from Stalin on have stressed the importance of reserves. For a country beginning to plan as Cuba was in 1962, adequate reserves are especially necessary. If reserves had been built into the 1962 Plan, it would have been less ambitious, but more realistic. Some of the effects of the inevitable deviations from the Plan would have been absorbed, instead of upsetting the dovetailing throughout the economy and creating general confusion. The Plan might have achieved a certain amount of control over the economy.

People are even more important in carrying out and controlling plans than in making them. The misunderstanding of these tasks during those early months of planning was especially great. Many people talked as if carrying out a plan was little more than a matter of following instructions—doing what the plan says—and as if control was simply seeing to it that instructions were followed.

These ideas are too simple. Carrying out a plan is not a mechanical detail. Plans fix key goals. Explicitly or implicitly, they provide key guidelines. They embody the solutions to key problems. But plans cannot cover everything, only essentials. For every one thing they cover, there are ten thousand they have to leave uncovered. Whatever the plans leave uncovered, has to be taken care of by people. True, the people have to work within plans; they have to try to fulfill plans. But plans do not run economies; people do.

A plan may fix the amount of goods that will be imported in a given year or quarter, but it cannot fix the exact day or even week when particular ships will arrive from across the seas. The scheduling of ships has to be done by people, taking into account the Plan, and— at each particular time—the goods ready for shipment and the ships available. People have to coordinate the work on the docks with the land transport to and from the docks, and the arrival and departure of ships. Even with plans, there is a great deal left for people to coordinate.

A plan can fix many targets and norms for mines, factories, and farms. But it cannot give advance answers to the thousands of problems that are always presenting themselves to the people who have to fulfill the targets and norms. In a mine, a wall caves in, the ventilating system breaks down, or the ore turns out to have a higher percentage of impurities than was expected. In a factory, the rate of absenteeism suddenly rises, the raw materials received fail to meet specifications fully, or the head of a key department turns out to be incompetent. The administrator of a farm finds that while manuals can make the setting up of work norms sound easy, it is often in practice an almost impossible task; the norms require standardization and much of the work on farms does not lend itself to standardization.

The erroneous conception of how economic plans are carried out helped make the 1962 Plan unrealistic. For a plan to be good, those who are constructing it must keep always in mind the task of carrying it out. They must try to envision the circumstances that will exist, the problems and difficulties that will be confronted; they must have a strong sense of responsibility for all aspects of the plan, not the feeling that carrying it out is somebody else's headache; they must deliberately try to make a plan that can be fulfilled. Not to do this is almost certainly to make a plan that cannot be fulfilled.

But the damage went beyond the Plan itself into the effort at execution. Before people can carry out an economic plan, they must understand how to work it. They must not expect more from the plan than it can give. They must understand that a plan can effectively guide the economy even if it covers only essentials; that it is possible to work within a plan even though it does not give complete instructions; that a plan can still be a plan even though it does not solve problems automatically. Even with a good plan, failure to understand these facts would have caused difficulties. As it was, the failure contributed to the disregard for the 1962 Plan that developed so quickly. In part, people disregarded the Plan because of its obvious errors. But in part they did so because the actual work of carrying it out did not fit their preconceptions. They saw no middle ground between a plan that would work exactly and automatically, and no plan at all. And so when it became necessary to deviate from the plan, they just forgot about it altogether.

Finally, the control of plans is not a mechanical task. If economic plans contained no errors and the unforeseen were not always happening, the task of control would be mechanical. With a perfect plan, there would remain only one thing to do: ram through its fulfillment. But economic plans are never perfect. They have to be adjusted and changed while they are being carried out. Controlling a plan is a mixture of tasks; it means not only enforcing discipline, but remaking the plan.

This idea is not new. Here are some statements on control from one of the Soviet planning manuals: "*Socialist planning implies the unity of the process of drafting plans, the creation of conditions for their fulfillment, control of their actual fulfillment, of specifying and adjusting the plans in the course of their fulfillment.* . . . Control helps to correct plans and specify them in greater detail. . . . Control of plan fulfillment should not be understood merely as a process of mechanically comparing statistics on the actual level of production with plan assignments in order to find out which branches do not carry out the plan. Such understanding of control is an expression of armchair bureaucratic methods of planning work."[19] Yet this idea was misunderstood by many in Cuba in 1961 and 1962, including the So-

[19] I. A. Yevenko, *Planning in the U.S.S.R.* Moscow, Foreign Languages Publishing House, pp. 203, 205, and 207. Emphasis in original.

viet technical advisor at the Ministry of Foreign Commerce, who constantly stressed the disciplinary aspect of control to the exclusion of the creative aspect.

The creative aspect is the more difficult and important of the two. When it becomes clear that part of a plan is not being fulfilled, the problem must be analyzed. Both the causes of the failure to fulfill and its possible effects throughout the plan must be determined. A number of judgments must be made: Is the fault in the execution or in the plan? Can fulfillment be attained by correcting the execution in some way, or must the failure to fulfill be accepted as irremediable, so that the plan itself has to be changed? And if it is the plan, can the changes be limited to the targets that have been missed? Can the effects of changing these targets be absorbed by the reserves, or will they be felt in other parts of the plan so that these too must be adjusted? When control is exercised in this way, an economic plan can be made to get ever closer to what is objectively right for an economy. It can be integrated with practical operations, both reflecting them and guiding them.

But if control is understood mechanistically, it becomes impossible to adjust the plan. Even with a good plan, mechanistic control would cause great difficulties. With the 1962 Plan in Cuba, it delivered the fatal blow. If control is limited to enforcing a plan and does not also mean correcting it, the only thing to be done with a bad plan is to disregard it.

With a true conception of planning and control, plans—even bad ones—should not simply be disregarded. They should be adjusted. The attempt should be made to salvage at least the fundamentals, if need be by making quick, broad changes in the plan. For example, even if it becomes necessary to disregard all the details in the plans for finances, foreign exchange, or construction, the attempt should be made to retain or rig up general controls and ensure some balance between the claims on resources and their availability. A tenacious effort must be exerted to guide the economy according to some plan—however general, however weak and imperfect. This would have been very difficult in Cuba in 1962; the manner in which the Plan had been constructed, without any distinction between details and fundamentals, made it so. When the time for action came, little attempt to stay with some sort of plan was made; people just reverted to *por la libre*.

This result was inherent in the mechanistic conception of planning, in the way in which all the different phases of planning—making the plan, carrying it out, and controlling it—were approached. The mechanistic approach cannot cope with imperfection. Either you can make the economy run like a clock, or you may as well give up altogether to disorganization. Since economies do not run like clocks, this view guarantees disorganization.

The *por la libre* with which the revolutionaries had handled the economy during the first two years of the Revolution had to be ended. But because of the method of introducing organization and planning, *por la libre* was overcorrected with the opposite extreme—bureaucracy, the mechanical adherence to rules and procedures the purpose of which has been forgotten. It was as if a rough-and-tumble fighter was given boxing lessons which taught him jabs and footwork to keep himself from being hit so often—and he became so obsessed with fighting scientifically and not being hit that he lost the knack for mixing it up with his opponent. The true purpose of jabs and footwork, however, is not to make shadow boxing impressive, but to help in fighting.

To begin to work well, organization and planning in Cuba would have to look away from arid formulas to the world and to people. The principles of organization and planning would have to be understood as principles, not as a set of mechanical how-to-do-it formulas. Forms and methods would have to be adjusted to Cuban circumstances. People would have to learn how to use the forms and methods, and not be dominated by them. Cuba's problems would have to be discerned and grappled with—by people. Throughout the economy, people would have to continue to work at the long hard task of acquiring the knowledge and skills required to run a socialist economy. And for organization and planning to work truly well, the sense of responsibility—the honest sense that means wanting really to do the job, not the bureaucratic sense that means fulfilling on paper—

already strong and widespread among the people, would have to grow ever stronger and more widespread. The best organization charts and planning methods cannot be made to work well, except by people.

I have called the 1962 Plan a failure in the interests of technical accuracy. Looked at technically and by itself, it was a failure. But it cannot merely be looked at technically or by itself—it was part of a process of revolution and learning. Looked at as part of a process, it can no more be called a failure than can the falls of an infant who is beginning to learn how to walk.

To help put the 1962 Cuban experience into perspective, here are a few comments from Anna Louise Strong's chapter on the first Soviet Five Year Plan in her book, *The Stalin Era*.[20] During this Plan, Miss Strong visited many construction sites and factories throughout the Soviet Union.

"American engineers who came to help the Plan on contract, liked to say that it wasn't really a 'plan' at all. Technically, they were right. The Plan was never a blueprint to be followed precisely—it was a challenge to be met and then surpassed."

Of the Stalingrad Tractor Works she writes: "Organization had to be built. They no sooner conquered one detail, than another slipped up to stop them. There were a thousand details to concentrate on at once. That had never been done in Russia. . . . They were building more storage warehouses—a year late. For lack of proper storage, nobody knew what spare parts were available. The line would stop for lack of a certain part; yet there might be hundreds of such parts stored somewhere a month ago."

A Soviet engineer working on the construction of the steel mill at Kuznetsk told her: "In America, you order ten carloads of firebrick by phone and get them in a few days. We ordered some of ours a year and a half ago. We waited without firebrick for the blast furnace for four months. Then it all came at once; there was no space for it and we dumped it everywhere in the way of other work. Our steel should

[20] New York, Mainstream Publishers, 1956, pp. 25, 26, 30.

have come in May; it came in September. Trainloads of equipment came from all parts of Russia and from abroad; cars get sidetracked and delayed."

The introduction of planning, especially in economically underdeveloped countries, is not easy.

The 1962 Plan in Cuba was an excellent training exercise. People began to learn the different planning jobs by doing them. The newly created or reconstructed organizations began to be broken in, to work more smoothly and effectively. As it became clear that the 1962 Plan was not working the way it should, people discussed why—and their idea of planning became more and more realistic.

The benefits began to show when the work on the 1963 Plan got started. There was far less rush and confusion. Meetings were fewer and shorter. Everyone felt less overwhelmed by the work on the Plan.

Because people knew their jobs better, they were more willing to assume responsibility, less wary of changing the planning forms. The forms began to be adapted to Cuba, to be stripped of unnecessary detail or requests for information that could not be obtained. The forms received by the Ministry of Foreign Commerce from *Juceplan* for the Financial Plans of its enterprises were good ones—adapted to trading and not to production enterprises.

Goals became more realistic. A person can defend an impossible goal once, saying that he personally guarantees its fulfillment. But when the ratio of fulfillment turns out to be 50 percent, he is less likely to make outlandish commitments the next time and still less likely to be listened to if he does.

It became clear that the 1962 Plan had tried to do more than the available resources would permit. *Juceplan* learned from its own studies that the construction goals went far beyond what could be done with the materials available. At the Ministry of Foreign Commerce, each passing month provided further data showing that the year would end with a large balance-of-payments deficit. For many months, these different pieces of information were not put together and analyzed as parts of a single whole. It took time for the full significance of the balance-of-payments deficit to be recognized. But even without a systematic over-all analysis, the separate indications of strain on resources began to have a healthy effect on planning for 1963. For example, efforts were made to hold down imports. The 1963 Plan was far more realistic than that for 1962.

The idea that plans automatically solve problems disappeared. People not only grappled with problems instead of avoiding them, but they began to move away from the *por la libre* way of doing so; they began to try to adapt and apply organization and planning to the problems. This can be illustrated by the construction industry.

Besides confusion in the distribution of construction materials, which had resulted from overambitious goals in the Plan, individual projects were sometimes badly managed. Sites were poorly chosen, materials and equipment were improperly handled, costs were excessive. Under the *por la libre* method someone in Havana would have tried to handle each specific problem as it came up—for example, by running from one site to another and trying to reduce costs. Now the Investment Division of *Juceplan* began to work out a general solution to the problem, which it felt lay in the organization of the projects. The head of the Investment Division once explained it to me at lunch: Does a plan, he asked, guarantee that a construction project will be carried out well? No, it doesn't. It allocates equipment, materials, and money. But does the plan prevent these resources from being used to start a housing project on a bad site—for example, on a site where, it turns out after work is well under way, there is no good water supply? And if this does happen who is to blame? The people in Havana? The people carrying out the project? There has to be a clear and full division of responsibility—apart from acts of God, nothing should be able to go wrong without somebody's being clearly responsible. Every project must have a project head who will see that it is carried out right. The project head will have to work within the plan. Certain standardized information will have to be worked up for all proposed projects before they can be approved by Havana. There will also be a system of reports and inspections on work in progress. But there are limits to what Havana can decide and control directly. It can standardize designs, fix building specifications, set up cost and work norms. But it cannot make the day-to-day decisions. Beyond what the plan and Havana say, the project head will bear full responsibility. No more of this business of ten or twenty people working on a project and none of them happening to think of water supply because the responsibilities are all mixed up. The project head will have to think of and worry about everything.

Several months later, the Investment Division arranged a two-day inter-Ministerial conference on the problems of organizing and planning construction. Not only were the proposals on how to organize construction projects discussed, but many other things as well, including the problem of coordination between the Ministry of Public Works and other Ministries, and the implications of the balance-of-payments deficit for the construction goals and plans.

Many people became interested in the broader problems of organization and planning. They began to ask themselves such questions as: How centralized does a socialist economy have to be? Which things should be centralized and which decentralized? When several of us from the Ministry of Foreign Commerce talked to the head of the Moa Nickel Plant, he complained strongly about overcentralization. Here I am, he said, heading an enterprise which earns several million dollars in foreign exchange, and I almost have to get Havana's approval when I need some pencils. We felt that this criticism was justified. He also thought that his enterprise should be permitted to send its own purchasing missions abroad to buy the parts and equipment it required; only people from the enterprise, not those of the Ministry of Foreign Commerce, could judge whether the parts and equipment offered were suitable or not. Here we felt that although he had a point, what he wanted was wrong. The technical judgments required, as he asserted, engineers of the enterprise; but this problem could best be handled by maintaining close contact between our Ministry and the enterprise and by allowing enterprise engineers to go along on Ministry purchasing missions. Otherwise, where would the dispersal of control over foreign exchange stop? The oil company, the electric power and telephone companies, and many other enterprises could ask to send their own purchasing missions with equal justification.

Foreign-exchange resources were scarce; they had to be centrally controlled by people who understood the over-all exchange situation and followed it closely.

From their own experience, many people learned of what some economists have called the problem of the "achievement indicators in a socialist economy." Major Guevara had mentioned the problem of quality at the production conference in the summer of 1961. "Quality," he had said, "is constantly being sacrificed in many sectors of our industry to assure savings, to assure production." By 1962, many people had become aware that the problem was not limited to industry. In somewhat different forms, it existed everywhere. For example, the statistics in our own Ministry were being judged more by their quantity than whether they meant anything. Or to take an example from transport: the fulfillment of the job of loading sugar on ships was measured by the weight of the sugar, not whether it got onto the boat in good condition; handling became careless and the Ministry began to receive reports of considerable sugar being spoiled because the sacks were somehow coming into contact with salt water. At one of the Ministry Council meetings during this period someone who had been on a trade delegation to the Soviet Union told a story he had heard there: A foreign visitor in a Moscow hotel sat down in an overstuffed chair next to a steam radiator. Finding it was too hot, he tried to move the chair, but couldn't budge it. So he called a hotel employee and together they moved the chair. Then he asked why the chair was so heavy. Well, was the answer, this chair was made at a time when we were measuring the fulfillment of the furniture plan by the weight of the furniture produced.

No quick solutions were found for the many problems of organization and planning: how to have centralization and decentralization where each is necessary and combine the two effectively; how to avoid the mechanical emphasis on quantitative goals that often results in poor quality or meaningless activity. There are no miraculous solutions —only a long, hard process of thinking, experimentation, education, and work. And this process was now under way in Cuba.

The Plan for 1963 was completed on time; the first version, the trade negotations with the other socialist countries, and the final revisions had all gone according to schedule. The Plan still suffered from countless flaws. For example, there was ambiguity in the figures for planned imports from the other socialist countries. Some of these countries were taking the figures in the trade agreements and contracts to mean that they had to *ship* the planned amount of goods to Cuba within the plan year, not that they had to schedule their shipping so that this amount of goods would *arrive in Cuba* in that year. Thus they could ship some goods on December 28 and these would count toward their export obligation for that year even though the goods would not arrive in Cuba till, say, January 28. Since the shipping time from the other socialist countries to Cuba is fairly long, this meant a large overhang of goods from one of Cuba's plan years to the next, which created confusion in the statistics and made control of the import plan difficult.

But none of the flaws in the 1963 Plan was comparable to those of the year before. The Plan was workable. And people had acquired a sense of how to work with a plan. So for the first time in 1963, the Cuban economy was operated according to an over-all economic plan.

6

Sugar Policy and the Long-run Orientation of the Economy

There are many aspects to the long-run orientation of the Cuban economy—the balance of payments, sugar policy, the relative roles to be played by agriculture and industry in economic development, the specific branches of agriculture and industry to be developed, the education of technical specialists and the people as a whole. Of these, I have first-hand familiarity with only two—the balance of payments and sugar policy. I worked on these aspects, in part because I headed during the second half of 1962 the little group at the Ministry of Foreign Commerce which began work on longer-run planning in foreign trade, and in part because of specific assignments I received from the Economic Secretary of the Integrated Revolutionary Organizations (ORI).

My familiarity with the other aspects comes mostly from helping to trace the significance of the balance-of-payments deficit for the various sectors of the economy, and is therefore limited. For example, I did not see any of the studies of the possible development of a large iron and steel industry, with discussions of costs and the problems of fuel and the high chrome content of the Cuban ores. Nor did I ever see more than two or three of the studies of agricultural development or attend any working meetings on this subject.

I shall therefore concentrate on the balance of payments and sugar policy, touching the other things only lightly. Even on the development of a new sugar policy—one which reversed the previous downgrading of sugar—I am mostly familiar with what took place at the Ministry of Foreign Commerce and among economists working on

181

the problem in various agencies of the government. My knowledge of how the decisions on sugar policy were taken by the leaders of the Revolution is based on hearsay and surmise; it is neither accurate enough nor important enough to be worth repeating, and besides, it would not be proper to do so. I shall tell what happened from the angle at which I saw it, and there will be some gaps.

How the new policies were forged is only part of the story. Even more important are the reasons behind these policies. I shall try to develop a line of analysis and argument that will illustrate these reasons. To do this, I shall have to borrow freely from the thoughts of others who worked on the problems. But, obviously, I cannot claim that what is presented here represents anybody's thinking but mine. And I should like especially to emphasize that in the sections on economic independence and the relative priorities to be given to agriculture and industry—both of which touch on potentially delicate matters —the reasoning is mine without significant conscious borrowing from co-workers in Cuba.

At the beginning, most of the long-run economic policies of the Revolution were those inherited from prerevolutionary days. Many are mentioned in Fidel's *History Will Absolve Me* speech. Others stemmed from ideas that were widely held among revolutionaries and radicals in Cuba.

The logic of most of the policies was natural and simple—to reverse what imperialism had been doing. Imperialism meant a Cuba of large plantations and idle land and labor; the thing to do was make a land reform and put the idle land and labor to work. Imperialism meant a one-crop Cuba; therefore diversify. Imperialism monopolized Cuba's foreign trade; Cuba must trade with all countries. Imperialism kept Cuba from more than token industrialization; Cuba must industrialize rapidly. Imperialism had made Cuba into an economic vassal of the United States; Cuba must try to create an independent economy.

As first and general approximations of what to do about the Cuban economy, these policies were excellent and the Revolution realized historic achievements by following them. Cuba needed to make a land reform and to break the trade monopoly of the United States. It needed to begin diversifying its agriculture and to move toward industrialization. And above all, it needed economic and political independence: it needed to control its resources, its markets, its governments, and its policies—otherwise it could not even begin to attack its problems.

But like all working hypotheses—like all theory—the initial policies were no answer to everything. Knowing that Cuba needs a land reform does not tell you whether the land should be divided into small farms, or organized into cooperatives or People's Farms. *Diversification* is a Latin abstraction; it carries a certain amount of meaning, but by itself, it does not tell you what to raise in greater quantities—tomatoes and cucumbers, rice and beans, chickens, pigs, cattle. That industrialization is required was clear, but what industries should Cuba develop? How fast should industrialization take place? What are the interrelationships between industrial and agricultural development? Everyone could see that Cuba ought to be freed from the iron grip of the United States. But beyond this, what does economic independence mean? Does it mean that Cuba must try to feed itself, to produce all the machinery and equipment it requires within its own borders? The initial policies had to be developed further.

The interplay between practice and theory began with the first actions of the Revolution in the Sierra. Practice was already beginning to teach lessons—for example, that it would not do to divide the huge cattle ranches into small farms because too many cattle would be eaten up by the *campesinos*.

When the Revolution took power, this process began to take place on a grand scale—the whole economy became a testing ground, the whole people became involved. Cooperatives and state farms were set up and people observed how they worked. Diversification began to be given ever more specific meaning; it meant growing rice, potatoes, and tomatoes, and raising more chickens, pigs, and cattle; and then, as experimentation and thinking went on, it began to mean specific kinds of rice and potatoes, chickens and cattle. As it was learned that conditions in Cuba are very favorable for cattle raising, it meant that this activity would be especially developed; and when the supply of lard from the United States was cut off, it meant that Cuba would try to raise large amounts of soy beans and peanuts for their oil.

There were innumerable discussions and memoranda, and after a while one or two studies began to appear. Sometimes people disagreed with something and said so. One person at the Bank of Foreign Commerce kept insisting that the plans for increasing rice production were too ambitious. Rice, he said, needs water—wet land or irrigated land —and we don't have that much. Often there were mistakes, such as neglecting to build warehouses for the storage of the increased potato crop. But practice is a tough teacher; next year, storage sheds began to appear on the cooperatives.

Industrialization also became more specific. Testing the possibility of setting up a large iron and steel industry began; decisions about such an industry cannot be made simply on the basis of general principles and the descriptions of ores given in geography books but require concrete engineering and economic studies. Specific factories began to be planned and placed under construction for producing pencils, knives and forks, picks and shovels, machine parts, stoves and refrigerators, and so on. Sometimes mistakes in planning were made, like the one mentioned by Major Guevara in one of his talks. We tried to choose industries, he said, that would save foreign exchange, that would produce substitutes for imports. But while we took into account the foreign exchange that would be saved by not having to import the finished product, we neglected to pay attention to the foreign exchange required to buy the raw materials for the new factories.

During the first two and a half years after the Revolution took power, practical work—for all its difficulty—meant simply applying the initial policies. Its main impact on the policies was to give them more specific content, not to qualify or change them significantly. The major decisions and programs flowed from these policies.

Here are two examples. In the spring of 1961, the leaders of the Revolution decided to cut back the acreage under sugar cane in order to free land for other crops—for diversification. They hoped by increasing yields to keep cane production up even while reducing the amount of land devoted to it. But, in addition, sugar was the symbol of imperialist slavery and less important than diversification. Fidel gave a television speech in which he discussed the decision. He explained that his own older brother, Ramón, disagreed; Ramón seemed to feel instinctively that for Cuba sugar was too important to be treated this way. Fidel criticized him strongly. After the 1961 sugar harvest of 6.7 million tons—second only to the 7.0-million-ton harvest during the Korean War in 1952—thousands of *caballerías* of caneland were ploughed under.

The other example is one of the early industrialization programs worked out in the Department of Industrialization of INRA and announced by Major Guevara in February, 1961, about the time the law creating the Ministry of Industry was promulgated. "In the next five-year period," said Major Guevara, "we shall invest in industry about one billion pesos—600 million of which will go for the importation of factories, machinery, and equipment, while 400 million will go for capital goods constructed in our own factories. We shall get the major part of the 600 million with credits from the socialist countries, although we shall also acquire factories in other countries. . . . By the end of 1965, our heavy industry will be very advanced."[1]

Both the decision to cut back cane acreage and the investment program announced by Major Guevara reflected the initial policies—diversification and rapid industrialization—and the early revolutionary élan which seemed to make it possible to accomplish all things simultaneously. Neither reflected grappling with the problem of scarce resources.

By the spring of 1961, the problem of scarce resources had already begun to appear in several areas of practical work; for example, dollar exchange was scarce, cement and other building materials were tight, and there was a shortage of workers for the sugar harvest. But nobody realized the full meaning of these scarcities. Dollar earnings were far smaller than they had been before the American embargo,

[1] *Revolución*, February 27, 1961.

but they were still substantial, and besides, hundreds of millions of dollars worth of goods could be bought from the socialist countries. A shortage of workers for the canefields was perhaps to be expected since the harvest was gigantic. And the scarcities were still limited to specific areas; they had not yet begun to affect the economy as a whole.

The production conference of August, 1961, was held in a time of transition. The problem of scarcity had spread to new areas and become more acute, and the leaders of the Revolution had begun to talk about it. But the old élan about the economy would not die easily. Everyone still clung to the old ambitious programs and the growth projections drawn up before the problem of scarce resources had become pressing. Nobody drew the meaning of the scarcities for the economy as a whole.

But the problem of scarcity kept spreading. And during the last few months of 1961, as people began to realize that the difficulties being faced by the economy were more general and intractable than they had appeared at first, the élan began to subside. For example, friends of mine working at the *Juceplan* began to voice doubts during our luncheon conversations that the economy would achieve an average growth rate of 10 percent during the next several years.

As I look back, it seems to me that many people engaged in the administration of the Cuban economy began to sense at this time that the initial economic policies of the Revolution were no longer adequate. It was not that these policies had been wrong. But new problems were arising. These problems had to be faced and solved. And the old policies simply did not provide the answers.

But for many months no one, from the leaders down, had much time to work systematically on basic policies. At first, there was the work of finishing the 1962 Plan which many people thought would automatically solve the problems. Then came the task of running the economy without a true plan, introducing food rationing, and arranging for additional food imports.

Even when there was a chance to discuss basic policies, it was hard to make progress. The Minister of Foreign Commerce, Major Mora, often tried to provoke such discussions during the meetings of his

Ministry Council. In the Soviet Union, he once said, the rapid development of heavy industry was the key. What's our key? We depend more on foreign trade than the Soviet Union. Can exports perform for us some of the functions of heavy industry? Even after this promising beginning, we all floundered.

Formally, it all looks easy. The manuals from the socialist countries stress the importance of guiding current economic planning and operations according to a longer-run "political-economic directive." By 1962 many people in Cuba had read, or were reading, the manuals. In conversations with different people around Havana, you would often hear: The trouble with the Cuban economy is that the leaders have failed to issue a political-economic directive. But if you asked the person who made this remark to give an example of what would serve as a political-economic directive for the Cuban economy, the answer usually was: I don't know; I can't do that; the political-economic directive is a decision for the leaders.

But everyone, and most of all the leaders, knew that a longer-run orientation was needed; the trick was to find the right one. Even though many technicians and others acted as if the problem were simply one of an act of will, of *deciding*, it was not; it was one of finding the answers to basic issues. In the Soviet Union, the early, long-run economic orientation toward rapid development of heavy industry did not come till a number of years after the Revolution won power in 1917. And it was not simply the result of technical work; it was hammered out in bitter political disputes.

Formalists have the whole world filed away in neat little drawers with labels on them, and can quickly find something to say about everything. But when you are struggling with reality, things are never neat and easy. When you don't know something, you can't hide behind textbook classifications; you have to grope.

From time to time during the meetings of our Ministry Council in the latter half of 1961, various people argued the need for making an analytic study of the world sugar market so that the Ministry would have a better idea of the future prospects for the export of sugar, the main factors causing prices to go up and down, and the like. In early 1962, the Minister asked the head of the Price and Market Studies Division and me to make such a study.

My co-worker and I found much that we thought interesting to put into our study. Much of the structure of international trade in sugar is determined by the division of the world into closed trading areas, into areas dominated by the various imperialist powers. And the so-called world free-sugar market is—for all its resounding title—a narrow, erratic, marginal market, which could not be counted on to absorb greatly increased amounts of sugar in the future.

Most of the world's sugar production is consumed in the countries in which it is produced. Total world production, cane and beet, had been running in recent years at 50 to 60 million tons. Only about 15 million tons entered into international trade. A country that can produce sugar generally does so, and gives the home industry tariff or other protection.

When a country does have to import sugar, it tends to do so from within the trading area or empire of which it is a part or which it dominates. Before the Cuban Revolution, the United States got over 95 percent of its sugar imports from Cuba, Puerto Rico, Hawaii, and the Philippines—its colonies. Britain got most of its imports from countries within the imperial preference area: Australia, Jamaica, and British Guiana. When France needed imports, it, too, turned to its colonies.[2] Of the 15 million tons of sugar that entered into international trade, more than half moved within closed trading areas.

Only about seven million tons of sugar—about 10 to 15 percent of the world's total production—had been traded in the so-called world free-sugar market; and the percentage had tended to decline throughout the 1950's. Most countries or trading areas used this market only as a buffer to take care of deficits in bad crop years and get rid of surpluses in good ones. Take Britain, for example. The large British sugar companies such as Tate and Lyle preferred to get their sugar

---

[2] Later we made a study of international trade in tobacco and found that much of it also followed imperial and trading-area lines.

from their own subsidiaries in British Guiana or Jamaica. Britain bought through the world free market only when it could not meet its requirements from countries within the empire. And it sold through that market in good years when the British companies had surplus sugar on their hands.

Of the large importing countries, only Japan got the bulk of its imports from the world free market. Japan had lost its empire and did not belong to any common market or other type of trading area. This is why it was a good customer for Cuban sugar.

Taken as a whole, the socialist countries had been self-sufficient in sugar before the Cuban Revolution. The Soviet Union had met most of its requirements with its own production, although sometimes, when its crop fell short, it imported sugar through the world free market. Several other socialist countries of Eastern Europe—Czechoslovakia, East Germany, and Poland—produced surpluses in most years and exported sugar to the world free market; but sometimes they too had to import. People's China had an extremely low per capita consumption of sugar, and although its domestic production of sugar was small for such a large country, it did not import significant amounts.

The structure of the sugar market changes with the formation of new trading areas or the entry of new countries into these areas, and the breaking off of colonies from their empires. Thus before the formation of the European Common Market, West Germany often used to import large amounts of sugar through the world free market, but it stopped doing so once the Common Market was formed. The Common Market set up a common tariff on sugar imports from outside countries, and West Germany began to meet its import requirements from within the area. Norway imports sugar through the world free market, but this would probably end if it were to become a member of the Common Market. On the other hand, Morocco became a customer for Cuban sugar in the 1950's when it began to break away from French domination.

Sugar prices in the world free market fluctuate wildly. In a few months, the price of sugar can easily rise from, say, 3.0 cents to 5.5

cents per pound or drop by the same percentage.[3] One reason for such instability is rigidity in the supply: it takes months to increase or decrease the output of beet and cane, to adjust the supply of sugar to the demand. Another reason is that the world free market is very narrow and is used by the participants as a buffer to absorb imbalances between the supply and demand for sugar in their own markets.

Surpluses and deficits of sugar arise from the balance between total world production and consumption of over 50 million tons; but their effects are concentrated in the world free market of six or seven million tons. The large producing and consuming areas control their own sugar markets to keep supply and demand in balance, to keep the markets stable. They transfer the surpluses and deficits—the instability —to the world free market. A total world sugar inventory of, say, three million tons and an increase of one million tons in that inventory represent modest amounts in relation to total world production and consumption. But when the inventory of three million tons and the increase of one million tons hang over a world free market of seven million tons, they loom large. This is why prices in that market seesaw.

Ability to produce sugar at a low cost does not by itself guarantee a large and expanding outlet for it. To be able to compete in a market, the low-cost sugar first must be allowed to enter.

Care must be exercised in judging how much sugar the world free market will be able to absorb in the future. The assumption made by some people in Cuba that this market will grow in simple proportion to the world consumption of sugar is unwarranted. Increases in world consumption do not have to result in a larger world free market; they can also be met by increases in production within the separate countries or trading areas. And if Britain and some of the other European countries that are not now members of the European Common Market were to join, the world free market could shrink significantly. It is also possible for the world free market to grow; for example, if countries were to break away from trading blocs instead of joining them.

[3] The price of sugar in this market soared to about 12 cents per pound in 1964, and then plummeted to less than 3 cents.

Aside from the socialist countries, however, the largest sugar-consuming countries in the world are the big imperialist powers. So long as they get most of their sugar imports from separate trading areas, the growth of the world free market will be limited.

The world free market cannot be counted on to provide an outlet which will absorb large increases in Cuban sugar in the future, especially with the United States working ceaselessly to isolate Cuba.

The balance-of-payments problem which appeared in 1962 not only quickly became Cuba's central economic problem, but also one of the main keys to its sugar policy, its agricultural and industrial policy, and to its longer-run economic policy in general.

At first, only a small group—the leaders of the Revolution and officials of the Ministry of Foreign Commerce and the National Bank—knew about the balance-of-payments problem. Often when others heard about it, they did not take it seriously. It seemed like a specialized financial problem which did not have much to do with their own fields of work—with, say, planning the development of agriculture or industry. And no one, even at Foreign Commerce or the National Bank, had any idea of its full implications at the beginning.

But it quickly became clear to those who had to grapple with the problem—leaders and technicians alike—that it was serious. The first estimates showed that the trade deficit for 1962 would be at least $150 million. (It actually turned out to be $170 million. See page 130.) Even before careful projections of future exports and imports were made, everyone could see that the deficit would continue for a number of years. Suppose there was a deficit of $150 million for the next four years. This would mean a total accumulated indebtedness from ordinary trade of $600 million. Now go back to Major Guevara's announcement of a billion-peso industry-investment program, of which 600 million would go for the importation of factories, machinery, and equipment. The "major part" of this importation was to be covered with credits from the socialist countries. Taking into account Cuba's ability to buy factories from capitalist countries for dollars, the part to be financed with credits would have to be about $500 million. Together, the deficit from ordinary trade plus the credits for industrial development would mean a total indebtedness by the end of 1965 of $1.1 billion. This is a large sum.

How large a sum, can be seen from the following figures. If a debt of $1.1 billion was to be amortized over a twelve-year period, just the amortization charge—without allowance for interest—would come to over $90 million a year. Added to a deficit on current trade of $150 million, this would make a total of $240 million by which annual exports would have to be increased to bring the payments into balance. Exports in 1962 were only $520 million—so they would have to rise by nearly 50 percent.

Nor was this all. The development of other sectors of the economy —agriculture, transport, and so on—would also require foreign exchange. And even without large credits for industrial and other development, a debt of $600 million from ordinary trade was a large amount in itself, and one to be taken seriously.

The first attacks on the deficit began at the Vice Ministry of Economy at Foreign Commerce, as soon as it became clear from the work on the 1962 Plan that there would be a deficit. The Vice Minister held meetings, often late into the night. "What should be done about the deficit?" he asked. How could it be eliminated or even reduced? There was no way of increasing exports quickly: the goods were not available. The only way of reducing the deficit was to cut imports. But which imports could be cut? Cutting imports was a heavy responsibility. It could result in shortages later which might seriously disrupt the economy and perhaps have undesirable political consequences. The head of the Office of Planning, which was responsible for preparing the export and import plans, was under pressure from the other Ministries to meet as many as possible of their requests for imports. He was reluctant to try to get agreement to large cuts. And overhanging everything was the pressure of time, the need to get the plan ready on schedule. So here and there the import plan was pruned. Requests from other Ministries that would have increased the deficit were resisted. But the deficit could not be greatly reduced, much less eliminated.

Months later, a small inter-Ministerial committee consisting of the Secretary of the Economic Commission of the Integrated Revolutionary Organizations,[4] a representative of *Juceplan*, and me, worked up a proposal for reducing imports. We scoured the lists of imports looking for such items as sporting goods, porcelain products, and tableware, which we felt could easily be cut. We questioned the quantity of imports planned for many items such as trucks and construction equipment. Our recommendations were ruthless. They were not accepted. It would not have made much difference if they had been. Differences of opinion are possible about the wisdom of specific reductions. But about the problem as a whole there could be only one judgment: Little was being spent on nonessential items such as sporting goods and porcelain; there was bound to be a deficit. For several years this deficit could not be eliminated, only contained. The solution had to be longer-run.

So thinking began about the longer-run aspects of the problem. Many people did the thinking; and there is no way of knowing what each one thought or of stating it exactly. But judging from the discussions at the Council of our Ministry and other meetings that I attended, I would say that the attention of most people turned first to the import saving that could be brought about by increasing the domestic production of various goods, especially foodstuffs. This tendency was natural; it flowed from the emphasis the Revolution had placed on agricultural diversification, industrialization, and economic independence.

But as discussions proceeded and memorandum succeeded memorandum, it became clear that while import saving could help, it could not by itself solve the problem. It was true that, under imperialism, Cuba had been spending tens of millions of dollars in foreign exchange on the import of tomato ketchup, eggs, milk, dairy products, meats, and other foodstuffs that it should have been producing for itself. But the import of most of these items had already been cut out or greatly reduced by the Revolution. Now one had to look at the

---

[4] This commission consisted of President Dorticós, Major Guevara, and Carlos Rafael Rodríguez of INRA. It was set up early in 1962 to coordinate the administration of the economy.

problem a little differently; one had to examine Cuba's food imports after the Revolution.

Cuba's total expenditures on the import of foodstuffs early in 1962 were running at an annual rate of about $125 to $150 million.[5] Even if it were possible to cut foodstuffs out completely, the balance-of-payments problem could not have been solved. But Cuba's food imports cannot be cut out completely. Cuba does not have a wide range of climate and some things do not grow there—wheat, for instance. In 1958, Cuba spent about $19 million on the import of wheat and wheat flour;[6] by 1962, the import of these items was running close to $30 million. Other foodstuffs eaten in Cuba but which do not grow there commercially are onions, chickpeas, and lima beans.

Besides wheat and wheat flour, the large food imports were fats and oils—lard, olive oil, soybean oil—and rice. Lard imports cost about $23 million in 1958 and vegetable oils, mostly olive oil, another $6.9 million.[7] Although the imports of lard dropped sharply after the last ferry from the United States stopped running in the summer of 1961, total imports of fats and oils were running higher in 1962 than in 1958. Here was a promising possibility for import saving by increasing local production of lard and of oils from soybeans, peanuts, and cottonseed. But it is one thing to begin reducing the drain on foreign exchange for the purchase of fats and oils, and another to eliminate it altogether. Cuba had been a uniquely heavy consumer of lard; with a population equal to about 3.5 percent that of the United States, it had been taking close to 10 percent of the lard produced by the highly developed American pig-raising industry. Even with Fidel campaigning against high consumption of lard as unhealthy, and with great increases in the domestic production of lard and the vegetable oil substitutes, the complete elimination of imports would be a difficult job. And even if it could be done, it would take a long time.

[5] Imports of "food products and beverages" had totaled $158 million in 1957 and $173 million in 1958. See Ministerio de Hacienda, República de Cuba, Comercio Exterior, 1959, p. 12. The Revolution cut out the luxury foodstuffs and liquors which made up much of these totals. But the total import bill for this category did not decrease much because, with the poorer sectors of the population eating much better, more imports of basic foodstuffs were required.
[6] Ibid., pp. 480-481.
[7] Ibid., pp. 472 and 505-506.

Rice imports cost $39 million in 1958, but they had been running lower since the Revolution came to power because of increased Cuban production. Just as—perhaps even more than—with fats and oils, reducing imports and eliminating them are two different things. Rice production requires wet land, and wet land was short. It quickly became clear from comments made by INRA people at meetings that the increase in the amount of irrigated land required to make Cuba self-sufficient in rice was tremendous, and that carrying out the irrigation projects was a task for many years.

Where else could import savings be made? Out of total imports of $600 to $700 million, roughly $300 million consisted of petroleum and raw materials and parts for industry. Petroleum imports were running at over $80 million per year. Geologists from the other socialist countries were prospecting for petroleum, thus far without success. A few small savings could perhaps be made in industrial raw materials. Cuba spent about $10 million on the import of raw cotton and cotton thread in 1958; because of increased domestic production, imports were planned at about $5 million in 1961. Perhaps two or three million more could be saved, but the limits were being approached. Cuba cannot produce all the types and qualities of cotton it requires. Perhaps Cuba could replace a little more of the imported pulp for its paper plants with bagasse from sugar cane and save a little more. But apart from three or four such possibilities, the import bill for industry was rigid. Cuba does not have a great variety of raw materials. And the structure given its industry by the foreign corporations made it heavily dependent on imports. The plants making fertilizer, paints, soap, rayon, tires, and so on ran on imported materials. Even the tomato-canning plants, using a local foodstuff, required imported tinplate.

How much foreign exchange could Cuba save by producing some of the industrial products it was importing? This cannot be answered simply, but here are some considerations. First, there is the capital cost in foreign exchange; the new industries have to be financed, either with cash or by going into debt. Then there is the cost of the imported materials and parts required by these industries. Even apart from the initial capital cost, many of the industries Cuba was setting up involved increased costs in foreign exchange rather than saving. Take the large household appliance and utensil plant at Las Villas, for example. The plant was designed, as Fidel mentioned at the production conference, to turn out 45,000 stoves, 40,000 refrigerators, 100,000 pressure cookers, 40,000 kitchen sinks, and 45,000 enamel wash basins per year. In 1962 Cuba was not spending any foreign exchange to import these items. To a considerable extent, the plant would have to work with and assemble imported materials and parts. As compared with 1962, the foreign exchange costs would be increased. The point about this plant is not that it saves foreign exchange, but that it provides work and an increased supply of industrial goods to the Cuban economy.

Even many plants that would produce goods being imported by Cuba would not result in saving. Take a tractor plant, for instance. Cuba imported 4,100 tractors in 1962 at a cost of $10.7 million. If the minimum-size tractor factory it was practicable to put up in Cuba had a capacity of, say, 10,000 tractors per year, there could easily be an increase rather than a decrease in foreign exchange costs. It would be useful to have the additional tractors, but the amount of foreign exchange required to buy parts and materials for the assembly of 10,000 tractors could be greater than the $10 million spent on 4,000 assembled units. This example is hypothetical, but it illustrates an important point that must be taken into account in planning new factories for Cuba. Cuba does not import just one size and type of tractor, but a variety. Importing allows flexible choice. Setting up tractor production in Cuba could mean either being restricted to one type of tractor or facing substantial increases in foreign exchange outlays. This difficulty arises from the structure of the Cuban economy, its shortage of raw materials, its smallness, and its low level of development and wealth.

It is true that there are some industries which could save foreign exchange. But because Cuba does not have a large variety of industrial raw materials, these industries would be limited to certain types. The savings would not be large and would take time to realize. And the problem of the capital costs of the plants—cash outlays or increase in debt—would present itself before any savings could be realized. So import saving through industrialization could not be considered a promising way of attacking the balance-of-payments deficit.

A final point about imports is that not only would import savings be difficult, but some factors in the economy would tend to make imports increase. The population was increasing; the standard of living would rise; the economy would grow. More people and a higher standard of living meant a higher demand for wheat, onions, and olive oil. Agricultural development meant larger imports of fertilizer or raw materials used by Cuban factories to make fertilizer. The large new electric power plants that were going up would mean increases in oil imports.

The discussions and memoranda on what to do about the balance-of-payments deficit therefore turned to exports. Previously innumerable discussions of how exports might be increased had been held both at Foreign Commerce and elsewhere. As it became clear that the United States would shut off its market for Cuban tobacco, the other possible outlets were canvassed, not once but many times. The foreign exchange earnings from building additional nickel plants to exploit Cuba's vast reserves came up now and then. The export possibilities for many specific products had been discussed during the work on the 1962 Plan.

But now the problem was not to assess the prospects for the export of this or that particular item. It was general: how to bring about a large, rapid increase in total exports, an increase that would quickly make a dent in the deficit and eliminate it within a few years. Just to formulate the question in this way almost led by itself to the answer —sugar.

The other possibilities for increasing exports were important. Cuba could try to develop the export of tropical fruits, canned seafood, and certain textiles. There would probably be some returns, and all returns are valuable. But no one—not even the most enthusiastic about the export prospects for these items—could argue that they would produce enough, even after five years, to reduce the deficit significantly. Increasing the production and export of nickel offered larger and more certain possibilities. Nickel is a strategic mineral; the market for it is assured, and its price seems to rise steadily. But it would take three to five years to get a new nickel complex planned, built, and into full production; the earnings of some $30 million would be very useful, but still not enough. The development of the Cuban cattle industry would open the possibility of large earnings from meat exports—after some years.

Everything pointed to increasing the export of sugar as the main solution to the deficit. Sugar was not subject to the uncertainties surrounding products in which Cuba was short of experience. Twice before she had produced seven million tons—some two million tons more than in 1962. Even at first blush it was clear that she could produce much more. And at the price of four cents a pound, which was then being received by Cuba from the Soviet Union, each million tons of sugar was worth about $88 million.

But supposing Cuba's sugar production was greatly increased—say, first to six or seven million tons and then to nine or ten—where could this sugar be sold? Again the question almost answered itself. Cuba herself would require about half a million tons. Sales in the world free market or under bilateral agreements with nonsocialist countries could not be counted on to absorb more than about two million tons. Where could the rest go? Only to the socialist countries.

So the Secretary of the Economic Commission of the ORI began to study the potential sugar market in the socialist countries. At first, the prospects for increased Cuban sugar exports to these countries seemed mixed. The Soviet Union was producing about six million tons of sugar in 1962, and its population was about 15 percent higher than that of the United States which was consuming 10 million tons of sugar. Taking into account increasing population and a rising standard of living, it would seem that the Soviet Union would soon be able to absorb more than the three million tons of Cuban sugar it had been taking. But the Soviet Union had long-standing plans to expand its own sugar industry; and the problem was complicated by the fact that parts of the sugar beet plant were used to feed cattle, so that a change in the plans for sugar production could affect cattle-raising as well. The potential consumption of sugar by China is, of course, enormous.

But it was not clear how fast China could allow sugar consumption to grow, or how much of her exports she would be willing to devote to paying for the import of sugar. The prospects among the other socialist countries did not seem promising since several were exporters of sugar themselves.

While working through the available data, the ORI Economic Secretary made an interesting discovery: the cost of producing sugar in the Soviet Union was much higher—several cents a pound higher—than in Cuba. And costs in Poland, Czechoslovakia, and East Germany were also higher, though not as much. The comparisons were a little blurred; some of the apparent differences in costs might have been due to statistical quirks arising from the use of exchange rates to convert various currencies to a common basis. But the differences were so great that there was little doubt about the essential point: Cuban cane sugar was cheaper to produce than Eastern European beet sugar. And further: with time, the cost comparison would become still more favorable to Cuban sugar. The loading and cutting of cane were being done by hand in Cuba; mechanization of these operations promised greater cost reductions than were possible with beet sugar. And the transport of sugar was only partly mechanized; with the development of mechanized sugar handling and shipment in bulk, with the sugar boats bringing oil or some other product on the return voyage, the cost of the long haul to the other socialist countries would be greatly reduced.

Why, then, shouldn't Cuba try to promote a large market for her sugar in the socialist countries? Even if Cuban sugar had not been cheaper than Soviet sugar, there would have been strong arguments for such an arrangement. The Soviet Union was financing Cuba's trade deficit. Unless sugar exports were expanded, the deficit would continue indefinitely. Before the Cuban Revolution, large sugar imports might not have been desirable from a Soviet economic point of view. But now the choices were not the same. Better to take sugar—even though there might be some disadvantages—than just to continue financing the deficit.

The low cost of Cuban sugar and the potential efficiency with which it could be produced greatly strengthened the case. The Soviet Union and some of the other socialist countries of Eastern Europe had recently become interested in a socialist international division of labor, and Premier Khrushchev had written an article on the subject. He had presented the argument that what was right from the point of view of a single economy might be wrong from the point of view of two or more economies. The larger whole must be taken into account. The socialist countries must try to divide their work rationally, to have each country produce those things for which its conditions are favorable, and which it can produce at low costs. Costs are important, said Khrushchev, because the lower the costs at which an economy produces what it needs, the more resources it will have for accumulation (investment) and development. The case of Cuba fitted all these arguments beautifully. Cuba could become the main source of sugar for the socialist countries.

Given these arguments, the plans of the Soviet Union to expand its own sugar industry should not present an unremovable obstacle. These plans had been formulated before the Cuban Revolution; it would be wise to review them now. A socialist market need not be taken as given in the same way as a capitalist market. The socialist market can be changed by conscious planning if there are good reasons for doing so. And meeting the needs of another socialist country, establishing a sensible, mutually beneficial arrangement between two socialist countries, *are* good reasons.

From the Cuban point of view, the socialist countries could provide Cuba with an incomparable sugar market—a planned, assured, growing market, with a fixed price, established by agreement beforehand. And the price could be a good one; apart from the consideration that the developed socialist countries should lean over backward not to exploit the weakness of the underdeveloped, their own high production cost makes it easier for them to pay a good price for imports.

But once the possibility of a large market for Cuban sugar in the socialist countries had been established, another problem had to be faced—the meaning that a large increase in sugar production had for agricultural diversification, and the proper balance between sugar and other products in agriculture. Because of the manner and degree to which they had accepted the policy of diversifying agriculture, many people would not even listen to talk of greatly increasing sugar production. When at a meeting someone broached the idea of a nine-million-ton goal for sugar output in 1970, the head of economic research at INRA threw his hands into the air and said, "But we can't do that; it will interfere with diversification." No amount of argument could get him even to consider the new idea. He was asked how he would attack the balance-of-payments problem without increasing sugar production, and he answered in effect that the balance-of-payments problem was not his responsibility. Someone argued that one had to look at the whole economy, not just isolated sectors of it. Someone asked how the goods required for agricultural and industrial development could be imported if the deficit continued. All to no effect. But this sort of thing did not stop exploration of a new sugar policy. It could not. There were problems and they could not be solved by the mechanical repetition of old formulas.

The economic assistant to the head of INRA became interested and began to work on the balance between sugar and other agricultural products. He showed a few of us who were working on sugar policy the Jesús Menéndez People's Farm, about two hours' drive from Havana. Several hectares of land that had formerly been used for sugar were now covered with neat little rows of peppers. This sort of thing had happened throughout Cuba; former sugar land was being used to grow peppers, tomatoes, cucumbers, and similar products. No one would have thought of spending foreign exchange to import secondary foodstuffs like these, but the use of sugar land to grow them, which also meant a loss of exchange, somehow seemed different. The unquestioning enthusiasts of diversification were not asking themselves whether the replacement of sugar with secondary foodstuffs might not be a mistake, whether the sugar could not be used to buy a larger quantity of foodstuffs—and more important foodstuffs—than the tomatoes, cucumbers, and peppers the land was yielding.

The problem became clear: It had been one thing to diversify at the beginning of the Revolution when idle labor and land abounded; it was another now that labor and land were tight. Now using the resources for one purpose meant not using them for another. The economist from INRA undertook to make a few rapid surveys comparing the costs and benefits of using a given amount of land for sugar and other important agricultural products.

The surveys began to appear in several weeks. What they showed can be illustrated by data Fidel gave in a speech in 1966 comparing sugar and rice. "To become self-sufficient in rice . . . we would have to use some 333,000 more acres of irrigated land and invest in them our scarce water supply. . . . Undoubtedly, it wouldn't be convenient for our country to stop producing one and one half million tons of sugar which is what we could produce on 333,000 acres of irrigated land planted to sugar cane, and which could increase our purchasing power abroad by more than $150 million, in order to produce on this land, with the same effort, rice valued at $25 million."[8]

As the results of the surveys flowed in, they showed that the yield from using land for sugar was higher than for most other agricultural products. But the policy argument in favor of raising sugar output had many aspects and did not depend just on mechanical comparison of yields. For example, it would not matter much if a given unit of land yielded a higher monetary value when planted to peppers, tomatoes, and cucumbers, rather than cane. Relative monetary yield is one element to be considered, not necessarily the definitive one. With peppers, tomatoes, and cucumbers, the important point was that they were not basic foodstuffs—that one could, if need be, do with less of them.

A policy judgment on sugar did not have to wait for precise statisti-

[8] *Granma*, Special Edition in English, Havana, January 3, 1966, p. 5. Fidel's figure of "more than $150 million" as the value of one and one-half million tons of sugar is not inconsistent with the figure of $88 million for one million tons which I gave earlier. My figure is based on a price of 4 cents a pound, which the Soviet Union was paying in 1962. But the price paid in 1965 by the Soviet Union and China was 6.11 cents a pound. Fidel's figure is conservative. At 6.11 cents a pound, the value of one and one-half million tons is $201 million. Even at a very low sugar price, the sugar-rice comparison would be extremely favorable to sugar. For example, at a price of 2.5 cents a pound, the value of one and one-half million tons of sugar would be $83 million—more than three times the value of the rice.

cal comparisons between yields from sugar and all other agricultural products. Speed was important. Sugar offered the fastest way of attacking the balance-of-payments problem, but it too would take time. Sugar planted in one year does not yield till twelve to eighteen months later, and the available labor supply limits the amount that can be planted in any one year during the two brief periods suitable for planting. Eventually, additional sugar mills would have to be built, and it takes several years to plan and build a sugar mill. The informal, inter-Ministerial committee—basing itself on a complex of considerations, including the payments deficit, the need for foreign exchange to pay for many of the goods required for economic development, the use of former sugar land to grow secondary foodstuffs, the yield comparisons between sugar and the most important alternative crops—decided to recommend that sugar production be increased to nine or ten million tons by 1970.

There were a few general arguments to be worked out. Several generations of enlightened Cubans had been educated on the evils of concentration on sugar. Their view was right historically. But Cuba was not now what it might have been if its economy had not been concentrated on sugar in the past, if it had not been made heavily dependent on imports. If the Cuban economy had been run rationally, its industry would not consist so largely of tire, paint, detergent, and other factories producing goods for the well-to-do with imported materials. But now that the tire, paint, and detergent factories existed, no one was suggesting that they be dismantled. Even a revolution has to begin with the economy it inherits.

The objection to concentration on sugar is not to concentration as such, but to its meaning and its consequences under imperialism. Before the Revolution, concentration on sugar was part of a broader system, part of the over-all domination of the resources, markets, policies, and governments of Cuba by foreign corporations and the United States Government. Concentration on sugar meant smothering the rest of the economy; it meant idle resources and stagnation. But now increasing sugar output would not mean unused land and unemployment. And it could be used to advance, instead of hold back, the rest of the economy, to buy machinery and equipment required for broad agricultural and industrial development.

Caution is necessary in interpreting the relationship between increasing sugar output and diversification. True, there is considerable contradiction between the two: more sugar means less land and labor for most other crops. But, still, production of these crops would be far greater than before the Revolution. Also, agricultural diversification in Cuba is much more than a matter of crops. There are programs for increasing the production of pork, chickens and eggs, and beef and dairy products. The programs for these products, especially those for beef and dairy products, are potentially far more important to Cuba than those for the crops. Increasing sugar production would not prevent the development of these other products.

Nor would increased sugar production be an obstacle to crop diversification forever. A great effort could be made to increase the productivity of the land and labor engaged in sugar production. After some years, even with much greater sugar production, land and labor could once again be switched to other crops. Meanwhile, efforts could be made to increase productivity in these crops, to produce more with fewer resources. After a few years—say by 1968—the payments deficit would be eliminated and replaced by a growing surplus. Increasing amounts of foreign exchange would become available to import machinery and equipment, factories and their raw materials. Agricultural diversification and industrial development could once again be accelerated.

Toward the end of 1962, the leaders of the Revolution—especially Fidel—began to pick up the various strands of the sugar problem. Discussions were undertaken with the Soviet Union which agreed to raise its future purchases of Cuban sugar by the amounts required to permit a large increase in production. The Soviet Union also agreed to pay a price of six cents a pound—two or three cents a pound more than the world market price had been running, and almost one cent more than the United States had paid for Cuban sugar under the quota system. In the spring of 1963, Fidel announced a sugar production goal of 10 million tons for 1970.

Discussions and meetings to work out programs for increasing sugar production began immediately. The decline in production from the peak of 6.7 million metric tons in 1961 had been sharp. Production was 4.8 million metric tons in 1962 and only 3.9 million in 1963. The decline was caused both by a reduction in the acreage under cane and a lowering of yields per unit of land.

It was not easy at that time to get accurate figures on cane acreage, but there was no doubt that it had declined considerably—roughly from 105,000 *caballerías* in 1960 to 85,000 in 1963. While I never understood all the reasons for this decline, the main one was the uprooting of cane in 1960 and 1961 to make way for diversification.

Average cane yields had dropped even more than acreage. Yields are given in Cuba in *arrobas* per *caballería*, each *arroba* being equal to 25 pounds and each *caballería* to 33 acres. The average yield fell from over 50,000 *arrobas* per *caballería* in 1961 to less than 40,000 in 1962 and less than 35,000 in 1963—a decline over the two years of at least 30 percent.

There were a number of reasons for the decline in yields. Technical norms for the cultivation of cane—for example, weeding—were being neglected. Often, where there was irrigation, it was not fully and properly used. There had been little replanting of cane in 1959 and 1960 when the landowners were expecting their lands to be taken away; sugar is a perennial grass which can last many years, but a certain amount has to be replanted each year—otherwise yields fall. Finally, 1962 and 1963 were years of drought.

Estimates of the additional land required for cane were rapidly made. They tended to be based on conservative projections of yield per unit of land so as to assure a rapid increase in sugar output. For example, one proposal was made to increase the area under cane to 120,000 *caballerías* as soon as possible. If yields rose faster than projected, no harm would be done and the appropriate action could be decided upon and taken later. The plantings to increase the area under cane got started at the end of the 1963 sugar harvest.

When the Soviet Union agreed to take larger amounts of Cuban sugar, it also offered to help develop machines for mechanizing the cutting and loading of cane. Machines were already being used on a small scale during the 1963 harvest. But the cutters had many defects, and although the loaders worked better, they still suffered from a few bugs which had to be eliminated. Now Fidel and Premier Khrushchev took a lively interest in the machines and the work of perfecting them was pressed forward with increased vigor.

To raise sugar production from 3.9 million tons in 1963 to 10 million tons in 1970 is an enormous task—one that requires a technical revolution in the Cuban sugar industry.

Even during the 3.9 million-ton sugar harvest of 1963, there was a shortage of labor. It would no longer be possible to harvest six million tons by hand; to harvest 10 million without widespread mechanization was inconceivable.

Although the area under cane would be expanded from the low level of 1963, most of the increase in output to 10 million tons would have to be brought about by intensifying cultivation, by greatly raising yields. How much cane yields would have to rise was later estimated. Per unit of area cut, they would have to rise by 24 percent over the average during the years 1954-1960. But relating yields only to area *cut* does not fully show the intensification. Before the Revolution, the landholders had left large areas of cane uncut each year; this would no longer be done. With an increase in yields *per unit of area cut* of 24 percent, yields *per unit of the total area under cane* would rise by 170 percent.[9]

To increase yields so greatly, many things would have to be done. The poorer cane varieties would have to be replaced by the best ones over the years. Cultivation practices would have to be improved—the preparation of the soil for sowing, the mulching of the cane plants, weeding, etc. The cane area under irrigation would have to be expanded; irrigation greatly increases yields, easily enabling them to double. Far more fertilizer would have to be used, and it would have to be applied more scientifically.

The length of the harvest would have to be increased by about a month and a half. This would permit the field work to be done with

[9] Raúl Herrera, "Problemas que plantea a la agricultura una zafra de 10 millones de toneladas," *Cuba Socialista*, March 1965, p. 5.

a smaller labor force and the capacity of the sugar mills and transport facilities to be utilized more fully. The previous views of many sugar experts on the proper length of the harvest are an interesting example of the limitations that sometimes affect expertise. These experts would solemnly explain that the harvest must be restricted to the period January through April when the sugar content of the cane is at its maximum; if it were started in December instead of January, a few percent of sugar content would be lost. But the inherited view about the length of the harvest is not—as many of the experts thought—eternally valid; it reflects the calculus of the private companies, rather than that of the economy as a whole. When these companies compared the alternatives—a larger labor force and a shorter harvest, or a smaller labor force and a longer harvest—it was only their own profits that they took into account. The loss of sugar content would cost them money. But the cost of having more people tied to sugar, of having more people who worked three months a year and were unemployed nine, was one they did not have to bear. The companies had no concern with making the economy as a whole more rational. But in a socialist economy, it pays to sacrifice a few percent of sugar content to obtain a more rational use of labor and the mills and transport facilities. Besides, early-maturing varieties of cane can probably be developed to cut down the loss of sugar content from lengthening the harvest.

The capacity of the sugar mills would have to be increased. Cuba's largest sugar harvest had been 7.2 million tons and the capacity of its mills was about 7.5 million tons. But because of the poor state of the equipment, this capacity was now theoretical. As a first step, the mills would have to be put into shape and brought up to their theoretical capacity. Then the capacity of these existing mills would have to be expanded. And finally, new mills might have to be built.[10]

Sugar requires tremendous amounts of transport. Each ton of sugar is produced from about eight times its weight in cane. In the 1960 harvest, 47 million tons of cane had to be moved in 87 days to produce 5.9 million tons of sugar. A sugar harvest of 10 million tons

[10] Orlando Borrego Díaz, "Problemas que plantea a la industria una zafra de 10 millones de toneladas," *Cuba Socialista*, April 1965, pp. 18-21.

would mean having to move 80 million tons of cane. Even with a lengthened harvest, the facilities for moving the cane to the mills would have to be expanded. And with three million tons more sugar than in any past harvest, the port facilities would also require expansion.

Not only would the transport facilities have to be expanded; they would also have to be modernized. Over 70 percent of the cane was hauled to the mills by railroads. Much of the cane was brought to the railroad loading stations by oxcart and transferred to railroad cars by slow-working hoists. In recent years a system of having a tractor haul a long line of cane carts had been developed and was proving advantageous. The tractors have a much larger transport radius than the two kilometers to which the oxcarts are limited and can often take the cane directly to the mill, eliminating the reloading onto the railroad cars. In the off-season, the tractors can be used for other purposes in agriculture. By further developing tractor transport much heavy investment in locomotives and railroad cars could be made unnecessary.[11]

The development of the bulk shipment of sugar would also become very important with a harvest of 10 million tons. The jute required to ship a harvest of this size in sacks could easily cost $40 to $50 million in convertible currency. Bulk shipment would not only save labor and lower costs, but help with an important sector of the balance of payments.

Planning and organizing the increase in sugar production to 10 million tons would involve many problems. The additional land to be planted to cane would have to be selected with a number of considerations in mind—its suitability for cane and for mechanized planting, cultivating, and harvesting; the possibility of irrigation; the availability of roads or railroads for transporting the cane to the mills. The increase in cane production and in the capacity of the mills and transport facilities would have to be carefully programmed and controlled to maintain coordination between many different factors. It would not be enough, for example, just to increase cane production

[11] *Ibid.*, pp. 24-25.

in general; the increases must be properly distributed geographically to correspond to the increases in the capacity of the various mills. And it would not do to have the new milling capacity ready a few years before the cane, or vice versa. A greatly increased number of technicians would be required by the sugar industry; education programs would have to get under way in time.

The task the Cuban people has set itself is difficult. But the prize is high. Instead of producing 5.5 million tons of sugar with 400,000 field workers, as it did in 1957 and 1958, the last years of Batista, Cuba would be producing 10 million tons with 150,000 workers—or even fewer. At the price of 6.11 cents which Cuba receives from the Soviet Union and China, the value of the additional 4.5 million tons is about $600 million—a large amount for a country whose gross national product in 1958 was $2.6 billion. The increase in sugar production would by itself make total export earnings go up to more than twice their 1962 level. The additional foreign exchange would permit many things to be done. It could be used in part to raise the standard of living, to ease the restrictions on the import of consumer goods. And it could be used to broaden and quicken economic development, to move more rapidly toward industrialization. In achieving their 10-million-ton sugar goal, the Cuban people will be writing an epic in the annals of socialism.

Along with the increase in sugar production would go the rapid development of cattle-raising. This also was decided in the months following the missile crisis of October, 1962, when the leaders of the Revolution were able to stand back and re-appraise longer-run economic prospects. Sugar and cattle-raising would be the main lines of agricultural development during the years 1963-1970. A tentative cattle goal was adopted: raising the cattle population from about six million in 1962 to ten million in 1970.[12] There would also be an increase in the average slaughter weight of the cattle.

[12] Albán Lataste, "El Próximo quinquenio económico 1966-1970," *Comercio Exterior*, July-September 1963, p. 40.

The development of cattle-raising would be given a high priority for several reasons. First, the natural conditions for cattle-raising are exceptionally good in Cuba. Many experts, including several from the Soviet Union, have confirmed this since the Revolution took power.

The U.S. Department of Commerce seems not so enthusiastic as these experts. It says: "Cuba possesses both natural advantages and disadvantages as a cattle-raising country. Pasture is available in all seasons of the year, natural grasses provide good grazing, there is no need for protection against extreme weather conditions, and Cuban cattle are relatively free of disease except for cattle tick fever. Conversely, the subtropical climate requires selection of adaptable breeds, the dry season frequently affects cattle weights, and birth rates average only two-thirds those in the United States. Poor grass management has led to considerable sheet erosion and weed and brush infestation. Complete dependence on pasture feeding greatly lengthens the time necessary to bring cattle up to slaughter weight."[13]

If read carefully, this quotation conveys an impression that differs from the one intended. The advantages are, as stated, natural. Most of the disadvantages, however, are due to the manner in which cattle-raising has been practiced in Cuba; and even those which are not man-made can still be overcome by the action of man. Thus "poor grass management" can be improved. "Complete dependence on pasture feeding" is not a law of nature, and Cuban agriculture since the Revolution has, in fact, been trying to move away from this practice. The loss of weight during the dry season is largely due to the dependence on pasture feeding and to the absence of silos. The low average birth rates result from poor breeding practices; the Cubans have been working to raise these rates. And while it is true that the subtropical climate requires "adaptable breeds," there seem to be such breeds. So, properly read, the statement from *Investment in Cuba* confirms that the conditions for raising cattle in Cuba are good.

The cattle industry would provide Cuba with increased amounts of milk and dairy products and meat. These foodstuffs are more important to Cuba than lard, which everyone agrees used to be consumed

[13] *Investment in Cuba*, p. 48.

in excessive and unhealthy amounts. After several years, the development of the cattle industry would permit the elimination of the rationing of milk and meat.

The cattle industry would also provide Cuba with increased supplies of raw materials for industry. Of these, hides are especially important. When the rate of cattle slaughter began to be controlled in the spring and summer of 1961, the supply of hides to the leather industry dropped sharply, and, in its turn, the production of shoes fell. The shoe industry had to work far below its full capacity because of the leather shortage. The development of the cattle industry would enable shoe production to rise and shoe rationing to be lifted after several years.

The cattle industry could provide important help to the balance of payments—the prospects for meat exports are good. The potential help from increasing meat exports is far greater than can be realized by the further reduction of food imports. For example, the complete elimination of rice imports—if it were practicable—would save $25 to $30 million. But meat exports of $50 million and eventually $100 million or more are easily conceivable.

Finally, cattle-raising, unlike most crops, does not conflict much with sugar, but rather tends to dovetail with it. The work is year round; there is no peak demand for labor—as with rice, for example—falling in the middle of the sugar harvest. Most cattle-raising is done on pasture land that is not suitable for sugar, and the increased cattle population would be supported by the intensified use of this land. Pastures could be fertilized. They could be divided into different sections that could be used in rotation to give the grass a chance to recover from trampling. Silos could be built to store grass and other feedstuffs for the dry season, and the use of artificial feedstuffs could be increased.

The development of cattle-raising would require investments. Expenditures in foreign exchange would often be needed, for example, for the import of breeding bulls. But almost all development in Cuba requires foreign exchange—cattle-raising less than most.

Again, as with sugar, the task would be big. It would take hard work and careful planning. And people trained in modern methods of cattle-raising—in scientific breeding and feeding, and the like. Cuba would have to educate agricultural technicians by the tens of thousands. The development of the cattle industry would be part of the continuing revolution in the Cuban countryside.

Sugar and cattle-raising are fine examples of Lenin's dictum about grasping the "main links of the chain" to understand and control a situation. They were main links. The fixing of policies on sugar and cattle-raising caused many things to fall into place and the general problem of longer-run economic orientation to become clearer.

For a number of years, the huge tasks imposed by the sugar and cattle-raising goals would take up much of the free energies and resources of the economy. A substantial portion of the total investment to increase the productive capacity of the economy would be going into sugar and cattle-raising or related activities.

While I have not seen any figures on the total amount of investment to be made in sugar, it is evident from the list of things required that the amount will be large—thousands of machines for planting, cultivating, cutting, and loading cane; locomotives and railroad cars and thousands of tractors and trucks; machinery and equipment to put over 150 mills in shape and expand their capacity; perhaps some additional mills; port facilities, including modern equipment for shipping sugar in bulk; sugar warehouses and storage tanks for molasses; and people, tens of thousands of additional sugar technicians.

Besides these investments directly needed to increase sugar production, other investments would indirectly be made necessary. For example, additional factories would have to be built to utilize sugar by-products—factories to turn the bagasse (cane pulp) into fiberboard, to produce alcohol from molasses, and the like. Work was being carried out to develop the use of the tops of the cane stalks as fodder for cattle; this could become an important feedstuff for the dry season. If this work proved successful, many factories would be required.

The dairy and cattle industry would also require heavy investments —in cattle, silos, feeding pens, milking stations, trucks and other equipment. Further investments would be required in equipment and facilities for handling the increased output—tank and refrigerator railroad cars, pasteurization plants, cheese factories, slaughterhouses, meat packing plants, and canneries.

Both the sugar and cattle industries (as well as agriculture in general) could be greatly helped by extending irrigation. So investment in irrigation works would also be needed.

Innumerable industrial products would be required for the expansion of sugar and cattle production. This would open up many possibilities for new industries that could mean large import savings by producing in Cuba fertilizers, pesticides, various implements and equipment, feedstuffs and vitamins for cattle, machine parts for the sugar mills.

Although sugar and cattle would receive the first priority, other branches of agriculture would continue to be developed—for example, the production of chickens and eggs, pigs, citrus fruits, and oil-producing crops. Again investments would be necessary both in agriculture itself and in factories to produce sprays for the plants and fruit trees, for packing or canning oils, fruits and juices, and so on.

Outside of agriculture, there were other candidates for a high investment priority. The port facilities needed redesigning to adapt them to the large, transoceanic vessels which were now carrying Cuba's imports and exports.[14] Many additional warehouses would be required, both at the ports and in the interior. The water supply systems of many cities and towns were in poor shape and urgently needed improvement.[15] The 250,000 private cars in use before the Revolution would not last forever; investments in busses would be necessary.

A large expansion of Cuba's electric power capacity was essential. According to the U.S. Department of Commerce in 1956, "Cuba, with approximately 103 watts of installed capacity per capita, ranks very high in terms of Latin American power development."[16] This statement, however, is misleading and almost meaningless. The high rank in installed capacity simply reflects the extent to which Havana was

[14] Albán Lataste, "El próximo quinquenio económico 1966-1970," *Comercio Exterior*, July-September 1963, p. 42.
[15] *Ibid.*, p. 42.
[16] *Investment in Cuba*, p. 104.

Americanized. With its neon signs, its air-conditioned hotels, restaurants, movie theaters, and office buildings, its handsome homes full of appliances, its concentration of factories, Havana consumed enormous amounts of electricity. But the rest of the country had a very low installed capacity, and large stretches of the countryside and many little villages had no electricity at all. Each youth marching into the countryside during the great literacy campaign of 1961 carried a kerosene lamp so that he could work at night.

Now Cuba needed additional generating capacity and transmission and distribution lines to spread electricity through the countryside, to bring it to the new farms and factories, to meet the requirements of economic and social development. The capacity of Cuba's public service power plants in 1961 was 550,000 kilowatts. In 1962, there were under construction a 200,000 kilowatt plant at Mariel about forty miles west of Havana, a 120,000 kilowatt plant at Nuevitas in the northeast of the province of Camagüey, and a 100,000 kilowatt plant in Santiago, Oriente. Work was also under way at a number of smaller plants, including a hydroelectric plant at Habanilla; and many still smaller Diesel plants were to be scattered throughout the provinces. It was planned to invest over $250 million in additional generating capacity during the years 1964-1969 when, it was estimated, electric power production would go up from about 2.3 billion kilowatt hours to over 5 billion.[17]

It was in this context—limited resources for development, a large share of which was required for sugar, cattle raising, electric power, and other high priority areas—that the question of Cuba's industrialization had to be considered. Before resources became tight, the possibilities for industrialization seemed almost infinite. But now it was clear they were limited and that they could only be determined by considering the total resources available and the other claims on them. The speed and timing of industrialization, whether to quickly set up a heavy industry, which other types of industries to install, were questions that could not be decided by themselves, but only as part of the development of the whole economy.

[17] Ministry of Foreign Relations, *Profile of Cuba*, Havana, undated, pp. 148-149.

Just to arrive at this understanding of the problem was to have moved a long way toward solving it. The balance-of-payments problem provided clear criteria as to the proper direction of economic development. Development should solve the balance-of-payments problem, not make it worse. This in itself meant limiting the speed of industrialization for a time, since industrialization depended in good part on burdening the balance of payments with debt charges, and many of the new industries would require imported materials to work with. Besides limiting the speed of industrialization in general, the balance of payments also provided an important criterion for selecting or rejecting specific industries. For example, the Director of Investments of *Juceplan* questioned—on balance-of-payments grounds —the advisability of rapidly setting up heavy industry. "Cuba has a very weak energy base. . . . The regular supply of fuels by the Soviet Union has tended to cause an underestimation of the critical dependence on this strategic item. . . . What would be the implications for the import of fuels . . . of an accelerated industrial program which included heavy industries that were high in fuel consumption? . . . . Sometimes, while looking for a way of reducing the dependence of the country on imported products vital for industrialization, people have thought of installing heavy industries with high import requirements in raw materials, machinery, equipment, and, of course, fuels. If this is not carefully studied, it can become a boomerang, which far from reducing dependence can increase it."[18]

The balance-of-payments problem, while the most critical, was not the only problem. By 1962, inflationary pressures had become strong, making financial order and prudence increasingly necessary. Investment programs for the different sectors of the economy could no longer be planned in isolation from one another as though the funds available for them were unlimited. The claims on the construction industry far exceeded its capacity; they would have to be reduced. Certain limits to the ability of the Cuban economy to organize and carry out specific projects were being reached; for example, imported

[18] Albán Lataste, "El próximo quinquenio económico 1966-1970," *Comercio Exterior*, July-September 1963, p. 41.

machinery sometimes arrived before the projects requiring it were organized. Piling up machinery in warehouses is a waste. Plans would have to be tailored to the ability to carry them out.

The problem of scarce resources had begun to trouble the Cuban economy toward the end of 1960. For many months thereafter specific scarcities erupted in different sectors of the economy and specific measures were taken to meet them. During 1962, both the scarcities and the measures became increasingly general. By the end of 1962, the problem had ripened to the point at which a fundamental choice had to be made, between giving first priority to the development of agriculture or of industry.

When the problem of a long-run orientation was raised during the preparation of the 1962 Plan, everyone groped but found no answer. Then the balance-of-payments problem, the sugar- and cattle-raising policies, and an electrification plan reduced the area of groping. As with a jigsaw puzzle, each piece put in place made easier the problem of placing the succeeding pieces. By the end of 1962, the answer to the question of long-run orientation was clear. It was decided and announced early in 1963 that for some years, agricultural development would receive first priority, that agriculture would be the base for Cuba's economic development.

The decision to give the development of agriculture first priority was, of course, not based solely on economic considerations. Almost no significant economic decision is ever based on economics alone; politics is almost always present. And a decision as fundamental as the one giving first priority to agriculture required looking at the *whole* of Cuba's strategic situation: not just the economic, but also the political, military, social, and revolutionary situation. The noneconomic considerations were often not made explicit, but they were there, interwoven with the economic.

Many people seem to think that the lesson of Soviet experience is that in all socialist countries and at all stages of revolution first priority must be given to industrialization. In the first years of the Cuban Revolution, many people almost unconsciously adopted the view that industry—especially heavy industry—must be developed as rapidly as possible. But why? Why must first priority always be given to industrialization? Think of the differences between Soviet and Cuban circumstances.

Here is what Stalin said about the need for rapid industrialization in the Soviet Union: "In order to secure the final victory of socialism in our country, we must . . . overtake and outstrip [the advanced capitalist] countries technically. *Either we do this, or we shall be forced to the wall.*

"This applies not only to the building of socialism. It applies also to upholding the independence of our country in the circumstances of capitalist encirclement. The independence of our country cannot be upheld unless we have an adequate industrial base for defense. And such an industrial base cannot be created if our industry is not more highly developed technically. . . .

"*The question of a fast rate of development of industry would not face us so acutely if we were not the only country but one of the countries of the dictatorship of the proletariat, if there were a proletarian dictatorship in other, more advanced countries as well, Germany and France, say.* If that were the case, the capitalist encirclement would not be as serious as it is now, the question of the economic development of our country would naturally recede into the background, we could integrate ourselves into the system of more developed proletarian states, we could receive from them machines for making our industry and agriculture more productive, supplying them in turn with raw materials and foodstuffs and we could, consequently, expand our industry at a slower rate. . . ."

Finally, Stalin pointed out that the reconstruction of Soviet agriculture on a new, large-scale technical basis, required the rapid development of industry.[19]

A few considerations can be added which Stalin took for granted,

[19] Joseph Stalin, "Industrialization of the country and the right deviation," in Spulber, *Foundations of Soviet Strategy for Economic Growth: Selected Soviet Essays, 1924-1930*. Bloomington, Indiana University Press, 1964. Emphasis added.

but which are necessary for a comparison of the Soviet Union and Cuba. The Soviet Union is a tremendous country, with a wide range of resources. It has a huge internal market. It possessed the conditions for the rapid development of a large, variegated industry, including heavy industry.

Cuba's situation is different. Cuba's ability to defend herself does not depend on the rapid development of her own industry. She cannot hope—at least for a long time—to produce the rockets, jet planes, tanks, patrol boats, and many other weapons needed to defend the Revolution. She can probably never hope to produce the whole range of necessary weapons. But Cuba can get weapons from the other socialist countries. The rapid development of industry in Cuba is not a matter of defense—of life and death—as it was in the Soviet Union.

Cuba is not the only socialist country. Her economic development does not depend—in the way that of the Soviet Union did—on building her own iron and steel industry, her own machinery industry. Cuba can import machines and equipment. The development of Cuban agriculture does not depend on building a large Cuban tractor industry. Agricultural equipment should be produced in Cuba whenever it is economical and convenient to do so. But Cuban agriculture can also be developed with imported equipment.

Not only does the need for rapid development of industry differ in Cuba from that in the Soviet Union, but so does the possibility. Cuba is a small country. Her resources are rich, but not varied. She lacks coal, including coking coal. So far no significant oil deposits have been discovered. Her iron ores contain chrome, and this poses technical problems. Cuba's internal market is small. It would be difficult for her—even with a far higher industrial development than she has now—to produce the whole range of types, qualities, and sizes of industrial products that a modern society requires.

Priorities are different in the Soviet Union and in Cuba. In the Soviet Union it was industrialize fast or be forced to the wall; but what will keep American imperialism from forcing Cuba to the wall will not be the rapidity of Cuban industrialization. In Cuba a high priority had to be given to providing an adequate food supply. Difficulties in the food supply could conceivably lead the United States to think that an attack on the Revolution might be successful. While the Cuban ration has not been meager, all rationing is unpleasant. It should not be allowed to go on indefinitely. The development of agriculture would increase the domestic production of some foodstuffs, make possible increases in the importation of others, and, after a while, eliminate the need for rationing.

What Cuba needs most to develop is the production of food, clothing, and houses. These are the things her people need most. Improving the life of her people is what will best enable Cuba to serve as an example to the rest of Latin America and other underdeveloped areas. It is more important for Cuba to expand her cement industry so she can build more houses than to start rapidly creating a large machinery industry. It is true that to develop the production of food, clothing, and shelter Cuba must give a high priority to those sectors of the economy that will provide her with the machinery and equipment required to do so. But this has been done. The highest priority has been given to sugar and cattle-raising because their foreign exchange earnings will pay for the machinery and equipment.

In her dependence on foreign trade, Cuba differs not only from the Soviet Union; she is unique among all the socialist countries. In no other socialist country are exports and imports equal to more than 30 percent of the gross national product. No other socialist country inherited such a specialized agriculture or an industry so dependent on imported materials. In Cuba, development does not depend only on the excess of total output over what is required for current consumption, on the production of a surplus that can be used for investment. Foreign trade must enter into the equation. Because so much of the capital equipment must come from abroad, development depends not only on the general surplus, but on the capacity to import beyond the level required to meet current needs. It therefore depends in large part on exports. Major Mora was right when he suggested that in a sense Cuba's heavy industry was her exports.

Cuba's dependence on exports will not long remain unique among the socialist countries. As the other countries of Latin America—with their heavy dependence on the export of a single crop or mineral product—revolt against imperialism and become socialist, Cuba will have company.

There remains the question of economic independence.

In the first years of the Revolution, many people in Cuba equated her political and economic independence with self-sufficiency. Some people outside of Cuba still do so. For example, the editors of *Monthly Review* have said: "Cuba's vulnerability to shifts in Soviet policy . . . is extreme and mortally dangerous. The conclusion seems obvious: If Fidel wants Cuba to be in a position to follow a relatively independent course . . . in the explosively tense and stormy period which lies ahead, he had better return as quickly as possible to a policy of agricultural diversification and self-sufficiency in foodstuffs."[20]

In this form, the argument about independence and self-sufficiency reminds me of a Will Rogers story. It was during the First World War and Will and a stooge were on stage discussing the large number of Allied ships that were being sunk by German submarines. Said Will to the stooge, "I don't see why the problem of the submarines should be so difficult. I understand that submarines can't exist in boiling water. So to get rid of them, all we have to do is bring the Atlantic to a boil." "But Will," asked the stooge, "how are we going to bring the Atlantic to a boil?" "I have given you the policy," answered Will. "Don't bother me with details."

The only major foodstuffs for which Cuba depends on the Soviet Union are wheat and wheat flour—and wheat does not grow in Cuba. Furthermore, why limit self-sufficiency to foodstuffs? What about oil, without which the economy of Cuba would quickly come to a halt? How do you grow the $100 million of oil which Cuba imports from the Soviet Union? What about the imported raw materials Cuba requires for her drug and pharmaceutical industry—raw materials she does not have? What about fertilizers or the raw materials necessary to make them? What about the tractors and trucks needed for agriculture? By far the bulk of Cuba's imports from the Soviet Union does

[20] *Monthly Review*, April 1966, p. 9.

not consist of foodstuffs, but of raw materials and capital equipment. And finally, what about weapons and the replacement parts for them, and ammunition?

Policy on self-sufficiency must meet the problems of reality and practice. The attainment of economic independence has rightly been one of the central aims of the Cuban Revolution. But economic independence cannot be mechanically equated with self-sufficiency; it has other aspects. And Cuba is not the Soviet Union or China; they have possibilities for self-sufficiency not open to her.

The problem goes far beyond Cuba. There is at present no realistic socialist theory of economic independence. It is important to begin constructing one.

Economic independence cannot simply depend on self-sufficiency. If it did, most countries would be doomed never to enjoy it—and the term loses meaning. Economic independence means that the people of a country control its economy and its destiny themselves, free of interference from abroad; they control its resources, its markets, its trade, its policies. They decide. They may decide to engage in certain forms of cooperation with other countries; or they may decide not to. But they decide.

Imperialism by its nature precludes such independence for the underdeveloped countries with which it deals. When the large corporations go into an underdeveloped country, they get control of resources, take over markets, and dominate foreign trade. They cannot avoid doing this and still function. And together with the governments that back them politically and militarily they cannot help but exercise political domination.

The socialist economy does not by its nature drive toward domination. Socialist countries do not invest in other countries and acquire ownership of land, mines, factories, railroads, docks, warehouses, stores, hotels, nightclubs, and gambling casinos. A socialist country may make a loan to another, but it does not thereby acquire property. When one socialist country exports to another, it does not get control of the internal market with a whole system of retail outposts. There are no private monopolies to bully foreign governments, and no external properties for the socialist state to defend.

This does not mean that there can be no abuses in the economic relations between socialist countries. There can be many. There is no iron guarantee against a socialist country's overcharging another. Or trying to use its trading strength or economic aid to get a weaker country to follow its political line. But even at the worst, there can be no comparison with the situation under imperialism. The abuses are not inherent in the system. They can be guarded against and corrected.

Self-sufficiency cannot be set up as a simple formula which will automatically solve the problems. For certain countries and at certain times a high degree of self-sufficiency may be possible and desirable. Even in countries for which general self-sufficiency is not possible, it may be worthwhile to strive for self-sufficiency in certain specific items. But the possibilities for self-sufficiency have to be assessed realistically. Self-sufficiency is one factor to be considered—to be balanced against others—in determining economic policy. It cannot be made into an absolute, a general policy for all socialist countries.

What sort of a general perspective would such a policy offer to the smaller countries of the world? Does it mean that Guatemala, with four million people, and the Dominican Republic, with three and a half million, to say nothing about still smaller countries, would also have to try to be self-sufficient? One of the greatest potential advantages of socialism lies in the possibilities a socialist organization of international trade offers to the underdeveloped countries, with their lopsided, one- or two-crop economies, heavily dependent on foreign trade. With socialism, a true international division of labor becomes possible.[21] And for the underdeveloped countries, a socialist international division of labor can open up possibilities for agricultural and industrial development that otherwise would not exist because of the lack of raw materials, the smallness of markets, and the shortage of capital and skills. Cuba is providing the first chapter of a great story to be completed in the rest of Latin America and elsewhere. All this is not to be given up lightly in pursuit of a self-sufficiency which for most countries is not possible.

[21] See Paul Baran, *The Political Economy of Growth*. New York, Monthly Review Press, 1960, p. 292.

Cuba has won her economic independence. She controls her resources, her markets, her trade, her policies. The obstacles to progress have been removed. And Cuba decides.

True, some three quarters of Cuba's foreign trade is with the Soviet Union. But it is nonsense to talk—as some do—of the Cuban economy being an appendage of the Soviet economy in the same way as it once was an appendage of the United States economy. Whoever says this shows that he does not understand what being an appendage of the American economy means. The trade between the Soviet Union and Cuba is socialist trade. The Soviet Union is not penetrating the internal Cuban economy. It is not monopolizing Cuba's foreign trade, preventing Cuba—as did the United States—from trading with any country it wants to. A large portion of Cuba's trade is with the Soviet Union because, given the United States embargo and the trade possibilities of the other socialist countries, there is nowhere else for it to go.

True also, Cuba's larger trading partners—the Soviet Union and China—can attempt to use their trade or economic aid to exert political pressure on Cuba. Cuba can, at considerable cost, grow more rice and reduce her trade dependence on China. But general economic self-sufficiency is out of the question. It would neither strengthen the Revolution in Cuba nor enhance its appeal in Latin America and elsewhere to move the Cuban economy sharply backwards, to condemn it to hopeless stagnation. This is what a serious attempt at self-sufficiency would mean.

The only policy for Cuba to follow is to develop her economy, trade freely with the socialist countries and any others that are willing, and be prepared to resist bitterly any pressures, any attempts to interfere with her decisions or actions, her sovereignty. This is the policy the Revolution has been following.

All beginnings are difficult, says a German proverb. Revolutionary beginnings are especially difficult.

Within four or five years from the time it took power, the Revolution accomplished many things. It smashed the old Cuban state and built a new one, kicked out the imperialists, made a land reform, freed Cuba's foreign trade, began to run the economy, introduced economic planning, and forged a long-run economic orientation. All in the teeth of the United States, all in the midst of crisis after crisis, all with the ordinary people of Cuba.

There were great difficulties and innumerable errors. But these errors were part of the deep upheaval that constitutes a true revolution. They were the manifestations of motion in a once stagnant economy. A cart that is standing still does not squeak.

During the first two years, the Revolution made great economic progress by correcting the blatant irrationalities and injustices of the old society. For the several million poor in the countryside and in the urban slums of Cuba, it opened up a new life. The difficulties encountered by the more comfortable classes with rationing, obtaining automobile parts, and the like, cannot come close to counterbalancing the benefits the Revolution has brought to the poor.

After the first two years, economic difficulties began to erupt. They were grappled with and Cuba found a road toward solving them. Rapid progress of the sort accomplished during the first two years was no longer possible. There were material limits. But there was great progress of a different sort—in organizing the economy, in beginning to build for the future.

The future will not be easy. To build a better life will take a great deal of sweat and thought and time. Hundreds of thousands of people will have to labor by hand in the canefields until the work can be mechanized. It will take years for organization and planning to be perfected. Problems will arise—one after the other—to which there are no answers in the textbooks. People will have to keep improving their ways of work so as to convert organization and planning into ever more living realities. Formal schooling takes time and accomplishes only part of the task. Much of what people need to know, including some of the most important things, can only be learned on the job. And everything will have to be done in the face of a shrewd and implacable enemy, who might seem to look away from Cuba for a while, but who will never give up the hope of somehow, someday, crushing the Revolution.

But by the end of this decade, the full benefits of socialism will begin to show themselves in Cuba. The dependence on American parts for the maintenance and repair of equipment will be far less acute. Increased output of sugar, nickel, and meat will have solved the balance-of-payments problem and begun to produce a surplus. Increased output of milk and meat, chickens and eggs, pork, and other agricultural products will have produced a big improvement in the diet. The output of shoes and clothing will be greatly increased. With a large expansion of the cement and construction industries, the building of houses will be under way on a grand scale. Fidel has said that by 1970 the rate will be 100,000 dwelling units per year—more than a fivefold increase over the 1959-1963 average. Programs of education and training will have produced many tens of thousands of technicians. This and the solution of the balance-of-payments problem will have permitted an acceleration of industrialization.

All this might take a year or two more, or a year or two less. But does this really matter except to those who get paid to score debater's points against socialism in bourgeois newspapers? In the perspective of history, the early economic difficulties of the Revolution will have covered a speck of time.

7

Some Conclusions

Cuba and Latin America

Even the half-blind can see that Cuba is one link in a broad chain of events. Latin America as a whole is in upheaval. The entire under-developed world is in motion. But many people will not go beyond this. Cuba, they say, is a special case, its Revolution unique. The other Latin American countries will have to solve their problems differently. What impresses such people is the specific characteristics of Cuba and its Revolution.

Innumerable specific characteristics distinguish the Latin American countries from one another. There are no general formulas for hand-ling the countless political and economic problems they face. Politi-cal tactics must depend on combinations of circumstances, both inside and outside the individual countries, that no one can entirely foresee. The practical answers to many economic problems depend on whether one is dealing with sugar, oil, copper, or coffee.

But in essentials there is unity. The root causes that produced the Cuban Revolution are present throughout Latin America. In all the Latin American countries, the central problem is not this or that spe-cific condition, but the United States—American imperialism. Every-where the conflict with imperialism is irreconcilable. Imperialism can-not be blunted or reformed. It must be kicked out. And it can only be kicked out by revolution.

Imperialism wields the ultimate power in Latin America. Some-times, as in the sending of troops to the Dominican Republic in 1965, American power is so visible that even American liberals are unable to deny it. Most of the time this power is skillfully hidden. But as a

Latin American representative to the United Nations once put it, when asked whether a unanimous vote by the Latin American countries in favor of a United States resolution had been obtained by American pressure: American power is like the sun; you don't have to see it to know it's there.

There are many means of influence and control short of American troops. In 1964, the mildly reformist, middle-class government of João Goulart in Brazil was overthrown by a military coup and General Humberto Castelo Branco took over as President. Here are some comments on this coup made before the Foreign Affairs Committee of the U.S. House of Representatives during hearings on the Foreign Assistance Act of 1964.

> MR. SELDEN [Armistead I., Congressman from Alabama]. You might explain more fully to the committee what you mean by [security deletion] theory that you have been operating under in Brazil.
> MR. MANN [Thomas G., Assistant Secretary of State for Inter-American Affairs]. Essentially, it is we should not give balance-of-payments and budgetary support to the National Government of Brazil because it was making no effort to help itself to promote long-term growth. [Security deletion.]
> MR. SELDEN. Do you feel this was helpful in the recent overthrow of the pro-Communist government?
> MR. MANN. Yes, sir.[1]

In 1966 Senator Robert F. Kennedy commented: "In Latin American eyes, rightly or wrongly, we bear a heavy responsibility for [the Castelo Branco government's] existence. Less than 3 weeks before the coup, it was reported in the press that, in private administration councils, our Assistant Secretary of State for Latin American Affairs [Mr. Mann] said that the United States would not automatically oppose every military takeover in the hemisphere. We recognized the new

[1] Hearings before the Committee on Foreign Affairs, House of Representatives, Eighty-Eighth Congress, Second Session, on H.R. 10502, Part II, p. 283.

government very quickly, within 3 days of the coup, and 3 months later gave it a special loan of $50 million."[2]

The rulers of the United States have no illusions about American power and how it is used. As Senator Kennedy said: "In Peru, an impasse in negotiations between the government and a U.S. oil company brought a slowdown of our development assistance; the same was true in Argentina; the Venezuelan economy depends in large part on oil company decisions whether to sell from their fields there, or from the Middle East. . . . These are but examples of the many ways in which Latin America is directly dependent on events and decisions made in the United States."[3]

Senator Kennedy did not mention the American-engineered overthrow of the Arbenz government in Guatemala in 1954. Most Americans do not remember this incident. All my Latin American friends remember it as though it happened yesterday.

The local authorities in Latin America have a certain amount of leeway. They can do many things so long as American interests are not injured. The American imperialists generally do not have to use open force any more than the corner policeman has to pull out his pistol at every little squabble. The response, says the official United States jargon, should be flexible. But once a Latin American government touches American property, the United States begins to consider its overthrow. Sometimes troops are not necessary. When they are, the local army is usually adequate. Why commit the central reserves of the empire unnecessarily? But the reserves are there, at American camps and bases in Panama, Puerto Rico, Guantanamo Bay in Cuba, and the United States.

The economic domination of Latin America by American imperialism is on a par with its political domination. The giant American

[2] "The Alliance for Progress: Symbol and Substance," Speech of Hon. Robert F. Kennedy of New York in the Senate of the United States, May 9 and 10, 1966, p. 15.
[3] *Ibid.*, pp. 13 and 14.

corporations own or control basic resources, foreign trade, and internal markets. Table 3 gives U.S. Department of Commerce figures on the value of United States direct investment in Latin America in 1965, by selected countries and industries.

Consider what an investment of $9 billion in an underdeveloped area like Latin America means. In 1965, total United States direct investment in the Common Market countries of Europe—Belgium, Luxemburg, France, Germany, Italy, and the Netherlands—was $5.4 billion. These countries have much stronger local economies than

Table 3
U.S. Direct Investment in Latin America, 1965
(in millions of dollars)

	Total	Mining & Smelting	Petroleum	Manufacturing	Public Utilities	Trade	Other
Total	9,371	1,114	3,034	2,741	596	1,034	852
Percent of total	100.0	11.9	32.4	29.2	6.4	11.0	9.1
Mexico	1,177	103	48	752	27	138	109
Panama	704	19	122	24	38	288	213
Other Central America and West Indies	621	35	152	60	147	30	197
Argentina	992	*	*	617	*	47	328
Brazil	1,073	51	57	722	37	162	45
Chile	829	509	*	39	*	24	257
Colombia	527	*	269	160	29	49	20
Peru	515	263	60	79	21	53	38
Venezuela	2,715	*	2,033	248	19	222	194
Other countries	219	8	89	40	21	21	40

* Combined in "other countries."
Source: U.S. Department of Commerce, Survey of Current Business, September, 1966.

those of Latin America, a combined gross national product many times greater. Yet France has been openly resisting United States economic penetration and the other countries are concerned about it.

Again, as in Cuba, the United States investment in Latin America results in foreign enclaves that are appendages of the American economy.

The American corporations have taken control of most of the valuable mineral and fuel deposits of Latin America and developed them for export, largely to the United States. Direct investment in mining and smelting in Latin America was $1.1 billion in 1965. But in the Common Market countries, it was $16 million, and in all of Western Europe, $55 million. Investment in petroleum was 32 percent of total United States direct investment in Latin America. Together, petroleum and mining and smelting accounted for 44 percent of investment.

Public utilities, a standard imperialist investment in underdeveloped countries, constituted another 6 percent of investment.

Trade constituted 11 percent of total direct investment. "Most of the [trade] investment," says the Department of Commerce, "is in wholesale trading, consisting mainly of enterprises distributing goods exported from the United States or produced by affiliated companies abroad."[4]

Notice that in Panama the figure for investment in trade is very high—over 40 percent of the total in that country. This investment has almost nothing to do with the economy in which most Panamanians live. Many international trading corporations have incorporated in Panama to take advantage of its liberal corporation and tax laws. Also, Panama is a free port where many enterprises have been set up to sell duty-free cameras, binoculars, and whiskey to travelers passing through.

Compare for different countries the items "Mining and Smelting" and "Petroleum" with "Manufacturing." You will notice that in only three countries—Mexico, Argentina, and Brazil—does investment in manufacturing exceed that in the other two categories. In Chile, in-

[4] U.S. Department of Commerce, *U.S. Business Investments in Foreign Countries*, 1960, p. 24.

vestment in mining and smelting is more than 13 times that in manufacturing; in Peru more than 3 times. In Panama, Other Central America and West Indies, Colombia, and Venezuela investment in petroleum is many times that in manufacturing.

Manufacturing accounts for 29 percent of total direct investment. Again as in Cuba, a large proportion of the plants are little more than disguised American export operations bringing in American goods for the local upper classes. Throughout Latin America, there are outpost plants for turning out soap, detergents, toiletries, bottles and cans, paint, rayon, automobile tires, and so on, from imported materials.

The same comment applies to automobile plants. Alfred P. Sloan, former President and Chairman of the Board of the General Motors Corporation, gives interesting information on his company's plants abroad. "In 1962 . . . about 59,000 cars and trucks were exported from the United States and Canada in what are called SUP's, or Single-Unit Packs. This means that the vehicles were shipped fully assembled, and could be made ready for the road with only minor adjustments. Another 46,000 were sent abroad as CKD's, that is, Completely Knocked Down, and they had to be put together at one of the ten General Motors assembly plants abroad. (Ordinarily CKD shipments do not include certain parts—upholstery and tires, for example—which can be supplied locally). . . . The assembly plants made it possible for us to identify ourselves with the local economies by using local management and labor. . . . This had another advantage over exporting complete cars in that it resulted in lower duty payments."[5] General Motors has assembly plants in Mexico, Peru, Venezuela, and Uruguay. By Mr. Sloan's own description these plants are little more than disguised American export operations. The only countries in which General Motors has manufacturing, as opposed to assembly, plants are Brazil and Argentina.

Direct ownership is one of the key ways in which the foreign corporations create enclaves, but there can also be enclaves without it. For example, in Ecuador and several Central American countries, the banana industry—plantations, railroads, ships, and ports—is an ap-

[5] Alfred P. Sloan, *My Years With General Motors*, New York, Macfadden Books, 1965, pp. 314-316.

pendage of the United States economy. Under the threat of land reform, the United Fruit Company has in recent years decided to transfer some of its land holdings to local owners who still supply it with bananas. This does not change the system, which still works as before. Similarly, varying the stock ownership in Chile's copper mines by a few percentage points does not change the system.

United States strength, both economic and political, can be used without ownership to bend Latin American economies to American purposes. The Brazilian coffee industry can be geared to the United States and dominated by American interests without American ownership of coffee plantations.

Basically, the imperialist economic system works throughout Latin America as it did in Cuba—to pull out agricultural and mineral raw materials and pump in finished products. Tables 4 and 5 give an idea of what Latin America means to the capitalist economy of the United States in imports and exports.

Table 4 shows selected categories of United States raw-material imports in 1965, by area of origin. Latin America was the leading supplier of coffee; sugar; fruits, nuts, and vegetables; and petroleum and its products—and the second supplier, after Canada, of ores and scrap metal, and nonferrous base *metals. It supplied 46 percent of total United States imports in the categories shown.

Table 4 also shows selected categories of United States exports in 1965, by destination. Latin America was an important market for United States industrial products, especially metal goods. For example, after Canada, Latin America was the second largest market for U.S. motor vehicles and parts. It absorbed 24 percent of the U.S. exports of motor vehicles and 19 percent of the exports of parts. Together, U.S. exports to Latin America of these two items amounted to over $600 million.

None of the figures in table 4 includes Cuba. If Cuba had not broken out of the U.S. empire, the figures showing Latin America's importance to the U.S. economy would be still greater.

For the United States, Latin America is a gigantic plantation, the

Table 4
Selected U.S. Imports and Exports by Region, 1965
(in millions of dollars)

	Total	American Republics	Percent of Total	Canada	Western Europe	Far East	Other Areas
IMPORTS							
Coffee	1,061	792	75			19	250
Sugar	443	219	49		2	118	104
Fruits, nuts, & vegetables	479	253	53	22	77	103	24
Ores and scrap metal	915	264	29	361	11	27	252
Nonferrous base metals	1,197	286	24	409	231	184	87
Petroleum and products	2,093	1,015	48	284	6	48	740
EXPORTS							
Chemicals	2,402	479	20	382	880	387	274
Machinery	6,705	1,116	17	1,711	2,022	828	1,028
Industrial machinery	3,939	713	18	981	1,102	491	652
Agricultural equipment	634	105	17	273	90	37	129
Electrical apparatus	1,661	265	16	380	580	232	204
Road motor vehicles	1,935	462	24	795	256	126	296
Automobile parts for replacement & assembly	750	145	19	452	65	29	59
Metals and manufactures	1,735	289	17	476	507	288	175

Source: U.S. Department of Commerce, *Statistical Abstract of the United States, 1966,* pp. 866-867.

most valuable part of its world empire. Latin America is by far the biggest supplier to the U.S. of tropical agricultural products. Together with Canada, it supplies most of the U.S. mineral raw-material imports. Nowhere in the world is U.S. penetration and domination as great as in Latin America.

Considering the extent to which they pre-empt local resources and markets, the American corporations contribute little to the creation of local employment, income, and a national market in Latin America. This is not an accident: it results from the way the monopolies—quite naturally—handle their Latin American operations as appendages of their United States operations.

In 1957, when United States direct investment in Latin America was $7.4 billion—about $2 billion less than in 1965—direct investment enterprises employed an estimated 950,000 people in all of Latin America. This figure includes cane cutters and banana pickers on American-owned plantations in Cuba, Central America, Ecuador, and elsewhere. The total bill for wages and salaries was $1.4 billion, including the pay of American employees working in Latin America.[6] Expenditures on materials and services totalled $3.6 billion.[7] The last figure, which is small to begin with, is swollen by the inclusion of imports from the United States and purchases from other American companies in Latin America; expenditures on materials and services from the local economies were much smaller. Finally, U.S. enterprises paid $1.1 billion in taxes in Latin America, of which more than half went to Venezuela.[8]

The American corporations controlled most of Latin America's resources and dominated its markets. But the jobs they provided were no more than enough to take care of the work force of a city about the size of Chicago.

The monopolies cannot create economies from which the people of Latin America can live. And by blocking them from their own re-

[6] U.S. Department of Commerce, *U.S. Business Investment in Foreign Countries*, 1960, p. 43.
[7] *Ibid.*, p. 115.
[8] *Ibid.*, p. 120.

sources, their own markets, and control over the policies and politics of their own countries, the monopolies prevent the people from creating such economies for themselves.

All the Latin American countries depend heavily on the export of a few raw materials to unstable international markets. Table 5 gives the leading Latin American exports as a percent of the total exports of each country for the period 1961-1963.

Coffee accounted for over 50 percent of total exports in four countries and between 40 and 50 percent in two more. Bananas accounted for more than 40 percent of total exports in three countries. Petroleum accounted for 93.3 percent of Venezuela's exports, and, together with iron ore, 98.3 percent. Tin accounted for 70.5 percent of Bolivia's exports, copper for 63.7 percent of Chile's. Even in Argentina, one of the more developed and diversified countries of Latin America, four commodities accounted for 65 percent of total exports.

Each one-cent fall in the price of a pound of coffee costs Brazil about $25 million a year and Colombia $6 million. If banana prices drop in the United States or West Germany, then Ecuador, Honduras, and Panama face difficulties. Between 1956 and 1958, the price of a pound of copper fell from over 50 cents a pound to less than 25 cents; each cent cost Chile $6 million a year in foreign exchange.

The effect of dependence on two or three commodities for exports is evident throughout the Latin American economies. Many countries depend on foreign trade for a large proportion of their taxes. Venezuela gets over 70 percent of its total revenues from its oil exports. Chile gets a large part of its revenues from copper. Several countries in Central America get much of their revenues from taxes on the export of coffee or from excise taxes on imports. So whenever the value of exports falls, there is not only a balance-of-payments crisis, but also a fiscal crisis. This is one of the reasons why the Latin American countries find it so hard to fight the galloping inflations from which most of them suffer. With such heavy dependence on see-sawing export revenues, it would be impossible for the Latin American governments

Table 5

Latin America: Leading Exports as a Percent of Total Exports, 1961-1963

	Argentina	Bolivia	Brazil	Chile	Colombia	Costa Rica	Dominican Republic	Ecuador	El Salvador	Guatemala	Haiti	Honduras	Mexico	Nicaragua	Panama	Paraguay	Peru	Uruguay	Venezuela
Coffee			52.2		65.3	49.9	11.0	12.1	53.6	57.9	44.1	13.4	6.9	18.9					
Bananas						27.1		62.5		7.8		47.9			42.3				
Cocoa						5.1	8.7	11.5											
Sugar							54.9						6.2				11.7		
Meat	22.0												7.0			22.3		19.5	
Cotton			8.3						22.1	14.4			20.7	33.5		6.5	16.8		
Wool	12.6																6.4	56.0	
Iron				10.7															5.0
Petroleum					17.1										30.5*				93.3
Copper				63.7													17.6		
Wheat	23.2																		
Hides	7.0																	10.1	
Tin		70.5																	
Fish meal																	19.9		
TOTAL	64.8	70.5	60.5	74.4	82.4	82.1	74.6	86.1	75.7	80.1	44.1	61.3	40.8	52.4	73.0	28.8	72.4	85.6	98.3

* refined

Source: Adapted from Table 1-5, pp. 22-25, in Pan American Union, Organization of American States, Latin America: Problems and Perspectives of Economic Development, 1963-1964. Baltimore, Johns Hopkins Press, 1966.

—even if their intentions were good—to achieve sensible fiscal and monetary policies.

Since the Cuban Revolution, many books discussing the land problem in Latin America have appeared in the United States. Worth repeating are a few of the main facts, as expressed by the United Nations Economic Commission for Latin America.[9]

"One of the features characterizing the Latin American agrarian structure is the concentration of a major proportion of the agricultural land in the hands of a few landowners, while the majority of farmers either own very limited tracts of arable land or are landless rural workers.

"Of the 32 million inhabitants constituting the economically active rural population, some 100,000 or less own two-thirds of the total agricultural area, about 2 million are medium farmers and approximately 30 million are *minifundio* farmers or landless agricultural workers. [This concentration] is greater than in any of the other large underdeveloped regions of the world."

The concentration, says the United Nations report, has several consequences:

"Poor utilization of the agricultural land. The large estates normally practice crop or stock farming by extensive methods, with a very low physical and economic yield per unit of area. . . . A particular sign of poor land use is the large area of agricultural land lying fallow or covered with natural pastures, which in many countries represents over half the arable land. . . .

"Proper supplementary crop rotation is rarely practiced, the normal procedure being single-crop farming which exhausts the soil and encourages erosion. . . .

"The underemployment of the rural population . . . *large-scale* seasonal unemployment. . . . [Emphasis in the original.]

"Wretched living conditions for the rural masses. . . .

[9] "Agriculture in Latin America: problems and prospects," *Economic Bulletin for Latin America*, Vol. VIII, No. 2 (October 1963).

"The stratification of Latin America's rural population into veritable separate castes."

Note in these observations the general similarities to Cuba—extensive agriculture, underemployment, wretched living conditions.

The average per capita income of $92 per year in the Cuban countryside before the Revolution is nothing special in Latin America. "A similar condition prevails in Brazil," says the United Nations report. "The average national income per active person in the agricultural sector is about 110 dollars . . . ; but in the North Eastern region where about one-third of Brazil's total population is to be found . . . . the overall average falls to about 85 dollars a year, while for the agricultural workers in the sugar growing areas it drops to approximately 50 dollars." In Ecuador, the highest-paid agricultural laborers work on the rich coastal flatlands—they get 60 cents a day; in the mountains of the interior, the daily pay is "equivalent to a little under 40 cents."

Not only does the agricultural setup waste land and labor, but it helps limit the growth of national markets. In Latin America as a whole in 1960, about 110 million out of a total population of 206 million lived in rural areas. Most rural dwellers were too poor to buy any significant amount of manufactured goods. In many countries, the bulk of them lived almost completely outside the money economy.

There are differences in the agricultural setup from country to country. In Cuba, the rural workers were proletarians who worked for wages. Agricultural wage labor also exists in other areas, for example, in northern Mexico, Central America, and parts of Brazil. But in many countries, for example Chile, rural workers are not paid mainly in money, but in kind—in the right to use a hut on the estate, to work a little land for themselves, to receive a few biscuits. In some countries, the large estates are export-oriented, in others not. In some countries, such as Peru, the land problem is associated with a nationality problem; the Indians of the highlands not only need land, but they are also an oppressed nationality with their own language, culture, and traditions.

These differences can be very important for specific problems. But they do not alter the general need for land reform. Throughout Latin America, the countryside is starving, the agricultural setup is a drag on general economic development.

Industry is developed to varying degrees in the different countries of Latin America. Argentina, Brazil, and Mexico have far more developed industries than El Salvador, Honduras, or Nicaragua.

But everywhere industry is limited and lopsided, squeezed between backward agriculture on the one side and the giant foreign corporations on the other. For all but a few goods the poverty of the countryside limits the effective demand to the cities, mostly to the oligarchy and its retainers. The foreign corporations take out cotton and cocoa, oil and iron ore that should be going to local industries. And they pump in their manufactured products, dominating the local markets for many goods, especially those made of metal.

In 1962, all of Latin America produced 5.8 million tons of unfinished steel and 3.4 million tons of finished steel.[10] Canada, with a population about 8 percent that of Latin America, produces one million tons more of finished steel.

Consider tractors. The Latin American market is limited by the backwardness of agriculture, and dominated by the United States which ships in about $100 million worth of tractors and parts each year. Tractors are produced in only two Latin American countries—Argentina and Brazil—which turned out about 20,000 in 1962.[11]

Table 4 shows that in 1965 the United States exported to Latin America $713 million of industrial machinery, $479 million of chemicals, $289 million of metals and manufactures, and $265 million of electrical apparatus. These exports dominated the local markets. Brazil is one of the two or three countries in Latin America that produce a significant amount of industrial machinery; the *Economic Survey of Latin America* calls it "outstanding" in this field. Yet in 1961, Brazilian

[10] Pan American Union, Organization of American States, *Economic Survey of Latin America, 1962*, Baltimore, Johns Hopkins Press, 1964, p. 169.
[11] *Ibid.*, pp. 180-181.

production of machinery met only 40 percent of the domestic demand.[12]

A vice president of W. R. Grace and Company, one of the most important American corporations on the west coast of South America, states: "The spindles and looms in our South American textile mills are made back in New England at Saco-Lowell shops, at Draper Corporation, and at Crompton and Knowles Loom Works. They are identical with the machines used in our North American textile industry. . . . This is true in our paper mill, our flour mill, our cement factory, our paint factory, and our other manufacturing enterprises."[13]

On top of everything else, the United States Government uses its power to prevent Latin American industrialization because it would hurt American corporations. United States foreign aid puts money into token projects in housing, education, public health, and the like—not factories. The charters of the United States foreign lending agencies, and the international lending agencies dominated by the United States, like the World Bank and the Inter-American Development Bank, all contain clauses that loans cannot be made for projects which private capital considers within its own domain. Most of the loans go to roads, railroads, and ports—adjuncts to the foreign agricultural and mineral operations. The United States insists that the Latin American countries not use their own public funds to build factories: that would be socialism.

Population is growing rapidly in Latin America. The stagnant agriculture cannot absorb the increase. Poverty on the land has been pushing people to the cities.[14]

But the cities cannot absorb the increase, either. Most of the flow from the land goes into enormous shantytowns which have risen around all the major Latin American cities.

[12] *Ibid.*, p. 163.
[13] Dan H. Fenn, Jr. ed., *Management Guide to Overseas Operations*, New York, McGraw-Hill Book Company Inc., 1957, p. 109.
[14] National Council of Catholic Women, "Urban Explosion," *Focus: Latin America*, Fact Sheet No. 4, Washington, 1962.

One of these shantytowns is briefly described: "Amidst Caracas's opulence roughly 35 percent of the population live in shacks made of cardboard, old boxes, tin and scrap."[15] Often the names of the shantytowns tell what they are like. The ones around Buenos Aires, Argentina, are known as *villas miserias*; those of Santiago, Chile are called *callampas* (mushrooms) because they sprout up so fast.

Most of the people coming in from the land cannot find steady work. The growth of industry creates some jobs, but nowhere near enough. Some people find work in construction. The upper and middle classes take on some as servants. But most of the people in the shantytowns have to live from part-time work, odd jobs, street hawking, begging, and prostitution.

The diary of a Brazilian woman who had to live from trash picking was found by a newspaper reporter: "We are poor, we came to the edge of the river. The river's edge is a place for trash and marginal ones. The people of the shantytown are considered marginal. You don't see buzzards flying over the riverbank near the garbage any more. Unemployed men have taken the buzzards' places."[16]

The shantytowns, with their odd-job workers and unemployed, are an important part of the social structure of Latin American cities. "The number of factory workers in relation to city population has been declining. Even in the most industrialized country of Latin America, Argentina, only 8.1 percent of the urban population is employed in manufacturing. In Mexico, the percentage drops to 4.9."[17]

As in Cuba before the Revolution, growth rates in Latin America, shown in Table 6, are highest during war; during peace stagnation sets in. The Korean War increased the prices of Latin American food and raw material exports, and during 1950-1955 gross product per capita rose by a yearly average of 2.2 percent. By 1960-1963, the growth rate had fallen to 0.7 percent. In 1964, it rose again; the United States

[15] *Ibid.*, p. 8.
[16] *Ibid.*, p. 5.
[17] *Ibid.*, p. 3.

Table 6

Growth Rates in Latin America, 1950-1964

(Cuba excluded)

Years	Gross Product	Real Income	Population	Gross Product Per Capita	Real Income Per Capita
1950–1955	5.0	4.8	2.8	2.2	1.9
1955–1960	4.7	4.3	2.9	1.7	1.4
1960–1963p	3.6	3.5	2.9	0.7	0.6
1964p	4.9			1.9	

p=preliminary

Sources: 1950-1963: Comisión Económica para América Latina, *Estudio Económico de América Latina 1963,* New York, United Nations, 1964, p. 6.

1964: Pan American Union, Organization of American States, *Latin America: Problems and Perspectives of Economic Development, 1963-1964,* Baltimore, Johns Hopkins Press, 1966, p. 8.

had been having a long economic upswing and the effects of the Vietnam War were beginning to make themselves felt.

There are of course significant differences among the individual countries. But as stated by the United Nations survey: "The decline in the rate of growth in the second half of the 1950's is a general phenomenon which occurs in almost all the countries although it varies in intensity and duration in some of them."[18]

The rate of economic growth in Latin America is low. Even with the 2.2 percent growth rate of the Korean War period, it would take over thirty years for Latin America's gross product per inhabitant to double. At the 0.7 percent rate of 1960-1963, it would take one hundred years.

But even when growth rates are high—as they are sporadically in individual countries—what does it mean? In 1961, Brazil's gross product rose by 7.7 percent and Peru's by 9.2 percent. But what does it mean to the shoeless agricultural laborers of Brazil's Northeast that skyscrapers are going up in São Paulo? What does it mean to the

[18] *Ibid.,* pp. 11-12.

melancholy Indians of the Peruvian Sierra that fine new stores have been built in Lima? Just as Havana is not Cuba, so São Paulo is not Brazil, Lima is not Peru, Caracas is not Venezuela. In all the Latin American countries, there are large sectors of the population to whom it does not matter whether growth rates are a little higher or a little lower—they starve at the same level as usual.

What is it that is growing in Latin America? The term "gross national product" is misleading. In Latin America, the gross products are not *national* because the economies are not *national*. The economies of Latin America are not integrated wholes; they are fragmented. They are agglomerations of separate pieces—foreign enclaves, local oligarchies, middle classes, workers, shantytowns, rural poor.

The American corporations expand mineral production or put in a few assembly plants, and there is *growth*. But what really happens? The American corporations make more money; the local oligarchy makes more money; a little trickles down to the local middle classes; a handful of jobs may be created. And for 85 percent of the population the increase in the production of copper or lead, refrigerators or automobiles, has as much significance as if it had taken place on the moon.

In Latin America, it is not whole economies that grow, but pockets within them. The pockets are smaller here, larger there. They grow at different rates in different countries and at different times. Sometimes the pockets get factories and other installations which are impressive to look at. Sometimes they give rise to modern apartment buildings and four-lane highways. But always they are pockets, nothing more.

Economic growth can make the pockets richer or enlarge them a little. But the kind of growth the Latin American countries get under imperialism—even when the rate is high—cannot begin to solve their problems.

How far can the problems of Latin America be solved by reform? What reforms could have any significant effect, and can they be carried through?

The 1961 Declaration of the Peoples of America announcing the Alliance for Progress promised to assure "fair wages." To whom? The Brazilian sugar worker who gets fifty cents a day? The unemployed in the shanty-towns? What can such a promise mean to the tens of millions who live outside the money economy?

The Declaration promised "to find a quick and lasting solution to the grave problems created by excessive price fluctuations in the basic exports." Like everything else in the Declaration, this is easier to talk about than to do. Aside from a coffee agreement which has not been able to prevent a sharp drop in coffee prices, nothing has been done.

To "reform tax laws" was another promise. But how do you get the people who run the Latin American governments to increase taxes on the privileged classes—that is, on themselves? If tax reforms had been carried out, the official reports could presumably explain them in clear, simple language. The reports could show that new, progressive income taxes have been passed, or that the rich Chilean landowners are being forced for the first time in history to pay some taxes. Instead the chapters on taxes in the last two annual economic surveys of the Pan American Union are transparent attempts to hide the fact that nothing significant has been done. The language on income taxes is always vague—"substantial modifications" are "under consideration." And the 1963-1964 survey is shameless enough to list as reforms, taxes which fall heavily on the poor: "Colombia and Honduras introduced general sales and excise taxes on goods and services. . . . Peru and Uruguay increased cigarette taxes."[19]

Setting up one or two international commodity agreements or increasing a few taxes will not solve any basic problem in Latin America. But even such measures as these are almost impossible to carry out. Clever liberals, both in the United States and Latin America, have found that there is political value in talk of reducing privileges. Each group involved is talking, however, about someone else's privileges, not their own. The United States Government is willing to have the Latin American oligarchies pay a little more in taxes to make the

[19] Pan American Union, Organization of American States, *Latin America, Problems and Perspectives of Economic Development, 1963-1964*, Baltimore, Johns Hopkins Press, 1966.

American position more secure against revolt from below. And the local oligarchs are willing to have the American companies pay more for raw materials to help safeguard (or enrich) themselves. Neither group is able to force the other to make the sacrifices necessary for real reform.

This situation is not unique. Just before the French Revolution, several ministers of Louis XV played at reform. One of them, Turgot, "prepared a plan for extensive reform. . . . Those in favor of reform were already hailing the dawn of a new era."[20] But the court wanted the nobility and the clergy to pay more taxes; the nobility and clergy wanted the court to reduce expenses; the nobility was willing to sacrifice the privileges of the clergy and the clergy was willing to sacrifice the privileges of the nobility. Turgot did not last long as minister and nothing ever came of his plan. Soon the Revolution came instead.

The Declaration of the Alliance also promised to encourage "comprehensive agrarian reform." But can a country dedicated to the protection of private property encourage land reform? The Pan American Union speaks of land reform in its Economic Survey of Latin America for 1962: "Any agrarian reform law, however, in seeking to both protect and extend the institution of private property, must incorporate certain basic decisions on method. The least common denominator of such laws includes answers, however imprecise, to the question which land is to be affected and which exempted by the program."[21] Below are some examples of "land exempted" in various land reform laws as stated in the Economic Survey:

Dominican Republic—All private property not voluntarily sold or donated.

[20] Gaetano Salvemini, *The French Revolution, 1788-1792.* New York, Henry Holt and Co., 1964, p. 12.
[21] Pan American Union, Organization of American States, *Economic Survey of Latin America, 1962.* Baltimore, Johns Hopkins Press, 1964. This and the following quotations and data are from pp. 211-235.

Guatemala—(a) Cultivated land; (b) land rented for at least five
    years with no personal service exacted.
Chile—Well-cultivated land or land of a six-year or more lease.
Costa Rica—To be determined by the Institute, [as] land fulfilling its
    social function.
Panama—Well-exploited.
Peru—Reserve to be specified by law for each zone; well-cultivated
    land.

Getting at the private land is difficult. "Once it becomes necessary
to expropriate privately owned lands, the detailed appraisals and negotiations, together with the possibility of a recourse to the courts, post-
pone settlement and may require large numbers of personnel as well
as large amounts of financial resources in order to compensate the
owners at an appraised price. Consequently, an agrarian reform program large enough in scope to be effective requires an enormous
budgetary allocation which could endanger the monetary stability of
the nation."

So the laws direct the "reforms" to public lands. But here too there
are problems: "Settlement on public lands is hindered by the fact that
these lands often require clearing, soil studies, and access roads before
they are usable, and such preparatory projects are extremely costly as
well as time-consuming."

How do the reforms work out? Chile is an example. Three hundred
thousand families, says the Survey, need land. "The goal for 1963 is
to settle 7,000 families" on public lands in the province of Magallanes.
Magallanes is at the extreme south of Chile, a cold and desolate re-
gion, more than a thousand miles from the nearest railroad.

Land reform can be carried out in only one way—by expropriating
the landholders. If the landholders have to be paid, there can be no
land reform. Land reform cannot be carried out with public land.
There isn't enough. And the problem of the laborers left on the large
estates would still remain. The large landholders will fight not only
measures which menace their land, but also those which threaten their
labor supply. They will no more stand by and watch their labor force

depart than did the slaveholders in the United States after the Civil War.

Neither the imperialists nor the local bourgeoisie can sponsor a true land reform in Latin America. The imperialists themselves own large amounts of land in a number of Latin American countries. In others, they have close economic ties to the local plantation owners who sell the coffee, sugar, cotton, bananas, and other export products. And the Latin American bourgeoisie has become increasingly intermingled with the traditional landholders: many of the bourgeoisie hold land and many of the landholders live in cities. Even where the landholders still constitute to some extent a separate class, the imperialists and the bourgeoisie need them for political reasons. The landholder governs and polices the countryside; he helps control legislatures. To do away with the landholder would upset the political balance.

A land reform is not a technical measure and it is not reform. It is revolution.

Other innocent-sounding measures of the Alliance also require revolution for fulfillment. The Alliance Charter promised "rational" industrialization; it called for "comprehensive and well-conceived national programs of economic and social development, aimed at the achievement of self-sustaining growth." But how can an economic colony of an imperialist power carry out such promises? To plan—in reality, not just on paper—you have to control. What kind of plans can you make when the foreign corporations dominate your resources, markets, policies, and politics? The precondition for meaningful industrialization and development in Latin America is true economic and political independence. And this requires revolution.

Even some of the imperialists dimly sense that Latin America needs revolution. "We propose to complete the revolution of the Americas," said President Kennedy in his speech announcing the Alliance for Progress. This is clever demagogy, but the idea is ludicrous. Imperialism cannot make a revolution against itself.

Can the local bourgeoisie lead the Latin American revolution? Can it lead the struggle against imperialism to victory? It cannot.

Everywhere in Latin America a large, powerful segment of the bourgeoisie lives from imperialism. Think of those in the export and import houses, the lawyers and accountants working for the foreign mines and factories, the hotel and restaurant owners dependent on tourism, the storekeepers selling foreign goods. And everywhere, the bourgeoisie is threatened from below and could not maintain its position without imperialism.

The national bourgeoisie which does not live from imperialism is significant in only four or five countries and even there its strength is limited. It sometimes squabbles with imperialism. In Chile, it tries to raise the local stock ownership in the mining companies. In Argentina it resists for a while giving oil concessions to the foreign corporations. In Brazil it tries to nationalize a foreign electric power or telephone company.

But national independence is not a matter of raising the local stock ownership in a few industries or even taking over one or two. Such actions will not solve anything basic. What is required is the complete elimination of imperialist power in Latin America.

To get rid of imperialism means a life or death fight. The only way for a Latin American government to win such a fight is to mobilize the people behind it as the Revolutionary Government of Cuba did. But the bourgeois governments cannot mobilize the people. They cannot take the measures that would make the people ready to defend them with blood. They cannot give the people arms.

Between imperialism and revolution, a bourgeois reformist government in Latin America has only a narrow area of maneuver. The best it can do is vacillate. It may start out with big talk. But it quickly becomes frightened of going too far. It may dream of winning some independence from imperialism, but it cannot accept the conditions for doing so. It needs popular support but cannot take the action necessary to get and keep this support. As the people become disillusioned with a reformist government that cannot reform, that government becomes increasingly vulnerable. Then it either refrains from offending the imperialists or they arrange for its overthrow.

In the Latin America of today only one kind of revolution is possible—a people's revolution. Only the people can stand up to imperialism, can carry the revolution far enough to solve the problems.

Who are the people? In his *History Will Absolve Me* speech Fidel talked about the people of Cuba. In the Second Declaration of Havana, he talks about the people of Latin America—the 32 million Indians, the 45 million mestizos, the 30 million blacks, the millions of poor whites; the peons on the great plantations; the miners of copper, tin, iron, and coal; the frustrated teachers, intellectuals, artists, and professionals. The struggle in Latin America will be "conducted by the masses, by the peoples."

And the revolutionary potential of the peasantry is crucial. "While it is true that in America's underdeveloped countries, the working class is in general relatively small, there is a social class which because of the subhuman conditions under which it lives constitutes a potential force which—led by the workers and revolutionary intellectuals—has a decisive importance in the struggle for national liberation: the peasantry. . . . No matter how hard the living conditions of the workers are, the rural population lives under even more horrible conditions of oppression and exploitation. But, with few exceptions, it also constitutes the absolute majority, sometimes even more than 70 percent of the Latin American populations."

The Declaration also says that "wherever roads are closed to the peoples . . . it is neither just nor correct to divert the people with the vain and fanciful illusion that the dominant classes can be uprooted by legal means which do not and will not exist." Those who talk about peaceful change in Latin America should be reminded that the problem is not one of remote theoretical possibilities. Apart from Cuba, there are nineteen countries in Latin America. In fifteen or sixteen, not even the forms of democracy exist. In the remaining three or four, the democracy is in good part sham; for example, in Chile, the peasants are disenfranchised by being kept illiterate. Everywhere there is an army ready to act if elections go the wrong way. And if the local armies cannot handle the problem, there are the troops of the imperialists.

One of the greatest lessons of the Cuban Revolution is the need for the people to capture state power, to smash the old state, armed forces and all. This is not just theory, but fact. How many governments haven't the imperialists been able to overthrow—Guatemala, Brazil, the Congo, and the rest. The imperialists worked harder against Cuba than any of the others, but Cuba stands.

When the people of any Latin American country have kicked out the imperialists, how much of the typical lopsided economy will remain in private hands? The people will take over the foreign plantations; the oil, copper, tin, lead, zinc; the railroads; the electric power and telephone companies; the foreign assembly plants. What will the economy of Venezuela be like when the people own the oil?

Kicking out the imperialists means taking over the foreign trade which they dominate. It means taking over the businesses of the local importers and exporters—close allies of the imperialists. These groups cannot be expected to work with a revolution. They cannot be allowed to sneak out capital or damage the economy. The power which their businesses give them must be taken away. Just kicking out the imperialists and taking over the businesses of their local allies will place the strategic parts of the Latin American economies in the hands of the state.

Strong government land-reform agencies—like Cuba's INRA—will be required throughout Latin America. Not only must the landholders be kicked out, but there must be a long vigorous follow-through to carry the land reforms to ultimate success. The revolutionary governments will have to bring schools, hospitals, and roads to the countryside; they will have to supply fertilizers, machinery, and credit. It is hard to conceive of private banks, operating on commercial principles, lending money to the semi-illiterate farmers of Latin America.

The revolutionary governments will have to carry out industrial development. Private enterprise cannot provide enough resources or assure growth of the type required. The Latin American bourgeoisies have never been strong on investing in industry, and they are even less likely to do so in a revolutionary situation.

The revolutionary governments will have to move quickly to economic planning. Only with planning will they be able to handle the lopsided economies and difficult problems. They will have to plan a basic redistribution of income, the use of foreign exchange in the interests of the people, the development of agriculture and industry—in short, the whole economy. And the planning will have to be real, not fake, not like what is called planning in the colonial economies of Latin America today. Planning does not mean having a few technicians concoct pretty programs, which are meaningless because there is no power to carry them out when the real powers of decision are in private hands. For the revolutionary governments to be able to plan, they—not the bourgeoisie—will have to control all the important parts of the economy.

Finally, what political power will the local bourgeoisie have after the imperialism which sustains it is gone? After the people have won state power with guns in their hands? After they have smashed the old state apparatus, as they must to hold on to what they have won? With the imperialists gone and the old state smashed there will be no counterforce capable of holding back a movement toward socialism. The armed struggle will give rise to the nucleus of a new revolutionary state. What can this be but a socialist state? The key cadres of the new state will come out of the armed struggle. They will have been formed in a fight to obtain not crumbs, but power—people's power. And how can the people's power be used to solve the people's problems, except through socialism?

As in Cuba, a revolution in Latin America cannot move, cannot grow and live, without being socialist. The choices are sharp. There is no middle ground. Either imperialism or socialist revolution.

Organization and Incentives in a Socialist Economy

Despite the superiority of socialism to capitalism, the task of running a socialist economy is anything but easy. Not only are the powers of socialism greater than those of capitalism, but also its aspirations. Socialism means running a whole economy rationally, constructing a new society, changing the very nature of man himself. None of this happens automatically. A vast task of organization and leadership is involved.

The basic responsibility for running a socialist economy must rest with the state. A revolution must not only win power but stay in power; it must defend itself against external and internal enemies. Control of the economy is an important weapon in the fight. Socialism will not construct itself spontaneously; the state has to direct nationalization, socialization, the creation of new organizational structures. Only the state can take into account all the people and all the different regions of the country, long-run interests as well as short-run interests, and social, political, and military considerations as well as economic considerations. Only the state can manage everything as a whole.

The literature of socialism has traditionally emphasized centralization. The economy will become "one single office, one single factory." Socialism will replace the anarchy of capitalism, the blind working of the market, with conscious central planning.

But even in an office or factory the manager does not decide everything himself—he has to delegate responsibilities to subordinates. Think of the millions of decisions required to run a whole economy in just a single day. Along with centralization, there must be decentralization. The problem is how to combine the two: what and how to centralize, what and how to decentralize.

Thus far, despite central planning, the market—the buying and selling of goods—continues to exist in all socialist countries. True, these countries have put limits on the operation of the market. But Engels' prediction that "The seizure of the means of production by society puts an end to commodity production," has not yet been realized.[22] No socialist country has been able, or at least found it advisable, to end commodity production—to wipe out the market altogether.

This is an impressive fact, since there are now many socialist countries. It may be that when the developed capitalist countries become socialist, they will be able to eliminate the market quickly. But socialism will be winning power soon in additional underdeveloped countries. These countries will probably be no more able to eliminate

[22] Friedrich Engels, *Anti-Dühring*, New York, International Publishers, 1966, p. 309.

the market quickly than the existing socialist countries. Clearly, socialism cannot permit the market to dominate the economy; it must be limited and controlled. Eventually the market will be eliminated in all the socialist countries, but it cannot be eliminated by words. The existing socialist countries and many—perhaps all—of those to come in the future will have to work with the market for some time. The problem is how to combine conscious socialist planning and the market, how to utilize the market without becoming its prisoner. Organizing and running a socialist economy includes the task of handling the market properly.

For some theorists—for example, some of the proponents of the input-output technique—the problem of combining centralization and decentralization does not arise. They assume that everything in an economy is interdependent with everything else; that ultimately every action, every error, affects everything; that only by weighing all the interrelations, all the consequences, can a scientific basis for action be provided.[23] Carried to extremes, this view makes decentralization impossible; it leads to the conclusion that the only scientific way to operate a planned economy is with a giant computer which somehow knows, weighs, and solves everything.

While some of the techniques developed from this view may be useful for specific purposes, it is erroneous when applied to whole economies. It is elegant and precise by the standards of mathematics, not by those of practical, working economics. In real economies, things are not so tightly interlocked. Some things are interdependent; others are—for practical purposes—independent. Some things are important because they have wide, lasting effects; others are trivial. Some things are important for one purpose and not another. It is on these differences that organization is based.

What is important is held at the top; what is less important is dele-

[23] See for example Wassily Leontief, "The Decline and Rise of Soviet Economic Science," in *The Soviet Economy*, edited by Harry G. Shaffer, New York, Appleton Century, 1964. Leontief writes that every change in the balance of supply and demand of one item is "bound to disturb the balance of many, and ultimately of all other goods and services."

gated to subordinate bodies or individuals; and these in turn do the same down to the lowest units. What is important for one purpose is made the responsibility of one line of organization; what is important for another purpose goes to a different line. There is division by industry, by territory, and by individual enterprise. There are a large number of bodies organized by function, responsible for planning and controlling finances, foreign exchange, prices, labor, and so on. The lines of organization often crisscross and the whole structure becomes complicated.

This organization cannot work with electronic speed. Problems have to be thrashed out from many angles by people from different organizational units, and this takes paperwork, telephone calls, conferences, special committees, discussions with superiors, and time. Representatives of planning boards have to hold conferences with representatives of ministries or regional authorities; people responsible for production have to hold conferences with those responsible for finances, foreign exchange, raw materials, labor supply. But for large organizations, the important practical goal is to avoid unwieldiness and bureaucracy. Just to do this is hard enough.

Nor can the organization work with absolute precision. All its units have only partial knowledge. But absolute precision is a matter of elegance; what is of practical importance is getting precision where it counts, to the degree that counts.

None of the basic problems of organization—centralization *vs.* decentralization; the role of ministries, territorial units, enterprises—can be understood unless one discards the chimera of absolute correctness and perfection. Each form of organization has advantages and disadvantages: the problem is to strike the best balance, and disadvantages have to be accepted in the interests of a larger advantage. For example, when tractors are scarce, the most important thing is to utilize them fully; and it is advantageous to hold them in central machine and tractor stations even though this means red tape for the farms every time a tractor is needed. When tractors become plentiful, it is better to put them on the farms. Those who set up organizations try to make them as good as possible. But a perfect organization—one without disadvantages—is inherently impossible. Conflicts between different considerations exist objectively; and trying to strike the best possible balance is the most one can do.

Obviously the basic organization of a socialist economy must differ from that of a capitalist economy. But this does not mean that there can be a single standard form of socialist organization suitable for all circumstances. Organizational forms must be adapted to the widely varying circumstances in the different socialist countries. And within each country circumstances are constantly changing. There has to be constant tinkering with the organizational forms—and occasionally major changes.

When a socialist country sets up ministries—of industry, agriculture, construction—is it centralization or decentralization? The answer depends in part on where you look from. Seen from a central planning board, ministries are a step toward decentralization. Ministers are usually people of stature, not just errand boys for a planning board. They are placed in charge of specific sectors of the economy because the operation of these sectors involves much more than the mechanical execution of plans. Problems of coordination will exist between ministries and planning board. The degree of decentralization can be varied by taking powers from the planning board and giving them to the ministries and vice versa.

But seen from regions and enterprises, ministries are centralized bodies. The greater their power in relation to regional and enterprise authorities, the greater the centralization.

The distribution of functions and powers between ministries and other bodies is a balance between conflicting considerations. Suppose, as in the first several decades of the Soviet Union, the rapid growth of industry is of overwhelming importance. The factories must be located in a variety of regions, but you cannot permit regional and local officials, moved by their special considerations, to interfere with them. So you set up separate ministries for defense industry, heavy industry, machinery production, and so on, with strong powers and with able, hard-driving people at their head. These ministries may entail certain disadvantages. Ministry factories may prefer to buy materials from far-away factories of the same ministry, even when local factories could supply them. They may feel more assured of the supply when the other factory is subject to the discipline of the same ministry. Strong centralization by branch of industry helps meet special problems of the industry, helps subject it to a uniform technical and economic policy, and helps assure that industry goals will be met, but such centralization is not conducive to the fullest utilization of regional resources. When industry considerations are overriding, the disadvantages of strong centralization along branch-of-industry lines are tolerated.

Even with this type of organization, territorial considerations cannot be disregarded and so there are territorial units in the ministries. With time, the territorial considerations become more important. The very growth of industry makes centralized control from a distance more difficult. The relative priorities and the balance of advantage and disadvantage shift. In 1957 the Soviet Union therefore carried out a reorganization that placed greater emphasis on territorial lines and gave greater powers to regional units. Branch-of-industry considerations do not disappear with such reorganization; they still have to be taken into account, and branch-of-industry divisions are set up in the regional planning boards, but their position is subordinate.

This reorganization is a move toward decentralization, but not in all respects. The strong industry ministries during the early years of planning in the Soviet Union also reflected the weakness of the central planning board. Only essentials were under planned control, not nearly the whole economy. But with time, more of the economy was effectively subjected to planning. In reducing the powers of the industry ministries, the 1957 reorganization strengthened not only territorial units, but also the central board. In this respect, the reorganization was a move toward greater centralization.

Experience presumably showed that the 1957 reorganization did not work well for defense industry, since in 1965 this industry was put back under centralized branch-of-industry control.

In the People's Republic of China, also, there has been experimentation to find the best combination between centralization and decentralization. To develop a large modern industry rapidly, many things have to be centralized. But China has an enormous, traditionally under-utilized population which, together with the many resources scattered throughout the countryside, constitutes a potentially tremendous economic force. An overcentralized organization would be difficult to manage and would fail to realize much of the potential.

Chou En-lai spoke, in 1956, of "excessive centralization" during the first five-year plan.[24] He laid down the principle that "all enterprises and public institutions which are vital to the national economy as a whole . . . should be administered by central authorities while the rest should as far as possible be administered by local authorities."

The policy of "walking on two legs" was developed. "In the past," says the *Peking Review* of April 15, 1958, "the lower levels depended for industrial construction on the relevant ministries and departments of the central government. These did a good job, but the enterprises built could not satisfy every need. . . . Now the arousing of the initiative of the local authorities and the people has revealed inexhaustible sources of strength. . . . In the past few months medium and small-scale industry have been springing up like mushrooms. Everywhere the enthusiasm of the people is high and unused potentialities are being brought into play."

The peasants invent a wooden rice-planting machine with which two men can transplant more rice seedlings than ten men working by hand. Local dams, canals, irrigation works, and roads are created. Industries rise based on local labor, materials, money, initiative, and enthusiasm.[25]

But the need for local initiative does not eliminate the need for unified central planning and control of certain things. Decentralization brings benefits but also problems. Once the rush of local construction gets under way it can draw men and materials into less

[24] *Report on the Proposal for the Second Five-Year Plan for the Development of the Economy*, Peking, Foreign Language Press, 1956.
[25] Edgar Snow, *The Other Side of the River*. New York, Random House, 1952, pp. 209-213.

important construction projects, leaving more important ones short. Urban commune workshops can draw too many skilled handicraft workers from the rural areas. Industry and construction can draw too many people from agricultural work. Corrective measures have to be taken.

The process of developing the organizational forms goes on—the attempt to get the best combination between the flexibility necessary for local authorities to function effectively and the central control necessary to assure the proper allocation of labor and key materials, and the proper balance between agriculture and industry, investment and consumption, exports and imports.

One of the most difficult problems in socialist economic organization is the relation of central planning bodies and ministries to individual enterprises. How much autonomy, authority, and responsibility should be given to such enterprises? Upon what criteria should they operate and be controlled? To what extent should emphasis be placed on centrally fixed targets for output, productivity, costs, and the like; to what extent on profits? What is the relation between economic planning and cost accounting?

The problem of the enterprise in a socialist economy is of course meshed with the problem of the market. Enterprises operate in markets—they buy and sell. Profits depend in part on the market. How much scope can markets be allowed to have? How far can markets and profits be allowed to determine what is to be produced? Or the direction of investment and future growth?

Lenin gave one of the classic reasons for having markets in a socialist economy. "There is no doubt that it is possible to carry out the socialist revolution in a country in which the small farmer producers constitute the overwhelming majority of the population only by means of a number of special transitional measures which would be totally unnecessary in countries with developed capitalism." The small farmers could not simply be expropriated; this would mean throwing them into the arms of the enemy. And these farmers were not ready for any form of exchange of goods other than purchase and sale. Time would be required to win them over to a different system. Lenin took into account the political implications of permitting markets. "Can we, to a certain extent, restore freedom to trade, freedom for capitalism for the small farmer, without at the same time cutting at the roots of the political power of the proletariat? Can it be done? It can, for the question is one of degree."[26]

In his *Economic Problems of the USSR*, Stalin carried the problem further. He said that Engels' statement about the end of commodity production under socialism "cannot be considered fully clear and precise because it does not indicate whether it refers to the seizure by society of *all* or only part of the means of production." He repeated Lenin's argument about the small farmers and gave an additional circumstance that might make it necessary to maintain commodity production—foreign trade.

Then Stalin went on to relate the market, not just to small farmers and foreign trade, but also to socialist enterprises. "It is sometimes asked," he wrote, "whether the law of value exists and operates in our country, under the socialist system. Yes it does exist and it does operate. . . . The operation of the law of value is not confined to the sphere of commodity circulation [the exchange of commodities through purchase and sale]. It also extends to production. True, the law of value has no regulating function in our socialist production, but it nevertheless influences production. . . . Such things as cost accounting and profitableness, production costs, prices, etc., are of actual importance in our enterprises. Consequently, our enterprises cannot, and must not, function without taking the law of value into account.

"Is this a good thing?" asked Stalin. "It is really not a bad thing, since it teaches our business executives to conduct production on rational lines and disciplines them. . . . It is not a bad thing because it teaches our executives to look for, find and utilize hidden reserves, latent in production and not trample them underfoot. It is not a bad thing because it teaches our executives systematically to improve

[26] V. I. Lenin, "The Tax in Kind," *Selected Works*, Vol. IX. New York, International Publishers, 1937, pp. 107 and 112.

methods of production, to lower production costs, to practice cost accounting, and to make their enterprises pay."[27]

"The profitableness of individual plants and industries," said Stalin, "is of immense value for the development of our industry. It must be taken into account both when planning construction and when planning production."[28]

But Stalin also strongly emphasized the limitations on the role of the market and market-type criteria under socialism. "The sphere of operation of the law of value under our economic system is strictly limited and placed within definite bounds." The law of value is subordinate to the central plans which are based on requirements for the balanced development of the economy. It does not function "as the regulator of production." It does not regulate the distribution of labor among the various branches of production. If it did, "it would be incomprehensible why our light industries, which are the most profitable, are not being developed to the utmost, and why preference is given to our heavy industries, which are often less profitable, and sometimes altogether unprofitable."[29]

And profits, said Stalin, are not just a matter of the individual firm. "If profitableness is considered not from the standpoint of individual plants or industries, and not over a period of one year, but from the standpoint of the entire national economy and over a period of, say, ten or fifteen years, which is the only correct approach to the question, then the temporary and unstable profitableness of some plants or industries is beneath all comparison with that higher form of stable and permanent profitableness which we get from the operation of the law of balanced development of the national economy and from economic planning."[30]

The Soviet Manual of *Political Economy* carries some of these thoughts further. "Economic accounting is based on a combination of centralized management of socialist enterprises by the state with the

[27] J. V. Stalin, *Economic Problems of the USSR*, New York, International Publishers, 1952, pp. 12-13, 18-19.
[28] *Ibid.*, p. 44.
[29] *Ibid.*, pp. 20-21.
[30] *Ibid.*, p. 22.

economic independence of operation of each enterprise. An enterprise is independent in its economic operation in that it receives and has at its disposal state-owned resources, both material and financial, and can exercise considerable initiative in the most rational use of them for the best possible achieving of planned targets.

"Economic accounting also implies that an enterprise is materially responsible to other enterprises for meeting its obligations. . . . Economic relations between enterprises are regulated with the aid of contracts. Enterprises acquire the means of production they need and sell their output by contracts which conform to the general state plan. . . .

"One of the most important requirements of economic accounting is that contract discipline should be strictly observed."[31]

The statements by Stalin and the Manual presuppose that there are organizational reasons for having enterprises and markets in a socialist economy. Why organize socialist production units into enterprises? And why have these enterprises buying and selling from each other? If the central authorities could plan and manage everything, neither enterprises nor buying and selling between them would be necessary. All the units of the economy would simply be separate departments of one big workshop; and goods would be transferred from one department to another without going through purchase and sale.

But the central authorities cannot plan and manage everything. Strong subordinate units are necessary to take care of what is left open. Why is it important for enterprise executives to find and utilize "hidden reserves latent in production"? Because much of this cannot be done by central authorities and plans. Why is cost accounting important? Because the enterprises need criteria beyond those provided by plans. Why are contracts between socialist enterprises necessary? Because central plans do not fully determine the interchange of goods between enterprises, and because agreements between individual enterprises are necessary to make the plans specific.

The statements by Stalin and the Manual constitute a general doc-

---

[31] *Political Economy*, Moscow, Akademia Nauk, Second English Edition, 1957, pp. 616 ff.

trine only. They disagree on the one hand with anyone who sees no role for profits and the market in a socialist economy; and on the other with anyone who denies that their importance is secondary, that they are subordinate to central planning. But the statements do not tell us exactly how central planning is to be combined with enterprises and markets and how the combination can vary with circumstances. They tell us that enterprises and markets cannot be given complete leeway and yet must be given some leeway. But they do not specify how much. They do not, for example, tell us whether—to meet the needs of central planning—enterprises should be subject to, say, twenty centrally-fixed targets and norms or whether two or three would be enough. A variety of specific forms and methods for operating a socialist economy is compatible with the general doctrine.

The system of organization and planning that grew up in the Soviet Union tended toward strong centralization of control over the enterprise. At first, there was centralization along branch-of-industry lines. But even when this particular type of centralization was altered by territorial decentralization or by increasing the role of central and regional planning boards, the enterprise remained subject to severe outside control.

The Soviet system was the product of many factors—Marxist theories, historical circumstances, traditional Russian methods of organization and administration. It must be judged in relation to the circumstances in which it arose and the tasks it faced. With it, the Soviet Union in a few decades turned medieval backwardness into a powerful, modern economy.

The Soviet system provided the first model for the other socialist countries. It was less specifically adapted to these countries than to the Soviet Union. But even for them it was without doubt extremely useful. There is a great difference between beginning with a model, even one that requires many adaptations to specific circumstances, and beginning with nothing at all.

But after a while, in many—perhaps most—of the socialist countries, a problem of excessive centralization developed. Yugoslavia was the first to react; it began to decentralize in the early 1950's. Yugoslavia, however, was a special case; the problem was not just how to organize socialism, but was connected with Yugoslavia's struggle with the Soviet Union and its economic dependence on the capitalist countries. In China, as we have seen, Chou En-lai was talking in 1956 of "excessive centralization"; the problem was being taken up by the State Council of China.[32] In this same year, Bronislaw Minc, a leading economist of the Planning Commission of Poland was writing: "First of all, we must substantially restrict the scope of the directives laid down by central authorities and accord a much wider measure of independence to enterprises and local organs."[33]

Since the early 1960's, economists of the USSR and other socialist countries have been debating whether and how to give greater leeway to enterprises. Ota Sik, a member of the Central Committee of the Czech Communist Party, has written of a widespread discussion of planning and management that took place in his country in early 1965: "The overwhelming majority felt that economic management had to be radically improved. . . . As the exchange of views developed, it became increasingly clear that the old system of management, based mainly on directives from central bodies handed down the administrative ladder, had to be replaced by a *comprehensive and economically sound system of management*."[34] In the Soviet Union, Czechoslovakia, and other socialist countries, new methods of planning and administration are being experimented with and put into effect.

The starting point for a discussion of the recent economic debate and experimentation in Eastern Europe should be recognition that the

[32] Besides Chou En-lai's report, cited earlier, see the chapters "China's New Economic Policy" by Franz Schurmann and "China's Economic Planning" by Audrey Donnitome in *Industrial Development in Communist China*, edited by Choh-ming Li, New York, Frederick A. Praeger, 1964.

[33] Quoted in John Jacob Montias, *Central Planning in Poland*. New Haven, Yale University Press, 1962, p. 263.

[34] Ota Sik, "Czechoslovakia's new system of economic planning and management," *World Marxist Review*, March 1965. Emphasis in original.

old methods have thrown up problems which must be grappled with. Reactions against excessive centralization have been too widespread to reflect simply differences in doctrine, although differences in doctrine enter into the picture. Overdependence on centrally imposed norms for the control of enterprises has been charged with many faults, and the charges repeat themselves in different countries: failure to make full use of factory capacity or local resources; waste in the use of materials, equipment, and labor; products of poor quality; hamstringing of factory managers in red tape. Anyone who has ever worked in or closely observed a socialist economy will know there are problems. There can be no question of the need to experiment with the methods of planning and management.

In Cuba, the nationalization of certain industries, for example, textiles, is accompanied by a decline in the quality of their products. Some of the decline, but not all, can be explained by problems of reorganization or faulty materials. You wonder how and why it has come about. Then in reading the literature of other socialist countries, you see references to the problem of quality in the USSR, China, and Czechoslovakia. The centrally-fixed targets are mostly quantitative; quality is often hard to control.

You visit a chrome mine in eastern Cuba in which you see a pile of unsold ore piling up near the dock. When you ask why, the Czech geologist tells you that the proportion of impurities in the ore is too high, so that the ore is unacceptable. You ask the administrator of the mine why this has been happening and he says that the plan for the mine is ambitious, that the miners have to strain to fulfill it and become careless. In discussions with technicians from the other socialist countries, you learn that this sort of problem also occurs in their countries.

You notice that sometimes imported trucks, machinery, and equipment remain a long time on lots or in warehouses before they reach their final user and are put to work. You feel instinctively that this is a waste and wonder what in the organizational arrangements allows it to happen. Doesn't somebody have to pay some sort of cost? Then you notice in the economic literature of the Soviet Union that there also machinery sometimes lies idle in factory storage rooms; that the system of calculating costs somehow permits this type of waste to occur.

Essentially these problems reflect excessive reliance in the management of enterprises on administrative targets and norms imposed from above. Such targets and norms have an important place in economic management, but they also have limitations. Descriptions of them sometimes create a misleading impression by stressing how scientific they are. In fact, the norms are often based—as anyone who has ever worked for a government or other large organization will know—on little more than the performance of previous years. And there are many problems.

One problem is that of measuring achievement. Some types of achievement are easy to measure—for example, the output of more or less homogeneous products such as electric power, steel, oil. But others, such as furniture or clothing, are not so simple. How is workmanship to be measured?

Suppose that in an attempt to measure quality, the output target for overcoats is fixed, not in physical units, but in value of production. And then one of the factories puts expensive—and unnecessary—fur collars on boys' overcoats to increase the value of its production. (This is not a hypothetical case; it comes from an article by a Soviet economist.)

The problem is not limited to production. It occurs in construction, transportation, distribution—everywhere. Suppose a construction enterprise whose work is measured by the length of sewer pipe it puts in place lays more pipe than is called for by its target, but much of it months before it can possibly be used. Is this an achievement or a waste?

Another problem is that targets and norms, no matter how well conceived and numerous, cannot provide automatic answers to everything involved in running an enterprise; and if targets and norms get too numerous, they can hamstring the people in the enterprise. The role of the people in the enterprise is basic. Generally they are the ones who know best what it can do, and their knowledge and cooperation is necessary to fix targets and norms in the first place. It is they who have to handle the day-to-day operations in such a way as to meet the targets and norms. Innumerable specific problems are always arising which can only be handled—or can best be handled—by them. To do their work well they need room for maneuver. They may discover that with a small increase in expenditure they can make a big improvement in the quality of their product—and then find out that a cost-reduction norm stands in the way. Or—to take another example from a Soviet article—they may be able to salvage $10,000 in metal with an expenditure of $2,500 in additional labor, but the plan does not permit the hiring of additional labor. In the recent Soviet economic literature, there are many references to the problem of "petty tutelage" of enterprises by the agencies over them.

Finally, a word on prices. Fixing prices centrally and holding them stable for long periods has certain advantages. The central authorities can use the price mechanism to favor industries important for development. They can protect the consumer against the enterprise. But there are also disadvantages. The ability of the seller to adjust to changes in cost or market conditions is lost. Sometimes centrally-fixed prices can unnecessarily create distribution problems, such as long lines at the retail stores or a piling up of unsold goods on the shelves. And when the authorities deliberately hold certain classes of prices high or low for reasons of policy, these prices lose some of their significance as measures of cost, and true cost accounting becomes more difficult.

These problems cannot be solved by textbook dogmatism—only by discussion, experimentation, and analysis. Changes in methods of organization and planning are inevitable. Such changes can lead to errors and excesses. But the danger that changes can be pushed too far is no proof that they should not be pushed at all.

A leading Soviet proponent of reduced centralized controls over enterprises is Y. G. Liberman, Chief of the Department of Political Economy of the Technological Institute of Kharkov. Professor Liberman argues that enterprises should be judged by their fundamental efficiency, not by a multitude of indices which regulate their operations in detail. Only fundamental indices should be handed down to enterprises. "What," asks Liberman, "are the principal demands that society makes of socialist enterprises? First, maximum output. Hence, the first thing that must be assigned to an enterprise is the volume of marketable output of a specified nomenclature and an appropriate quality. This should be the principal index of the work of the enterprise. . . . Second, maximum efficiency in production and the sale of the output. . . . And since efficient operation increases the profitability of production . . . the profits index of an enterprise should be assigned as its second fundamental task."

Professor Liberman also asks: "What guarantee is there that with this the enterprises will give preferential attention to state interests?" And he answers: "What is profitable for society as a whole will also be so for each production collective, and on the other hand, what is anti-economic from the point of view of public interest will also be so in greater degree for all enterprises. In principle, there should be no place in socialism for contradictions between the interests of society and those of an enterprise."

Professor Liberman also includes in his proposals methods of giving the managers and workers of an enterprise a "material interest" in its profits by allowing them to participate in the profits through bonuses.[35]

Another Soviet economist who proposes decentralization is V. S. Nemchinov, the director, before his death a few years ago, of the Institute of Applied Mathematical Economics. Nemchinov's analysis is broader and more systematic than Liberman's. He sees the economy as a combination of different systems—an over-all "macro-system" and various "micro-systems" such as regions, enterprises, and their subunits. For these systems to "coexist and work harmoniously," it is not necessary that the sum of the parts coincide with the whole with arithmetic exactness. "It is enough that the priority of the macro-system be preserved. . . . *The essential is to coordinate the mechanism of planning with the autonomous management of the enterprises.*" (Emphasis in original.)

---

[35] Y. G. Liberman, "Dirección y Planificación Industrial," *Comercio Exterior.* La Habana, October-December, 1964.

Nemchinov argues that not all prices have to be fixed centrally, just a few which have an important influence on the standard of living or costs of production. The rest can be controlled by price limits. Nemchinov proposes that the Soviet Union should begin replacing the centrally controlled, direct allocation of raw materials among enterprises by "state wholesale trade." He also recommends that fixed capital and inventories should not be considered cost-free, that a rent should be charged for their use by the enterprise. This, he says, will constrain the enterprise to handle these items with a certain minimum efficiency.

Finally, Nemchinov also speaks of the principle that "all that which is useful and advantageous to the whole of the economy should also be so to the enterprise charged with executing the task."[36]

Some Soviet economists disagree with Liberman. How, they ask, can the necessary over-all balances in the economy be maintained if the central authorities give up their controls? How, for example, can the over-all balance between the supply and demand for labor be maintained if individual enterprises can vary their labor force at their own discretion? How can the supply and demand for consumer goods be maintained if enterprises can vary their wages and salary payments according to their profits?

Enterprises, say some, are ignorant of the over-all interrelationships in the economy. They are not in a position to evaluate regional considerations in the distribution of investment. The regional distribution of investment can only be carried out by planning on a national scale.

Objections are also raised to Nemchinov's proposals. An economist named Kosiachenko argues that reserves of many materials are not large enough to warrant shifting from centralized administrative allocation to state trade. For example, bad harvests can cause shortages of agricultural raw materials for the food and light industries and direct allocation of materials becomes necessary to cope with the shortages.[37]

[36] V. S. Nemchinov, "Gestion et Planification de la production en U.R.S.S.," *Economie et Politique*, Paris, February, 1965.
[37] Kosiachenko, "Important Condition for Improvement of Planning," in *Problems of Economics*, selected articles from Soviet economics journals in English translation, New York, International Arts and Science Press, April, 1963.

Ota Sik of Czechoslovakia explains in detail why a new system of planning and management became necessary in Czechoslovakia and how it is expected to work. "There are times," he says, "in particular the transition from capitalist to socialist economy, when strict centralized management is necessary. Centralization helped us to accelerate the socialist structural remolding of the economy. . . . But as socialist economic development gradually got into its stride, the rigid centralized planning and management became the main impediments to greater efficiency."

Investment funds were centralized and channeled into *new* factories and *additional* machinery. Less and less was left for *renewal* and *modernization* of the existing plant. "The newly-built capacities, however, did not compensate for the diminishing returns caused by the aging of the old plant." Investments proved less and less effective and economic growth slowed down.

"The one-sided drive for more output, for quantitative targets was accompanied by a lack of sufficient stimuli to improve technology, go over to the use of new materials, and turn out better and more up-to-date goods. . . . The central managerial bodies were unable either fully to reveal or make systematic use of all the levers for improving quality."

The balance between supply and demand was upset. "On the one hand, the output of less essential and even unnecessary items often expanded . . . (as can be seen from the steady piling up of unplanned stocks) and on the other hand, the list of items in short supply grew longer."

Under the new system, "the long-range prospects of economic development will be mainly determined by the general state plan. . . . Only a central body is able to ensure, through a *long-range* plan, the proportional development and the necessary structural changes in the economy. The long-range plan deals primarily with basic capital construction . . . [the] volume of output of the most important items . . . [the] international division of labor and the Czech economy . . . the structure of the labor force . . . the distribution of national income."

But "as distinct from hitherto existing practice, the new system . . .

allots only a minor role to directives from the top. . . . The interests of the enterprises and the interests of society will be harmonized by means of the over-all state plan and a system of rules and levers necessitated by the commodity-money relations. . . .

"The new system provides for radical change in supplier-consumer relationships. In concluding agreements between supplier and consumer plants, not only will the role of the state plan indices be restricted or reduced to nil, the consumer will have a much bigger say. . . . The consumer plant will be in a position to choose its supplier and to go over to different materials, change technological processes, and even to amend the production program if what the supplier plant offers is not to its advantage. . . .

"The new system underscores the role of prices, which should help to channel production along lines expedient to the whole of society. . . . Fixing of prices . . . should be flexible. Prices for the new and modernized goods, and also for goods in great demand, should be fixed, temporarily, higher than price of production, and, conversely, prices for obsolete goods or those for which there is little demand, should be below the price of production. It goes without saying that in Czechoslovakia, with its vast nomenclature of output, flexible prices cannot be fixed by one central body. On the other hand, arbitrary price formation cannot be countenanced. Therefore the new system provides for three categories of prices: fixed prices, limited prices, and free prices."

Finally it may be noted that, according to Sik, "the decisive role in production planning by enterprises is played by the *material interests* of its workers. . . . The new system of management is aimed at creating an economic climate in which the workers, when taking relatively independent decisions concerning the production program, will have the maximum material incentive to work for the fullest possible satisfaction of the requirements of society. . . . The new system aims at ensuring that enterprises and workers have a stake in the newly-created value of output sold."[38]

[38] Ota Sik, "Czechoslovakia's new system of economic planning and management," *World Marxist Review*, March, 1965. Emphasis in original.

Liberman, Sik, and others have tied the questions of decentralization and material incentives together. But these are really two separate questions—related at certain points, but still separate. You can have greater or lesser stress on material incentives combined with either greater or lesser centralization. You can base a system of bonuses on centrally-fixed norms of output, productivity, or costs; and you can use profits as an indicator of efficiency without having a system of bonuses. Decentralization and material incentives will therefore be taken up separately in what follows.

People engaged in theorizing about economic administration generally have a stronger bias in favor of centralization than those engaged in the practice of administration. There is a reason for this. Running an economy involves both big things and little things—a few big things and an infinity of little ones. Those who are theorizing tend naturally to think of the big things, and it is these that need to be centralized. Those engaged in practical work have to cope with thousands of little things and are forced to try to think of ways to divide the work.

Some economists in the socialist countries take the mechanistic view that it is not possible to give enterprises greater flexibility without destroying the whole planning system. It is true that a socialist economy requires the maintenance of many over-all balances—in materials, equipment, labor, foreign exchange, finances. But it is not true that the only way of assuring the balances is for a central body to prescribe rigidly and in detail the amounts of these items the enterprises can use.

Central balances do not have to be exact to the third decimal. The flexibility given to enterprises can be held within limits which permit calculation of its over-all effects. The central authorities can maintain reserves to serve as cushions against the uncertainties created by additional flexibility. Often the cost of the reserves would be far outweighed by the advantages of the flexibility. This would be following the basic principle: control of essentials, flexibility on details.

Take, for example, the foreign-exchange balance in Cuba. It was necessary to set up strong central control of dollar exchange at the end of 1960. But the need for such strong control is not an absolute; it flows partly from the scarcity of dollars. Once these become more plentiful, the central control can be relaxed. With more dollars, there would be nothing wrong with allowing larger enterprises a sort of petty cash fund in dollars which they could spend without having to go through other agencies.

The same principle holds for materials, equipment, and so on. The socialist economies all started as scarcity economies. It is natural that as they become wealthier there should arise a tendency to ease central controls. And it is possible to ease controls without giving them up. For example, investment should be centrally controlled, but this does not mean that enterprises cannot be allowed a small investment fund which they can use for small expenditures without having to go through the bureaucratic chain.

Centrally fixed targets and norms are important. But for many purposes they cannot substitute for cost accounting. How can you keep enterprises from allowing machinery to lie around idle in storage rooms or from laying pipe too soon? It is often impossible to handle these problems with targets and norms. The targets and norms just cannot be made to cover everything. But assigning a cost to the time that machinery and pipe lie idle can help.

Even though Lenin spoke about the importance of cost accounting almost fifty years ago, the development of socialist cost accounting is still in its infancy. This is shown by the very debates in the socialist countries about whether to assign a cost to the use of machinery and other fixed assets. As the socialist economies become richer and more complicated, it will become less and less possible to run them according to a few simple overriding priorities, and cost accounting will become more and more important.

Within limits, profit has certain advantages as a criterion of rationality and efficiency in an enterprise and offers a simple, practical method of lifting the burden of too many targets and norms. It can serve the firm as a comprehensive criterion in a way that targets and norms cannot. The targets and norms measure separate aspects of performance: production, costs, thrifty use of materials, etc.; but they do not provide a means of balancing them against one another. Suppose a firm finds it can improve the quality of its product, but only by increasing its costs—should it do so? Whether or not to introduce a new machine has to be decided: it improves the quality of the product and requires less labor, but it is costly and uses more expensive raw materials—what should be done? The targets and norms often provide no answers or lead in practice to clearly irrational decisions.

Also within limits, there is nothing wrong with increasing the role of the market in socialist economies. What is the good of producing dresses that women don't want? Why shouldn't *sales* sometimes be a better index of achievement than *output*?

And why do *all* prices have to be fixed centrally? Is the price of thumbtacks, say, that important?

Economies are many-sided and complex. The parts vary in importance and have different specific characteristics. They need not all be handled in the same way. Investment determines the structure and direction of the economy for many years to come and must be subjected to a high degree of central control. Current production does not have to be controlled as tightly as investment. And enterprises producing dresses do not have to be handled in the same way as those producing electric power or steel. For some goods, the control of quality and design can depend mainly on centralized bureaus of standards and quality, for others on the preferences of consumers. Controls can be relaxed over many specific parts of an economy without giving up the essentials of control over the economy as a whole.

But there is also another side. It is possible to push decentralization too far and lose important controls over the economy. All sorts of difficulties—inflation, disruption of the orderly distribution of materials and labor, etc.—can result. This is not just a theoretical possibility; it has happened.

In Poland, for example, the decentralization carried out by the Gomulka regime after it came to power in 1956 brought benefits, but also caused the government to lose control of the balance between consumer purchasing power and the supply of goods available for consumption.

"The inflationary pressures generated by a vigorous investment drive in the second half of 1958 were reinforced by the decentralized outlays of the state enterprises, cooperatives, and local people's councils. . . . Another contributing factor in the financial crisis was the breakdown in 'wage discipline'. . . . A high level of investments, planned or un-planned, would have been tolerable if the output of food and other consumers' goods had kept up with the wages and other incomes from investment projects being injected into the income stream. But targeted increases in the output of consumers' goods were the smallest in five years . . . [and] poor weather conditions brought on an ab-solute decline in crop output. . . . Higher incomes from wages, sal-aries, and pensions converged on reduced stocks of meat. . . . Informal rationing and queues formed. . . . The lesson Gomulka drew from this embarrassing affair was that decentralization had gone too far, that it had led to a breakdown in financial discipline and a falling off in the coordination of plans."[39]

Some socialist economists who argue in favor of decentralization seem to see only the advantages of their proposals and not the possible difficulties. This is poor analysis which can lead to erroneous policy. The advantages and disadvantages of the alternative methods must be seen simultaneously and weighed against one another.

Liberman writes: "The interest of enterprises in attaining the max-imum result with the minimum outlays assures the fulfillment of the control targets for the whole area, including fundamental indices such as labor productivity, salaries, and costs of production." This is just not so. Interest in profits does not automatically assure fulfillment of over-all norms. The Soviet critics of Liberman are right in pointing out that profits can often be increased by raising prices or by produc-ing high-priced but unnecessary goods.

Giving greater leeway to enterprises will make it more difficult to establish over-all balances in labor, materials and finances. Ota Sik says that under the new system, "There will obviously no longer be any need to determine by directives from the top the size of the wage fund and the number of workers employed in the enterprise." He

[39] John Michael Montias, *Central Planning in Poland*. New Haven, Conn., 1962. pp. 316-319.

does not explain how an over-all labor balance will be attained other than to hint that the market will automatically produce one. But we know that the market does not automatically produce balance; it can also produce unemployment.

Decentralization is justified in spite of the problems it will bring, not because such problems do not exist. Even in the heat of partisan argument, these problems must always be kept in mind. Only thus can ways of meeting them be devised. And only thus can decentralization be kept from going too far.

An example of going too far is the argument by Liberman and Nemchinov that what is profitable for society will be profitable for the enterprise and vice versa. This argument—unless it does not mean what it seems to mean—is simply false. Any number of examples can be given in which it will not hold. A lumber enterprise may be able to make more money by ruthless cutting of forests, but the interests of society lie in conservation. An enterprise may find it cheaper to use an imported raw material when the interest of society lies in conserving foreign exchange and making the fullest possible use of domestic materials. An enterprise may be able to promote its own interests by hoarding labor which is short in other parts of the economy. And so on—without end.[40]

In some articles by socialist economists, the term "correct prices" crops up: the firm and market will automatically operate in the interests of society, but for this prices must be "correct," that is, based on costs. It is true that price structures sometimes need reforming. They often reflect decisions taken over a long period of years which have not been altered to meet changing circumstances. For example, prices fixed at a deliberately low level to subsidize basic industry may be allowed to continue at this level long after the subsidy has become unnecessary. When this practice is widespread and continues for a long time, the interrelationships among prices for different types of goods can become distorted. Nevertheless, there is no such thing as "correct" prices.

[40] Even bourgeois economists began to recognize the falseness of this argument years ago, for example, Arther Pigou in *The Economics of Welfare*.

To base prices on costs seems easy. But the concept of costs is much less simple than it seems. Often it is difficult to say what the cost of something is. What is the cost of providing electric power during an off-peak period? Should overhead be included? Or should it be excluded on the ground that the facilities would have to be there anyway to meet the peak demand? There is no mechanical answer. The allocation of costs reflects not only what happens physically, but policy, accounting conventions, and the tax structure.[41]

And while costs are an important element in fixing prices, they cannot be the only one. For example, the prices of automobiles in the Soviet Union and imported watches in Cuba are fixed not at cost, but much higher. Why? Because these goods are scarce and setting the price above cost is necessary for orderly distribution. And also because taxing luxury goods can be a useful way of sopping up excess purchasing power. On the other hand, the only way of getting rid of certain goods sometimes is to sell them below cost. Prices are an instrument of policy. They are a compromise among a number of considerations.

To go back to the enterprise. There is no reason why the actions of the enterprise, which has only a partial vision of the economy and has to operate within an imperfect price mechanism, should necessarily coincide with the interests of society. To argue otherwise is to introduce capitalist metaphysics into socialist economic theory. It should be the aim of socialist organizational arrangements to make the actions of the enterprise coincide as much as possible with the interests of society. But this is an ideal. In practice, there will always be deviations between the two—often of great significance.

So in a socialist economy, even with decentralization and greater roles for enterprises and markets, the state and its central bodies must remain in control. Conscious reason, conscious planning and control to promote welfare and balanced economic development, must remain dominant over the workings of the enterprise and market. Central plans must provide the basic guidance and control. The state must

[41] Once again a book by a bourgeois economist might be cited: John Maurice Clark's *Economics of Overhead Costs*.

determine the rules within which enterprises and markets operate and be able not only to widen their autonomy, but also to narrow it. Enterprises and markets must be thought of as subordinate instruments for running a planned economy—necessary because economies cannot be run perfectly. And the influence of profits and markets must be "strictly limited." It is not through overemphasis on profits and markets that the problems besetting Latin America and the other underdeveloped areas can be attacked.

Basically, the problem of centralization or decentralization in the enterprise is the same as in the economy as a whole. The problem is not one or the other but how to combine the two.

Sometimes people talk as though new techniques—input-output, mathematical economics, etc.—now permit enterprises to be managed in a completely centralized manner. Some people also say that the leading capitalist enterprises, which have been grappling with the problems of organization for several generations, are fully centralized and that the socialist countries would be wise to learn how they do it. It would be nice if those who make such claims for the new techniques would provide concrete evidence of how they are being used to manage whole enterprises. And if those who say that capitalist enterprises are fully centralized would name the enterprises and explain how they work.

The idea of centralized control through mathematical techniques has a certain theoretical allure. But running an enterprise means much more than programming materials through automated machinery. It means deciding policies; organization; capital investment programs; the design, size, and location of plants; the design and quality of products. It means coordinating different things—for example, finances and engineering, engineering research and production work. It means meeting the unforeseen problems that are always arising. There are no techniques for doing these things automatically. People have to grapple with them.

And it is not true that the typical capitalist enterprise is highly centralized. General Motors, for example, is not. Alfred P. Sloan, the person most responsible for the organizational structure of General Motors, has stated the philosophy behind it: "Good management rests on a reconciliation of centralization and decentralization, or decentralization with coordinated control. . . . From decentralization we get initiative, responsibility, development of personnel, decisions close to the facts—in short, all the qualities necessary for an organization to adapt to new conditions. From coordination we get efficiencies and economies."[42]

The production and sales operations of General Motors are decentralized in divisions—automobile divisions such as Chevrolet, Buick, and Cadillac; and parts and accessories divisions such as A.C. Spark Plug and Hyatt Roller Bearing. Specific operations "are under the absolute control of the General Manager of [the] Division, subject only to very broad contact with the general officers of the corporation."[43]

How can the top officers allow so much independence to the divisions without losing control? Sloan and the others grappled with the problem and concluded "that if we had the means to review and judge the effectiveness of operations, we could safely leave the prosecution of those operations to the men in charge of them."[44] So a number of financial controls and measures of performance were developed, and the division managers were required to submit regular reports. "The figures did not give automatic answers to problems. They simply exposed the facts with which to judge whether the divisions were operating in line with expectations as reflected in prior performance or in their budgets."[45]

But General Motors is a single corporation. Centralization of many things is unavoidable. For example, the individual divisions cannot be allowed to produce any type of automobile they might want to; the various General Motors cars must be planned in relation to one an-

[42] Alfred P. Sloan, *My Years With General Motors.* New York, Doubleday and Co., 1964, p. 429.
[43] *Ibid.*, p. 106.
[44] *Ibid.*, p. 140.
[45] *Ibid.*, p. 142.

other to form a coherent whole, without gaps or duplications. Often different divisions use the same parts and there are advantages in the standardization and central purchasing of such parts. There would be little point in having each division carry on its own basic scientific research when a central research laboratory can serve them all.

So there is a central management responsible for coordination and over-all policy. Central management determines the authority and responsibility of the division managers—the limits within which they operate. It fixes the boundaries and relations between the divisions; and, where necessary, it tries to fit their activities into a unified whole. It allots capital investment funds among the divisions. It thinks ahead for the whole corporation; for example, it decides whether to expand into new lines.

Central staffs perform many specific functions for the whole corporation. There is a central legal staff and a central financial staff. There are central technical staffs: a Research Laboratory, an Engineering Staff which develops new product designs, a Manufacturing Staff which works on machine design and automation, and a Styling Staff. All patent work is done in a Patent Department attached to central management.

This type of organization is not unique. General Motors was one of the pioneers in working out the organizational structure of the modern American corporation. It has been imitated by many other corporations, including Ford.

The Westinghouse Electric Corporation can serve as another example. Until 1935, Westinghouse was highly centralized. Then in the period 1935-1939 a radical reorganization was carried out which introduced a high degree of decentralization.[46]

The company had a number of plants in different cities. "But all major decision making—and much that was minor—as well as all basic financial and cost knowledge were concentrated in a small group of top executives" located in East Pittsburgh. The company was organ-

[46] "Centralization versus Decentralization: The Reorganization of the Westinghouse Electric Corporation, 1935-1939," in Ernest Dale, *The Great Organizers*. New York, McGraw-Hill, 1960.

ized by functions. There were four vice presidents in charge of manufacturing, sales, engineering, and finance. "Each . . . had direct authority over his functions in the 'field,' that is, in each of the individual product units or plants."

How did this system of centralized control by function work? Suppose the engineers in one of the plants wanted to get the sales department to move faster on new products. They couldn't just talk to the sales people directly. They "had to go all the way up the engineering ladder and then all the way down again on the sales ladder."

Each of the plants had several bosses. As the head of one of the plants put it: "There were more executives in my plant not working for me than there were working for me." Before making even a minor decision he had to deal with a large number of different departments, located at other plants in other cities. The lines of authority and responsibility were unclear. There was a tangle of interrelationships. No one was in full charge of a plant; no one could be held responsible for its operation.

The reorganization broke up the one large administrative unit into a number of smaller ones. Divisions and companies were set up composed of plants producing similar products. The manager of each division or company "could run his unit partly as though it were a separate business, subject only to the overriding policies and controls of headquarters."

The heads of the different functions at headquarters ceased being line commanders directing field operations. They became staff people whose job was to advise and help. "Thus the vice president in charge of manufacturing at headquarters no longer directed production; his function was to help the divisions improve manufacturing procedures, to coordinate jobs and rates, to set up tool and machinery specifications, and to provide some inspection." Despite the autonomy given to the divisions, the headquarters staff was expanded. It could undertake much useful staff work that under the old system had never been done.

General Motors and Westinghouse are only two enterprises out of many. And they are *capitalist* enterprises. Care must be taken in drawing conclusions from them about the organization of a socialist economy. Yet some of the problems and principles of organization are similar. For example, the logic of putting a single person in charge of an operating division to produce automobiles or electrical equipment is similar to the logic in Cuba of putting a single person in charge of each construction project instead of trying to run them all from Havana.

Cutting up work into functions to be directed from far away has disadvantages. It complicates and blurs responsibilities. Everyone has the responsibility for a function; no one, except at the very top, has the responsibility for a whole job.

And yet in enterprises as in whole economies, many operations must be centralized. There can be no real grant of "complete autonomy" to operating divisions, or of "absolute control" to their managers—these are shortcut phrases. The autonomy and control are limited. One-man management is a meaningful principle, but it is a matter of degree. There can be no such thing as absolute one-man management. No unit exists by itself in the world; all must be subject to outside controls. The advantages and disadvantages of one-man management and division of work into functions must be balanced against one another.

There is no simple answer to the problem of combining centralization and decentralization in the enterprise. The right balance will vary with many factors—the size of the enterprise, its geographic structure, the variety of its products, its technology, the skill of its management and work force. Sometimes a high degree of centralization is desirable; sometimes a high degree of decentralization. Far more important than a rigid view about highly centralized or decentralized organization is a sense of the principles to be used in judging what and how much to centralize, what and how much to decentralize.

This holds not just for enterprises, but for all organizational units down to the smallest. The head of the smallest office must wrestle with the problem of what work to do himself, what work to delegate, and how to control the work that he delegates. Organizations are not run just by leaders, but by everyone in them.

While organizational forms and planning methods have great importance, there are limits to how far the problems of running socialist economies can be solved by changing them. Economies also depend on people. No organizational form or planning method—even the best—will work well unless people work it well.

No general forms and rules can provide automatic solutions to the concrete problems that are always arising. For an organization to work well, the people who compose it must understand its purposes and be dedicated to them. They must want the organization to work well. They must want to do their own jobs well—not only mechanically well according to the rules, but truly well. They must be willing to accept responsibility and make decisions even when there is personal advantage in avoiding responsibility. This is not socialist romanticism. Even capitalist theorists on organization stress these precepts.

Many of the problems of running socialist economies are caused or made worse by simple bureaucratism. Take the enterprise that put unnecessary fur collars on boys' coats to swell its apparent output. There is another way of dealing with this problem, besides adjusting the achievement indicators of the enterprise—firing the managers who would do such a thing.

There are no bureaucrat-proof organizational forms. The construction of socialism—and then communism—means not only the development of the economy, but also the development of people.

This leads to the question of incentives. The Soviet Union, Czechoslovakia, and other socialist countries in Eastern Europe are tying the problem of relaxing central controls over enterprises to that of material incentives. The two problems, however, are separate.

The heavy-handed and increasing emphasis on material incentives raises the gravest questions. It is a formula answer to problems which can only be solved by slow patient work on organization and education. It will create its own problems; for example, how to avoid differences in remuneration due to luck, not to effort or efficiency. And—most serious for a socialist society—it will focus everyone's attention in a petty manner on his own remuneration and the bureaucratic mechanism by which it is determined.

Liberman proposes detailed arithmetical formulas for participation of enterprises in the profits they realize. They would get a certain proportion of profits of 0 to 5 percent, an additional proportion of those from 5.1 to 10 percent, and so on. Other Soviet economists object to this as unfair. One agricultural enterprise may have higher profits than another, not because it is more efficient, but because it has better land or is closer to the market. One mine may have more easily worked seams than another. And profits can be increased not only by raising efficiency, but by producing certain goods instead of others, or by charging higher prices.

Liberman answers that the problem can be met by setting up "profitability norms" which take account of varying circumstances in different enterprises and industries. Whereas Liberman is quick to criticize other norms, he is blind to the defects of his own. You just set up "scientific" norms and that's that. Try to imagine what such a system means in practice—a proliferation of paper work, conferences, and arguments between those setting the norms and those receiving them, bureaucratic maneuvering to get better norms or higher prices.

Under the new system in Czechoslovakia, says Sik, the fund from which workers are paid will vary with profits. This fund will be used "for basic wages and bonuses for fulfillment of quotas, as well as for additional bonuses and special premiums." Again a complicated system and a glossing over of problems. Workers doing the same work, and with equal efficiency, in different enterprises, will find their wages far apart. How will this problem be handled? No discussion. Workers will now have an interest in the maneuvering of their enterprises to get higher prices. No discussion. Is it good in a socialist society to enmesh everyone in a complicated set of indices on which pay depends? Is this the way to develop people for a communist society? No discussion. Just one or two formula-like statements that "moral factors" and "socialist attitudes" remain important.

But criticism of the way in which the socialist countries of Eastern Europe are stressing material incentives should not lead to the opposite extreme—a rigid melodramatic stress on moral incentives. This one-dimensional approach to a many-dimensional reality, for example, in Adolfo Gilly's book *Inside the Cuban Revolution*, makes for exciting reading, but it avoids grappling with the problems.

The leaders of a socialist economy do not pick their problems or the choices open to them. The problems come and the range of choices is limited—often severely so. The leaders must remember where the economy and the people should be headed. But they must also meet the problems.

Suppose, as in Cuba, you have a hundred thousand small farmers who support the Revolution but are not yet ready to give up their private farms and form collectives. What do you do? Force them into collectives at the point of a gun? And how do you get these private farmers to deliver their goods to market? You try to exert leadership; you appeal to patriotism and revolutionary enthusiasm. But you also need realistic farm prices.

Suppose certain members of privileged groups—say doctors and dentists—cooperate with the Revolution and make a contribution to it. The march of events by itself forces a reduction in their standard of living. Would it make sense to go beyond this and embark on a rigid program of further cutting it down?

Suppose there is a shortage of cane cutters. Volunteer labor helps, but cannot solve the problem. Many of the volunteers do not know how to cut and often damage the cane plants. Mechanization will—after several years—greatly reduce the need for cane cutters. But not all of the cutting can be mechanized. A certain number of hand cutters will still be required. Fidel is right when he says: "There remains to us the recourse that cane cutting be one of the best paid types of work; if it is one of the hardest, it is correct that it be one of the best paid."

It may be worthwhile to go back to one or two fundamentals on the question of incentives and equality. "What we have to deal with here," said Marx in a famous passage of his *Critique of the Gotha Program*, "is a communist society, not as it has *developed* on its own foundations, but, on the contrary, just as it *emerges* from capitalist society; which is thus in every respect, economically, morally, and intellectually, still stamped with the birth marks of the old society from whose womb it emerges." (Emphasis in original.) In the first phase of such a society (the phase which today we would call socialism) payment is according to work and therefore unequal. This means defects in the new society. "But these defects are inevitable in the first phase of communist society as it is when it has just emerged after prolonged birth pangs from capitalist society. Right can never be higher than the economic structure of society and its cultural development conditioned thereby." Only in a higher phase can "society inscribe on its banners: From each according to his ability, to each according to his needs."

Lenin in *State and Revolution* repeated Marx's argument. "If we are not to indulge in utopianism, we must not think that having overthrown capitalism, people will at once learn to work for society *without any standard of right;* and in fact the abolition of capitalism *does not immediately* create the economic premises for such a change." (Emphasis in original.)

But it is worth noting—especially for those who like to call emphasis on material incentives a "Leninist principle"—that this statement does not exhaust Lenin's thinking on the subject. Lenin also thought that government employees should receive the same pay as workmen —and no more. And he was enthusiastic about the Subbotniks (free volunteer labor originally on Saturday—*Subbota*). "The *Communist subbotniks* organized by the workers on their own initiative are of enormous significance. Evidently this is only a beginning, but it is a beginning of unusually great importance. It is the beginning of a revolution that is much more difficult, more material, more radical and more decisive than the overthrow of the bourgeoisie, for it is a victory over personal conservativeness, indiscipline, petty-bourgeois egoism, a victory over the habits that accursed capitalism left as a heritage to the worker and peasant. Only when *this* victory is consolidated will the new social discipline, Socialist discipline, be created; only then will a reversion to capitalism become impossible and Communism become really invincible."[47]

Much depends on how the principles laid down by Marx and Lenin

[47] V. I. Lenin, "A Great Beginning," *Selected Works*, New York, International Publishers, 1937, IX, pp. 423-424.

are applied. There are no principles that cannot be perverted in their application. It is one thing to pay cane-cutters well, but another to provide fancy villas for officials and bureaucrats. It is one thing to vary pay according to work, according to a simple criterion such as the weight of cane cut; another to tangle everyone, as General Motors does with its executives, in systems of bonuses, special bonuses, and premiums tied to profits. It is one thing to have small differentials in pay; another to set up differentials in which the best paid get ten or twenty times as much as the poorest.

Many examples could be given from Cuba to show how profound was Marx's insight that the new society will bear the birthmarks of the old. Fidel gave one in a speech. Havana, which has less than 15 percent of Cuba's population, receives 43 percent of its income. As Fidel pointed out, this inherited deformation, unjust though it is, cannot be removed overnight. Other such defects exist, some of which may last many years.

And yet Marx's insight cannot be understood mechanically. The Revolution did change some things overnight. Despite differences in income, housing, and the ownership of cars, there is a fundamental equality in Cuba today—an equality which overshadows the differences. People feel equal.

Prerevolutionary Cuba was cursed with racism. Now only faint traces remain—in the minds of a few remnants of the old order. The Revolution got rid of racism with amazing speed.

A few people have argued on "Marxist" grounds that the Revolution raised the income of the peasantry too quickly. Their heavy-handed interpretation of Marxism has blinded them to one of the Revolution's chief accomplishments.

The problems are many-sided. A socialist economy must be made to work, produce, develop. This cannot be done just with speeches and declarations of principles. It takes practical work. Read those who have led their countries during socialist construction—Lenin, Stalin, Mao—with this in mind and you will see how they come back again and again to the importance of practical work—ordinary, prosaic, day-to-day, practical work.

Those who lead a revolutionary economy must be practical, realistic, responsible. They cannot afford illusions about what people will do. The effects of their decisions show up in practice—and this is a hard test. The use of material incentives cannot be fully renounced. It is sometimes necessary.

And yet the advancement of socialism means the development not only of the economy, but also of man himself. The development of man will not happen automatically. It is not a matter of simply waiting for a communist man to emerge from a higher economic stage of society—and meanwhile misusing Marx's principle that "right can never be higher than the economic structure" to justify ugly abuses.

On September 28, 1966, the *New York Times* carried a story about criticism by Yugoslav newspapers of privileges enjoyed by party and state officials in that country. Among the privileges were seaside villas, hunting preserves, and foreign exchange benefits. A leading party official answered the critics by accusing them of ignoring the "fact that morals emerge from existing social-economic relations." Perhaps the *Times* account was inaccurate. But if not, there is only one way to characterize the party official's argument: it is a mechanistic perversion of Marxism.

Privileges and overemphasis on material incentives can create large groups of people who are no credit to socialism. They can generate harmful political attitudes, both on internal and external affairs. They can become an impediment to the whole future development of socialism.

The development of man cannot be postponed to a later stage in which it will supposedly come about without conscious effort. This is to avoid the problem. It must be planned as the development of the economy is. It must be worked on constantly.

Great leadership will be required—leadership that combines realism with vision. The same Fidel who pointed out that it will take time to establish the proper balance between Havana and the rest of the country inspired the youth of Cuba to march into the countryside and teach the *campesinos* how to read. The same Fidel who thinks cane-cutters should be well paid argues for the elimination of rents on housing by 1970.

To sum up: Easy little formulas—at one extreme or the other—will not solve the problems. A world is being changed. This takes the effort of millions of people from many different countries, with different histories and traditions, different ways of doing things, to some extent different standards of what is fair, what is appropriate. It takes patience and practical work, realism and good sense. And yet recognition that inequality cannot be eliminated in a day is not the same as extolling it. Making realistic use of material incentives is not the same as centering socialist economies on them. Trying to make economies that work well now does not mean forgetting the kind of society socialism is trying to build. Material incentives must be used; and yet there must be an unremitting effort to create a society in which they will no longer be necessary. Here again, there is a basic unity: the highest idealism has its roots in reality and the highest practical sense has vision and ideals.

Epilogue

"Es una revolución hermosa," said my friend Jaime one night as we sat back after a long session on some problem. He was right: It's a beautiful revolution. Its beauty is not that of a painting or a piece of fancy needlework. It is the beauty which only a revolution can have.

The Revolution did the seemingly impossible. Who would have said before hand that such a revolution could succeed? Yet it did. This was not an accident.

The great leaders of the Cuban Revolution—Fidel, Major Guevara, and the others—understood revolution. Engels once wrote: "Never play with insurrection unless you are fully prepared to face the consequences of your play. . . . The insurrectionary career once entered upon, act with the greatest determination, and on the offensive. . . . Surprise your antagonists while their forces are scattering, prepare new successes, however small, but daily; keep up the moral ascendancy which the first successful rising has given you. . . . In the words of Danton, the greatest master of revolutionary policy yet known, *de l'audace, de l'audace, encore de l'audace."*

The Cuban leaders brought these principles to life. The Cuban Revolution is not the lucky result of adventurous gambles, but of a careful assessment of possibilities and dangers. To use another phrase of Engels, the Cuban leaders acted with "that courage which is the result of clear insight into the state of things."*

It was an inspiring thing to see the Cuban people grow taller and taller as the Revolution developed. There before your eyes was daily proof of how people can change, of what they can do. Who would have said that the Cuban people would turn to socialism so quickly

---

* Friedrich Engels, *Germany: Revolution and Counterrevolution*, New York, International Publishers, 1933, pp. 100 and 112.

and profoundly? Who would have guessed the depths of their courage in confronting the mighty United States? As the Revolution moved from crisis to crisis, the Cuban people found qualities which they themselves had not known they had.

But the Cuban Revolution is only one overflow of a deep tide. The other oppressed and exploited peoples will also find ways to do the impossible. Seeing the Cuban people in Revolution gives a glimpse of what great things are latent in all the peoples of the world.

Index

Index